Know Your
BIBLE

A Self-Guided Tour through God's Word

Know Your
BIBLE

A Self-Guided Tour through God's Word

By PAUL KENT and ED STRAUSS

BARBOUR BOOKS
An Imprint of Barbour Publishing, Inc.

Published by Barbour Books, an imprint of Barbour Publishing, Inc., P.O. Box 719, Uhrichsville, Ohio 44683, www.barbourbooks.com

Our mission is to publish and distribute inspirational products offering exceptional value and biblical encouragement to the masses.

Member of the
Evangelical Christian
Publishers Association

Printed in the United States of America.

Introduction

Welcome to *Know Your Bible: A Self-Guided Tour through God's Word*, a book dedicated to the basic facts and principles of the Bible. This reference is ideal for new believers as well as older Christians who want to know their Bible better, and its goal is to lead you into a deeper understanding and appreciation of the Word of God.

The Bible is the source of all wisdom and life, and "whatever was written in earlier times was written for our instruction, so that through. . .the encouragement of the Scriptures we might have hope" (Romans 15:4 NASB). So we do well to know the Bible better.

Know Your Bible is based on a small volume of the same title, with sales of well over two million copies. This expanded, illustrated edition contains four separate courses you can follow:

- a one-month course containing "Basic Surveys" of the Bible's sixty-six books
- a three-month course including the sixty-six Basic Surveys and twenty-four "Heart of the Book" entries—for a total of ninety readings
- a six-month course featuring the Basic Surveys and Heart of the Book entries, along with an additional ninety "Closer Look" readings, and
- a twelve-month course of all of the above plus 185 "Hidden Treasure" readings.

The one-month course will give you a quick overview of God's Word; the three-month course will go into more detail; and the six-month and one-year courses each give increasing amounts of information.

At the end of each day's study are two or three chapters of scripture we suggest you read. We pray that you will be blessed as you meditate on God's words directly from the Bible.

(cont. next page)

How to Benefit from This Book

ONE-MONTH COURSE—If you choose this course, read the **Basic Surveys** of *two Bible books per day*. For example, start by reading the Basic Surveys for Genesis and Exodus. In thirty-three days you will have read these basic introductions to all sixty-six books of the Bible.

THREE-MONTH COURSE—If you select this course, for ninety days you will alternate between reading (1) the **Basic Survey** pages and (2) the **Heart of the Book** pages.

SIX-MONTH COURSE—If you follow this course, for 180 days you will alternate between reading (1) **Basic Survey** pages, (2) **Heart of the Book** pages, and (3) **Closer Look** readings.

TWELVE-MONTH COURSE—If you take the complete course, for 365 days you will read every page in the book, alternating between (1) **Basic Survey** pages, (2) **Heart of the Book** pages, (3) **Closer Look** pages, and (4) **Hidden Treasure** readings.

To help you follow the reading course of your choice, each of the four features (Basic Survey, Heart of the Book, etc.) appears in a distinct color, to help it stand out from the other features.

In addition, after you finish each reading, you'll see a note directing you to the page that your next reading can be found on. (For example: "One-Month Course: your next reading is on page 14.") There are no such directions at the bottom of the Hidden Treasure pages, because if you're reading them, you've chosen the twelve-month course and are reading every page in the book, one after the other.

Note: The Hidden Treasure readings are shorter than the others, taking up only half a page each. Nevertheless, you should only read one of these per day, and save the second reading on the page for the following day.

May God reward you richly and open the eyes of your understanding as you devote yourself to knowing and understanding His Word better.

Paul Kent and Ed Strauss

BASIC SURVEY

GENESIS

AUTHOR: Not stated, but traditionally attributed to Moses.

DATE: Moses lived around the 1400s BC, but the events of Genesis date to the very beginning of time.

IN TEN WORDS OR LESS

God creates the world and chooses a special people.

DETAILS, PLEASE

The Bible's first book never explains God; it simply assumes His existence: "In the beginning God. . ." (1:1 KJV). Chapters 1 and 2 describe how God created the universe and everything in it, simply by speaking: "God said. . . and it was so" (1:6–7, 9, 11, 14–15 KJV). Humans, however, received special handling, as "God formed man of the dust of the ground, and breathed into his nostrils the breath of life" (2:7 KJV), and woman was crafted from the man's rib. Those first two people, Adam and Eve, live in perfection, but ruin paradise by disobeying God at the urging of a "subtil" (crafty, 3:1) serpent. Sin throws humans into a moral freefall, as the world's first child—Cain—murders his brother Abel. People become so bad that God decides to flood the entire planet, saving only the righteous Noah, his family, and an ark (boat) full of animals. After the earth repopulates, God chooses a man named Abram as patriarch of a specially blessed people, later called "Israel" after an alternative name of Abram's grandson Jacob. Genesis ends with Jacob's son Joseph, by a miraculous chain of events, ruling in Egypt—setting up the events of the following book of Exodus.

QUOTABLE

> And God said, Let there be light: and there was light (1:3 KJV).

> Then the LORD said to Cain, "Where is Abel your brother?" He said, "I do not know. Am I my brother's keeper?" (4:9 NKJV).

> But Noah found grace in the eyes of the LORD (6:8 KJV).

> Abram believed the LORD, and he credited it to him as righteousness (15:6 NIV).

UNIQUE AND UNUSUAL

Genesis quickly introduces the concept of one God in multiple persons, a concept later called the *Trinity*: "God said, Let *us* make man in *our* image, after *our* likeness" (1:26 KJV, emphasis added). Also early on, God gives a hint of Jesus' future suffering and victory, when He curses the serpent for deceiving Eve: "And I will put enmity between you and the woman, and between your offspring and hers; he will crush your head, and you will strike his heel" (3:15 NIV).

SO WHAT?

Genesis answers the great question of "where did I come from?" Knowing that can give us meaning in a world that's otherwise hard to figure out.

READ GENESIS 1–2.

● One-Month Course: your next reading is on page 14.   →

● Three-Month Course: your next reading is on page 9.   →

● Six-Month Course: your next reading is on page 9.   →

HEART OF THE BOOK

ABRAHAM—FATHER OF A MULTITUDE

Abraham was a Hebrew, born in Ur in southern Babylonia. His father, Terah, led their family north to Haran, and after he died, God told Abraham to head to Canaan. There Abraham spent the next one hundred years as a shepherd, but God promised that his descendants would inherit the entire land of Canaan (Genesis 17:8)—and they later did.

Abraham, who is seen here in *Abraham's Journey from Ur to Canaan* by József Molnár (1821–1899), was told by God that he would be the father of many nations.

Abraham had great faith. He believed that God could give him and Sarah a son in their old age (Genesis 15:1–5). The scripture says, "He believed in the LORD, and He accounted it to him for righteousness" (Genesis 15:6 NKJV). Sure enough, Sarah became pregnant and gave birth to a son called Isaac. When Isaac was a lad, God tested Abraham by telling him to sacrifice his son (Genesis 22). Abraham passed the test, and Isaac, fortunately, was spared.

Abraham was originally named Abram ("high father"), but when he was ninety-nine, the Lord renamed him Abraham ("father of a multitude"). God said, "Your name shall be Abraham; for I have made you a father of many nations" (Genesis 17:5 NKJV).

God promised: "In your seed all the nations of the earth shall be blessed" (Genesis 22:18 NKJV). Paul explains, "The Scripture, foreseeing that God would justify the Gentiles by faith, preached. . . , 'All the nations will be blessed in you.'" So "if you belong to Christ, then you are Abraham's descendants" (Galatians 3:8, 29 NASB).

Abraham is listed as a great hero in the Hall of Faith (see Hebrews 11:8–12, 17–19).

READ GENESIS 15 AND 22:1–19.

● Three-Month Course: your next reading is on page 14.   →

● Six-Month Course: your next reading is on page 10.   →

CLOSER LOOK

Jacob and the Birthright

In ancient times, the firstborn son was the chief heir of his father and ruled the family. This right was called the "birthright." Godly fathers also conferred a blessing upon this son.

Isaac married Rebekah, and before their twin sons were born, God told her, "The older will serve the younger" (Genesis 25:23 NIV). The first son

to be born was called Esau ("hairy") because he was covered with reddish hair. The second son came out holding Esau's heel, so he was called Jacob ("he grabs the heel").

Esau was the firstborn, but he grew up into a self-centered, carnal man, caring little for God. He also didn't take his role as firstborn seriously. So one day when he came home famished from a long, exhaust-

Jacob deceived his father in order to gain Isaac's blessing, as shown in the painting *Isaac Blessing Jacob* by Gerrit Willemsz Horst (c.1612–1652).

ing hunt, he thoughtlessly promised his birthright to Jacob in exchange for a bowl of red lentil stew.

Years later when their blind father, Isaac, thought he was dying, he told Esau to go hunting and cook some of the venison for him. Then Isaac would give his blessing. Rebekah heard, quickly cooked two goats, and told Jacob to go to his father, pretending to be Esau. Jacob did, and Isaac pronounced the blessing of the firstborn over him.

Jacob inherited the birthright and blessing because he passionately desired them. The Bible warns, "Make sure that no one is immoral or godless like Esau, who traded his birthright as the firstborn son for a single meal" (Hebrews 12:16 NLT).

READ GENESIS 25:19–34 AND 27.

● Six-Month Course: your next reading is on page 11.   →

CLOSER LOOK

Building a Nation

After Jacob deceptively gained Esau's blessing, Esau was furious and wanted to kill him, so Rebekah talked Isaac into sending Jacob far north to Haran to "find a wife" from her own Hebrew relatives. When he arrived there, Jacob fell in love with Laban's youngest daughter, Rachel, and arranged to work seven years in exchange for marrying her. But on Jacob's wedding night, Laban slipped his older daughter, Leah, into the dark bridal chamber, and Jacob lay with her.

When Jacob realized the deception, it was too late, so he was forced to work another seven years for Rachel. He now had two wives. But though Jacob loved Rachel more, she bore no children. Leah, meanwhile, gave birth to several sons. In desperation, Rachel followed an ancient custom and gave her handmaid to Jacob as a wife, to bear children for her. It worked, and soon her handmaid was pregnant.

She found that two could play that game, however, when Leah also gave *her* handmaid to Jacob as a wife. Within thirteen years, Jacob had four wives, twelve sons, and an unknown number of daughters. By the time Jacob entered Egypt, many years later, he had a whole tribe of descendants. Then "the children of Israel were fruitful and increased abundantly, multiplied and grew exceedingly mighty; and the land was filled with them" (Exodus 1:7 NKJV). After 430 years in Egypt, the Hebrews were a nation about two million people strong.

READ GENESIS 29:1–30:24.

 Six-Month Course: your next reading is on page 14.   →

ISAAC—THE MIRACLE CHILD

When God told Abraham that ninety-year-old Sarah would become pregnant, Abraham fell to the ground laughing at the idea (Genesis 17:17). He likely staggered with mirth before he actually fell over. Despite this reaction, however, he "staggered not at the promise of God through unbelief; but was strong in faith, giving glory to God" (Romans 4:20 KJV). Later, when the Lord visited Abraham's camp disguised as a passing stranger and announced

that Sarah would give birth, Sarah laughed, too. But God had the last laugh, because Sarah did indeed become pregnant and give birth. She said, "God has brought me laughter, and everyone who hears about this will laugh with me" (Genesis 21:6 NIV). This is why Abraham named his son Isaac ("laughter").

Abraham was told by strangers that Sarah was expecting a child. The scene is depicted in the painting *Abraham and the Angels* by Aert de Gelder (1645–1727).

READ GENESIS 17:15–21; 18:1–15; 21:1–7.

JACOB WRESTLES AN ANGEL

After twenty years away from home, Jacob was returning to Canaan. When he heard that Esau was riding to meet him with four hundred armed men, Jacob became sick with fear. Sending his flocks and family ahead, he stayed behind to pray. That night, a stranger attacked him. Jacob began fighting with him, and their struggle lasted till dawn. Eventually, Jacob re-

This image by Gustave Doré (1832–1883) is titled *Jacob Wrestling with the Angel*, and it illustrates the pivotal moment in Jacob's role in Israel's future.

alized the stranger was an angel, so even after he threw Jacob's hip out of joint, Jacob refused to let go until he blessed him. For this reason the angel said, "Your name shall no longer be called Jacob, but Israel [Prince with God]; for you have struggled with God and with men, and have prevailed" (Genesis 32:28 NKJV).

READ GENESIS 32–33.

HIDDEN TREASURE

JOSEPH'S PRIDE

Jacob had a son by his favorite wife, Rachel, and named him Joseph. Jacob showed preferential treatment to Joseph and gave him "a coat of many colours" (Genesis 37:3 KJV). This aroused his older brothers' jealousy. To make matters worse, Joseph brought bad reports about his brothers' shepherding to their father. Finally, Joseph began having vivid prophetic dreams about his brothers bowing down before him. Unfortunately, because of his pride, he couldn't resist telling them his dreams. So one day they ripped his cloak from him, threw him into a pit, then sold him as a slave to some Midianite merchants going down to Egypt. There God blessed Joseph then humbled him by allowing him to be falsely accused and thrown into prison.

READ GENESIS 37 AND 39.

HIDDEN TREASURE

GOD EXALTS JOSEPH

One night, Pharaoh had disturbing dreams. In one, seven starved cows rose out of the Nile and devoured seven well-fed cows. In the other, seven shriveled heads of wheat ate up seven full heads of wheat. None of Pharaoh's wise men could explain the dreams. Then his cupbearer (who had been in prison with Joseph) told him that Joseph could interpret them, so Joseph was rushed from prison. He informed

Joseph gained power in Egypt when he interpreted dreams for Pharaoh, which is illustrated in the painting *Joseph Interpreting Pharaoh's Dream* by Peter von Cornelius (1783–1867).

Pharaoh that God was warning that there would be seven prosperous years followed by seven years of famine. Pharaoh therefore made Joseph vizier to prepare Egypt. Overnight, Joseph became the second most powerful man in the land. Later, his brothers came to Egypt to buy grain and did indeed bow down to him (Genesis 42:6–9).

READ GENESIS 41–42.

BASIC SURVEY

EXODUS

AUTHOR: Not stated, but traditionally attributed to Moses. In Exodus 34:27 (NASB), God told Moses, "Write down these words," and Jesus, in Mark 12:26, quoted from Exodus as "the book of Moses."

DATE: Approximately mid-1400s BC.

IN TEN WORDS OR LESS

God delivers His people, the Israelites, from slavery in Egypt.

DETAILS, PLEASE

The Israelites prosper in Egypt, having settled there at the invitation of Abraham's great-grandson Joseph, who entered the country as a slave and rose to second-in-command. When Joseph dies, a new pharaoh sees the burgeoning family as a threat—and makes the people his slaves. God hears the Israelites' groaning, remembering "his covenant with Abraham, with Isaac, and with Jacob" (2:24 KJV), and raises up Moses as deliverer. God speaks through a burning bush, and Moses reluctantly agrees to demand the Israelites' release from Pharaoh. To break Pharaoh's will, God sends ten plagues on Egypt, ending with the death of every firstborn child—except those of the Israelites. They put sacrificial blood on their doorposts, causing the Lord to "pass over" (12:13) their homes. Pharaoh finally allows the Israelites to leave the country (the "Exodus"), and God parts the Red Sea for the people, who are being pursued by Egyptian chariots. At Mount Sinai, God delivers the Ten Commandments, rules for worship, and laws to change the family into a nation. When Moses delays on the mountain, the people begin worshipping a golden calf, bringing a plague on themselves. Moses returns to restore order, and Exodus ends with the people continuing their journey to the "promised land" of Canaan, following God's "pillar of cloud" by day and "pillar of fire" by night.

QUOTABLE

> And God said to Moses, "I AM WHO I AM." And He said, "Thus you shall say to the children of Israel, 'I AM has sent me to you'" (3:14 NKJV).

> Thus saith the LORD, Let my people go (8:1 KJV).

> When I see the blood, I will pass over you (12:13 KJV).

> "You shall have no other gods before Me" (20:3 NASB).

UNIQUE AND UNUSUAL

God told the Israelites to celebrate the "Passover" with a special meal of bread made without yeast (12:14–15). Three thousand years later, Jewish people still commemorate the event.

SO WHAT?

The story of redemption is on clear display in Exodus, as God rescues His people from their slavery in Egypt. In the same way, Jesus breaks our bonds of sin (2:15).

READ EXODUS 1 AND 34.

● One-Month Course: your next reading is on page 21. →

● Three-Month Course: your next reading is on page 16. →

● Six-Month Course: your next reading is on page 16. →

HEART OF THE BOOK

MOSES THE DELIVERER

Pharaoh commanded the Hebrews to cast all their newborn boys into the Nile, but Moses' mother set him in the river in a basket among the papyrus instead. Pharaoh's daughter saw him and adopted him, and Moses was raised in the royal palace as a prince of Egypt.

When Moses grew up, he became convinced that he was called to deliver his people (Acts 7:25), so when he saw an Egyptian taskmaster beating a Hebrew slave, he killed the overseer. This became known, and Moses was forced to flee. He took refuge in the land of Midian, where he worked as a shepherd for forty years.

One day God appeared in a burning bush on Mount Sinai and told Moses, "I am sending you to Pharaoh to bring

Moses was chosen by God to lead His people out of Egypt and into the land He had promised them. Moses is shown here in *Moses with the Tables of the Law* by Guido Reni (1575–1642).

my people the Israelites out of Egypt" (Exodus 3:10 NIV). Back in Egypt, Moses performed miracles and called down devastating plagues. After the death of all the firstborn Egyptian sons, stubborn Pharaoh finally yielded and let the Israelites go free. Later, when Pharaoh's charioteers chased them, Moses raised his staff and God parted the Red Sea. The Israelites escaped, but the sea came crashing back down and drowned the pursuing chariots.

On Mount Sinai, God gave Moses the Ten Commandments and the books of the Law. Moses led the Israelites forty years in the wilderness, all the way to Canaan. God promised Moses, "I will raise up for them a Prophet like you" (Deuteronomy 18:18 NKJV), and Jesus is that Prophet and Deliverer (Acts 3:22–23; 7:37).

READ EXODUS 2–3.

● Three-Month Course: your next reading is on page 21.   →

● Six-Month Course: your next reading is on page 17.   →

CLOSER LOOK

THE PASSOVER

Even though the first nine plagues had devastated the land of Egypt, Pharaoh still hardened his heart and refused to let the Israelites leave Egypt. So Moses warned that the Lord would send one final plague. He commanded the Israelites to sacrifice a one-year-old lamb at twilight on the fourteenth day of the first month. They were then to roast it and eat it after sundown.

He also instructed them to smear some of its blood on the doorframes of their homes (Exodus 12:7). Moses warned that they must then stay indoors all that night. "For the LORD will pass through the land to strike down the Egyptians. But when he sees the blood on the top and sides of the door-

This painting, *The Sacrificial Lamb* by Josefa de Ayala (1630–1684), shows the importance of the Passover Feast, which is in honor of God's grace and the deliverance of the Israelites.

frame, the LORD will pass over your home" (Exodus 12:23 NLT). This is how the Feast of Passover got its name.

Just as God had warned, at midnight the Angel of the Lord passed throughout Egypt. He passed over the houses of the Israelites and didn't harm them, but killed all the first-

born males of both people and animals. After this, Pharaoh finally set the Israelites free.

For the next nearly fifteen hundred years, the Jews celebrated Passover. Then in AD 30, Jesus was crucified during the Passover Feast. He was the ultimate Passover lamb. As Paul wrote, "Christ, our Passover, was sacrificed for us" (1 Corinthians 5:7 NKJV). And John the Baptist declared, "Behold! The Lamb of God who takes away the sin of the world!" (John 1:29 NKJV).

READ EXODUS 11–12.

 Six-Month Course: your next reading is on page 18.   →

CLOSER LOOK

God Parts the Red Sea

When the Israelites left Egypt, God didn't instruct them to head west through the desert, by the northern road. Instead, He directed them to take a southern route that brought them to the shores of the Red Sea. It seemed to be a mistake. Worse yet, Pharaoh changed his mind and sent his chariot army after them. And there the Israelites were, trapped! But God had a plan.

God astonished them by miraculously parting the waters before them. "The floods stood upright like a heap; the depths congealed in the heart of the sea" (Exodus 15:8 NKJV). Since *congealed* means "hardened," it appears that God performed an outright miracle, causing the normal laws of nature to bend to His omnipotent power.

He could also have divinely amplified natural means. Exodus 14:21 (KJV) specifies, "The LORD caused the sea to go back by a strong east wind all that night. . .and the waters were divided." Even today, a phenomenon called "wind setdown" (sustained east-west winds) at the Bitter Lakes, north of the Red Sea, pushes the waters aside, exposing the lakes' bottom. After all the

Israelites had crossed the sea, God may then have stopped the wind abruptly, causing massive walls of water to rush back with punishing force, drowning Pharaoh's charioteers.

However God did the miracle, He did it. The Israelites escaped slav-

God delivered the Israelites from Pharaoh's army by parting the Red Sea so that His people could cross to safety. This deliverance is illustrated in *Passage of the Jews through the Red Sea* by Ivan Aivazovsky (1817–1900).

ery, and Egypt's chariot army was destroyed. And for centuries, this miracle was referred to as the greatest of God's wonders of old—a pivotal event in their history.

READ EXODUS 13:17–22 AND 14.

● Six-Month Course: your next reading is on page 21.   →

GOD SENDS MANNA

Soon after the Israelites headed into the desert, they ran out of food. So God said, "I will rain down bread from heaven for you" (Exodus 16:4 NIV). The next morning thin flakes like frost covered the ground. The Israelites asked, "*Manna?*" which is Hebrew for "What is it?" Then "the people. . .boiled it in a pot and made it into flat cakes. These cakes tasted like pastries baked with olive oil" (Numbers 11:8 NLT). The Bible calls manna "the bread of heaven" (Psalm 78:24 NKJV), and God supplied it for forty years. Some Jews told Jesus that God gave their ancestors bread from heaven and asked what miracle *He* would do. Jesus replied, "I am the bread of life" (John 6:35 NKJV).

READ EXODUS 16 AND JOHN 6:22–69.

THE TEN COMMANDMENTS

"Now Mount Sinai was all in smoke because the LORD descended upon it in fire. . . and the whole mountain quaked violently" (Exodus 19:18 NASB). Then the Lord called Moses to the top of the mountain and for the next forty days gave him laws to govern His people. "And when He had made an end of speaking with him on Mount Sinai, He gave Moses two. . .tablets of stone, written with the finger of God" (Exodus 31:18 NKJV). These tablets contained the Ten Commandments. While all the many ceremonial laws of Moses were fulfilled in Christ and are now passed away, these ten commands remain in effect. Paul said that

This statue, showing Moses holding the tablets, is found in St. Martini Church in Braunschweig, Germany.

"the entire law is fulfilled in keeping this one command: 'Love your neighbor as yourself'" (Galatians 5:14 NIV).

READ EXODUS 19–20.

THE GOLDEN CALF

When Moses had been many days on the mountain, the people told Aaron, "Come on. . . make us some gods who can lead us. We don't know what happened to this fellow Moses" (Exodus 32:1 NLT). Aaron was in charge while Moses was absent, but he yielded to the pressure and made a golden idol of a calf. Then the people announced, "This is your god, O Israel,

The Golden Calf as in Exodus 32:4 by James Tissot (1836–1902) illustrates how the Israelites disobeyed God while Moses was away.

that brought you out of the land of Egypt!" (Exodus 32:4 NKJV). They then began partying. When Moses came down, he "saw that the people were running wild. . .out of control" (Exodus 32:25 NIV). God was prepared to wipe out everyone, but Moses pleaded with God, so He spared them. Nevertheless, three thousand of the worst offenders died.

READ EXODUS 32–33.

THE ARK OF THE COVENANT

This relief appears in the Auch Cathedral in France and portrays the Israelites transporting the ark of the covenant.

The ark of the covenant was a small chest made of acacia wood and covered with gold inside and outside. A golden lid called the "atonement cover" was on top, with two golden cherubim with outspread wings sitting on that. The two stone tablets of the Law, a gold jar of manna, and Aaron's rod were stored inside (Hebrews 9:4). When the Israelites were in the wilderness, the ark was kept in the tent of meeting. When Solomon built a temple of stone, it was in a special room called the holy of holies. God sometimes appeared and spoke from between the two cherubim (Exodus 25:22). That's why the Israelites considered the ark to be a symbol of the presence of God.

READ EXODUS 25 AND 37.

BASIC SURVEY

LEVITICUS

AUTHOR: Not stated, but traditionally attributed to Moses.
DATE: Approximately mid-1400s BC.

IN TEN WORDS OR LESS

A holy God explains how to worship Him.

DETAILS, PLEASE

Leviticus, meaning "about the Levites," describes how that family line should lead the Israelites in worship. The book provides *ceremonial* laws as opposed to the moral laws of Exodus, describing offerings to God, dietary restrictions, and purification rites. Special holy days—including the Sabbath, Passover, and Day of Atonement ("Yom Kippur")—are commanded. The family of Aaron, Moses' brother, is ordained as Israel's formal priesthood. Leviticus lists several blessings for obedience, and many more punishments for disobedience.

QUOTABLE

> "You shall be holy; for I [God] am holy" (11:44 NKJV).

> "For the life of the flesh is in the blood, and I have given it to you on the altar to make atonement for your souls" (17:11 NASB).

UNIQUE AND UNUSUAL

Leviticus's blood sacrifices are contrasted with Jesus' death on the cross by the writer of Hebrews: "He does not need to offer sacrifices every day. . . . Jesus did this once for all when he offered himself as the sacrifice for the people's sins" (Hebrews 7:27 NLT).

SO WHAT?

Though we don't live under the rules of Leviticus, we still serve a holy God—and should treat Him as such.

READ LEVITICUS 4–5.

● One-Month Course: your next reading is on page 25.   →

● Three-Month Course: your next reading is on page 25.   →

● Six-Month Course: your next reading is on page 22.   →

MANY CEREMONIAL LAWS

Many Christians avoid reading Leviticus because it's full of ceremonial laws, detailed descriptions of animal sacrifices, and lengthy admonitions on ritual purity. But God emphasized purity to teach His people to revere Him and to cause them to dedicate themselves to Him. He said, "You shall be holy; for I am holy" (Leviticus 11:44 NKJV).

Also, the many details about animal sacrifices were to convince them that they were sinners, unable to approach a holy God—in constant need of repentance and forgiveness. It also taught the necessity of blood sacrifice to cover sin (Leviticus 17:11)—of which Jesus

The Israelites had many ceremonial laws to follow, including the offering of burnt sacrifices as shown in this illustration.

Himself was the ultimate fulfillment. Many Jews, however, focused on following the tiny details of the Law and missed its core message. Jesus rebuked them for thinking they were righteous by tithing the tiniest spice while they "omitted the weightier matters of the law, judgment, mercy, and faith" (Matthew 23:23 KJV).

But even when the Law of Moses was in effect, those who truly loved and knew God lived by faith. "The just shall live by his faith" (Habakkuk 2:4 NKJV). "For by it [faith] the men of old gained approval" (Hebrews 11:2 NASB).

Jesus died for our sins, fulfilling all the laws concerning purity and forgiveness, and established a new covenant in His blood (Luke 22:20). "By calling this covenant 'new,' he has made the first one obsolete; and what is obsolete and outdated will soon disappear" (Hebrews 8:13 NIV). And it did disappear in AD 70 when the temple was destroyed.

READ LEVITICUS 20 AND HEBREWS 10.

● Six-Month Course: your next reading is on page 25.   →

CLEAN AND UNCLEAN FOODS

In Leviticus 11, God detailed which foods were *kosher* (clean and acceptable) and which were unclean, and faithful Jews scrupulously followed this list. In particular, they avoided pork. There were commonsense reasons for God's prohibitions: in the days before modern feeding regulations, pigs devoured all kinds of unclean food, including dung—and their meat had to be well cooked to avoid passing on the parasite *Trichinella spiralis*. Crabs and shellfish are still the garbagemen of the oceans; oysters and clams often

contain pathogenic bacteria. Many Christians believe that these dietary prohibitions were done away with in Acts 10; other believers insist that these dietary laws are still in effect— and that Acts 10 refers to the spiritual cleansing of the Gentiles, not of unclean foods.

The Israelites did not eat pigs, which were deemed unclean.

READ LEVITICUS 11 AND ACTS 10.

BLOOD MAKES ATONEMENT

In Leviticus 17:11 (NASB), God said, "The life of the flesh is in the blood, and I have given it to you on the altar to make atonement for your souls." The word *atonement* (at-one-ment) was invented by English Bible translators in the 1500s to describe a restoration of the relationship between God and man. The Hebrew word used here is *kaphar,* which means "to cover." The picture is of blood flowing out from the sacrificial animal and covering the

sin; God then sees the blood, not the sin, and forgives the sinner. By dying on the cross, Jesus made us "at one" with God. "In Him [Jesus] we have redemption through His blood, the forgiveness of sins" (Ephesians 1:7 NKJV). (See also 1 John 1:7.)

READ LEVITICUS 17 AND HEBREWS 9.

The Israelites made the sacrifices on horned altars similar to this one, which was reconstructed according to the remnants of the original altar.

LOVE YOUR NEIGHBOR

Jesus said that the two greatest commands in the Bible were "Love the Lord your God with all your heart" and "Love your neighbor as yourself" (Matthew 22:37, 39 NIV). The command to love others is only briefly mentioned in the book of Leviticus, where God's instruction to not bear grudges ends with, "You shall love your neighbor as yourself" (Leviticus 19:18 NKJV). While this powerful directive isn't listed

One rule sums up all the commandments: Love your neighbor as yourself.

in the Ten Commandments, it's certainly implied there. Paul tells us, "The commandments, 'You shall not commit adultery,' 'You shall not murder,' 'You shall not steal,' 'You shall not bear false witness,' 'You shall not covet'. . .are all summed up in this saying, namely, 'You shall love your neighbor as yourself'" (Romans 13:9 NKJV).

READ LEVITICUS 19 AND PROVERBS 28.

AN EYE FOR AN EYE

Leviticus 24:20 (NASB) states, "Fracture for fracture, eye for eye, tooth for tooth; just as he has injured a man, so it shall be inflicted on him." God directed Moses to set up a civil code to deter crime, but over the centuries, many Jews used this law to avenge themselves. So Jesus said, "You have heard that it was said, 'An eye for an eye, and a tooth for a tooth.' But I say to you, do not resist an evil person; but whoever slaps you on your right cheek, turn the other to him also" (Matthew 5:38–39 NASB). We can avail ourselves of the legal system, as Paul did repeatedly (Acts 16:35–39; 22:24–29; 25:11–12), but we're not to seek vengeance.

READ EXODUS 21 AND MATTHEW 5.

BASIC SURVEY

NUMBERS

AUTHOR: Not stated, but traditionally attributed to Moses.

DATE: Approximately 1400 BC.

IN TEN WORDS OR LESS

Faithless Israelites wander forty years in the wilderness of Sinai.

DETAILS, PLEASE

Numbers begins with a census—hence, the book's name. Fourteen months after the Israelites escape Egypt, they number 603,550 men, not including the Levites. This mass of people, the newly formed nation of Israel, begins a march of approximately two hundred miles to the "promised land" of Canaan—a journey that will take *decades* to complete. The delay is God's punishment for the people, who complain about food and water, rebel against Moses, and hesitate to enter Canaan because of powerful people already living there. God decrees that this entire generation will die in the wilderness, leaving the promised land to a new generation of more obedient Israelites.

QUOTABLE

> The LORD is longsuffering, and of great mercy, forgiving iniquity and transgression (Numbers 14:18 KJV).

UNIQUE AND UNUSUAL

Even Moses misses out on the promised land, punishment for disobeying God by striking, rather than speaking to, a rock from which water would miraculously appear (20:1–13).

SO WHAT?

God hates sin and punishes it. We can be thankful that Jesus took that punishment for us.

READ NUMBERS 1 AND 6.

● One-Month Course: your next reading is on page 30.   →

● Three-Month Course: your next reading is on page 30.   →

● Six-Month Course: your next reading is on page 26.   →

Doubters Get Their Wish

The older generation of Israelites constantly doubted that God cared for them. As a result, they didn't think that He'd protect or provide for them. This belief caused them to imagine the worst. Once they did that, of course they began to murmur. Every time they ran into a problem, this cycle repeated. This happened *ten* times! (Numbers 14:22).

When the Israelites doubted God, He prevented them from entering the land He promised them. *Moses Seeing the Promised Land* by Christian Rohlfs (1849–1938) depicts Moses gazing upon the land that he would not be allowed to enter.

Finally, the Israelites arrived at the oasis of Kadesh Barnea on the southern border of Canaan. From there they were to march into Canaan, but first they sent twelve spies to scout out the land. They soon learned that its cities were highly fortified and its people powerful (Numbers 13). The Israelites moaned, "If only we had died . . .here in the wilderness!" Then they completely lost it, wailing, "Why is the Lord taking us to this country only to have us die in battle? Our wives and our little ones will be carried off as plunder!" (Numbers 14:2–3 NLT). Far from being overcoming warriors, they wanted to dump Moses and choose a new leader to take them back to slavery in Egypt.

God had heard enough. He said, "I will do to you the very things I heard you say. You will all drop dead in this wilderness!" The Lord added, "You said your children would be carried off as plunder. Well, I will bring them safely into the land, and they will enjoy what you have despised" (Numbers 14:28–29, 31 NLT).

Sure enough, the entire older generation wandered forty years in the Sinai desert until they died. Then their children went boldly in and conquered the promised land.

READ NUMBERS 13–14.

● Six-Month Course: your next reading is on page 27.　　　　→

CLOSER LOOK

Korah Leads a Rebellion

One day Korah, Dathan, Abiram, and 250 Israelite rulers confronted Moses and Aaron, saying, "The whole community is holy, every one of them, and the LORD is with them. Why then do you set yourselves above the LORD's assembly?" (Numbers 16:3 NIV). They were accusing Moses of exalting himself to be leader. But he had never wanted to be God's spokesperson (see Exodus 4:10–15). Aaron and Moses were only doing their jobs because God had called them.

The rulers were disguising *their* own lust for more power under the pretext that "the whole community is holy," so Moses declared, "In the morning the LORD will show who belongs to him and who is holy" (Numbers 16:5 NIV). He also told them,

Maria Hadfield Cosway (1760–1838) depicted God's wrath in the painting *The Judgement of Korah, Dathan and Abiram.*

"The LORD is the one you and your followers are really revolting against! For who is Aaron that you are complaining about him?" (Numbers 16:11 NLT).

Moses told the 250 rulers to take their censers, put burning coals and incense in them, and appear before the Lord. So the next morning they did. Korah, Dathan, and Abiram were standing with their families beside their tents when Moses shouted. "Quick!" he told the people. "Get away from the tents of these wicked men" (Numbers 16:26 NLT). The next instant the ground opened beneath Korah's tents and swallowed them all up. Then fire from the Lord consumed the 250 rebellious rulers offering incense.

As those whom Christ has cleansed, we *are* all holy—but we still have to respect those whom God has appointed as leaders (Hebrews 13:7, 17).

READ NUMBERS 16–17.

● Six-Month Course: your next reading is on page 28.   →

CLOSER LOOK

Moses Loses His Temper

Moses brought water from a rock, but he did it with such fury that he may have broken his rod in two. Nicolas Poussin (1594–1665) painted this image titled *Moses Striking Water from the Rock.*

People wonder why God wouldn't let Moses enter the promised land just because he lost his temper once. Nearly forty years earlier, just after the Israelites had come out of Egypt, God had told Moses to strike a rock with his staff. Moses obeyed and water gushed out (Exodus 17:1–7). Paul compared this rock to Jesus, saying, "They drank from the spiritual rock. . .and that rock was Christ" (1 Corinthians 10:4 NIV).

Forty years passed. The Israelites had just rebelled in Kadesh Barnea. They began wandering in the desert and camped in a desolate, waterless region. In His great love and mercy, God prepared to do a miracle.

This time He commanded Moses to simply *speak* to a rock. But Moses was angry and shouted, "Hear now, you rebels! Must we bring water for you out of this rock?" (Numbers 20:10 NKJV). Then he whacked it with his staff . . .*twice*! Water gushed out, but God said that because Moses didn't believe Him, and didn't respect Him in front of the Israelites, he couldn't lead them into the promised land. (See Deuteronomy 3:23–27; Psalm 106:32–33.)

This answers another question: the ark of the covenant was only about 3¾ feet long (Exodus 25:10). Moses' staff, which was an ordinary shepherd's rod, would have been 5 to 6 feet long (Exodus 4:1–4). Yet Moses was able to place it *inside* the ark (Hebrews 9:4). How did it fit? Moses apparently struck the staff against the rock with such fury that it broke in two! *That* had to have looked bad.

READ NUMBERS 20:1–13 AND JOHN 4:1–42.

● Six-Month Course: your next reading is on page 30.   →

HIDDEN TREASURE

BALAAM THE DISOBEDIENT PROPHET

The younger generation of Israelites finally prepared to invade Canaan from the east. They camped north of Moab, and Balak, its king, sent messengers to the prophet Balaam, urging him to come curse the Israelites. Balak promised him a great reward. But God warned, "Do not go with them. You are not to curse these people" (Numbers 22:12 NLT). Balaam really *wanted* to

go, so God let him. However, on the way there, God almost killed him. Shaken up, Balaam didn't curse the Israelites. But later on, to earn that reward, he advised Balak to tempt the Israelite men to sin so that *God* Himself would curse them and send a plague on them. That's why the Israelites killed Balaam (Numbers 31:16; Joshua 13:22).

Balaam was prevented from disobeying God, which John Linnell (1792–1882) portrayed in his painting *The Prophet Balaam and the Angel.*

READ NUMBERS 22–23.

HIDDEN TREASURE

MOSES TAKES A CENSUS

At the beginning of the time in the wilderness, God told Moses to "count. . .all the men in Israel who are twenty years old or more and able to serve in the army" (Numbers 1:3 NIV). They took a census and counted 603,550 men, not including the priestly tribe of Levites (Numbers 1:47–49; 2:32). Forty years later, because of Balaam's evil advice, the Israelites sinned, so God sent a plague. Some 24,000 people died. (These were mostly men, since it was they who had sinned.) After this, God told Moses to take another census. This time there were only 601,730 men (Numbers 25:9; 26:1–2, 51). After forty years they were 1,830 *fewer.* Why? There had probably been some 22,000 *more*, but they had died in the plague.

READ NUMBERS 25–26.

BASIC SURVEY

DEUTERONOMY

AUTHOR: Traditionally attributed to Moses. Chapter 34, recording Moses' death, was probably written by his successor, Joshua.

DATE: Approximately 1400 BC.

IN TEN WORDS OR LESS

Moses reminds the Israelites of their history and God's laws.

DETAILS, PLEASE

With a name meaning "second law," Deuteronomy records Moses' final words as the Israelites prepared to enter the promised land. Forty years have passed since God handed down His laws on Mount Sinai, and the entire generation that experienced that momentous event has died. Moses reminds the new generation of both God's commands and their national history as they ready their entry into Canaan. The invasion will occur under Joshua, as Moses will only *see* the promised land from Mount Nebo. "Moses the servant of the LORD died there. . . . And [God] buried him in a valley in the land of Moab" (34:5–6 NKJV). Moses was 120 years old.

QUOTABLE

> "And you must love the LORD your God with all your heart, all your soul, and all your strength" (6:5 NLT).

UNIQUE AND UNUSUAL

The Ten Commandments, most commonly found in Exodus 20, are restated in full in Deuteronomy 5—with slight differences, however.

SO WHAT?

Deuteronomy makes clear that God's rules and expectations aren't meant to limit and frustrate us, but instead to benefit us: "Therefore hear, O Israel, and be careful to observe it, that it may be well with you" (6:3 NKJV).

READ DEUTERONOMY 4:1–40 AND 8.

● One-Month Course: your next reading is on page 34.   →

● Three-Month Course: your next reading is on page 34.   →

● Six-Month Course: your next reading is on page 31.   →

CLOSER LOOK

A STORY TWICE TOLD

Is the dry old book of Deuteronomy worth reading? Yes, definitely! Jesus Himself not only read and studied it, but meditated upon it and memorized key passages from it.

The New Testament quotes from Deuteronomy dozens of times, and in the story of Jesus' temptation in the wilderness in Matthew 4:1–11, He defeated Satan by quoting exclusively from Deuteronomy. Jesus restated Deuteronomy 8:3 (NKJV) ("Man shall not live by bread alone; but man lives by every word that proceeds from the mouth of the LORD"). He quoted Deuteronomy 6:16 (NKJV) ("You shall not tempt the LORD your God") and Deuteronomy 6:13 (NLT) ("You must fear the LORD your God and serve him").

Deuteronomy retells the history of the Israelites.

Deuteronomy is basically a retelling of the Israelites' history, and sometimes we wonder why the Bible duplicates entire books. Why, for example, do we need 1 and 2 Chronicles when they cover most of the same material as 1 and 2 Kings? Why do we need the Gospels of Mark and Luke when basically the same story is told in Matthew? Why does Acts 11:1–17 repeat Peter's trip to Caesarea in Acts 10?

Some people guess that when something is repeated, it's because it's more important than other things in the Bible, but this isn't the case. Rather, the benefit is that in the retelling, much that is new is brought out. Also, we discover amazing truths when we compare two separate accounts, lay them over one another, and draw conclusions from the differences. It's like seeing a movie in 3-D.

READ DEUTERONOMY 5–6.

● **Six-Month Course: your next reading is on page 34.**   →

HIDDEN TREASURE

ISRAEL'S MANY REBELLIONS

In Deuteronomy 9, Moses reviewed the constant rebellions of the Israelites and pointed out that they were a stubborn, disbelieving generation. They had seen God do mighty miracles in Egypt, bringing down devastating plagues. They rejoiced and believed for a while, but as soon as they hit another obstacle, they lapsed into disbelief and accused God of not caring for them. Then they began complaining and imagining the worst. When they found themselves trapped at the Red Sea, they doubted again. God did a miracle and delivered them—but later when they had no water, and when they ran out of food, they doubted again. And they backslid by worshipping the golden calf. They simply didn't trust God, and their hearts weren't dedicated to Him.

Moses recounted many of the Israelites' rebellions against God, which are found in the ninth chapter of Deuteronomy.

READ DEUTERONOMY 9 AND 1 CORINTHIANS 10:1–22.

HIDDEN TREASURE

DESTROYING THE "HIGH PLACES"

When the Israelites prepared to enter Canaan, God ordered, "You shall utterly destroy all the places where [the Canaanites]. . .served their gods, on the high mountains and on the hills" (Deuteronomy 12:2 NKJV). "Destroy all their. . .idols, and demolish all their high places" (Numbers 33:52 NIV). If the Israelites left the idols standing, they'd be tempted to worship them (Exodus 23:32–33). The Canaanites often worshipped on top of mountains and hills. That's where the altars to their demon-gods were, and that's where the Canaanites did their disgusting worship, so God told the Israelites to desecrate these spots. God didn't even want His people to worship *Him* on these defiled high places. He wanted them to worship Him at His temple wherever He chose to have it (Deuteronomy 12:10–11).

This statue of Baal would have been one of the many things that God ordered the Israelites to destroy when they entered Canaan.

READ DEUTERONOMY 12 AND PSALM 78:52–72.

Loving, Merciful Laws

First John 4:8 (kjv) says, "God is love," and many of God's laws were directly related to the command to love our neighbor as we love ourselves. For example, in Deuteronomy 22:1–4, God commanded the Israelites to look out for one another and to help lift an overloaded donkey or ox if it fell down. He even commanded, "If you meet your enemy's ox or his donkey going astray, you shall surely bring it back to him again. If you see the donkey of one who hates you lying under its burden. . .you shall surely help him with it" (Exodus 23:4–5 nkjv). He also commanded them to care for a stray animal till its owner arrived. He even commanded them to help runaway slaves escape (Deuteronomy 23:15–16).

READ DEUTERONOMY 22:1–6 AND EXODUS 23.

Blessings or Curses

God made a covenant with the nation of Israel. He said, "The Lord your God has chosen you to be a people for Himself, a special treasure above all the peoples on the face of the earth" (Deuteronomy 7:6 nkjv). This was a tremendous privilege and would provide unprecedented blessings. "The Lord has declared today that you are his people, his own special treasure. . .and that you must obey all his commands. And if you do, he will set you high above all the other nations he has made" (Deuteronomy 26:18–19 nlt). But they had to

Joshua encouraged the Israelites to stay true to God, which is depicted in this lithograph titled *Joshua Renewing the Covenant with Israel.*

be faithful to uphold their end of the agreement—to love and obey God—to receive these blessings. On the other hand, if they willfully disobeyed, God would judge them severely. The choice was theirs.

READ DEUTERONOMY 7 AND 11.

BASIC SURVEY

JOSHUA

AUTHOR: Traditionally, Joshua himself, except for the final five verses (24:29–33), which describe Joshua's death and legacy.

DATE: Approximately 1375 BC.

IN TEN WORDS OR LESS

The Israelites conquer and settle the promised land of Canaan.

DETAILS, PLEASE

With Moses and an entire generation of Israelites dead, God tells Joshua to lead the people into Canaan, their promised land. Joshua leads a successful military campaign to clear idol-worshipping people from the land. Major cities subdued, Joshua divides the land among the twelve tribes of Israel, reminding the people to stay true to the God who led them home: "Now therefore. . .put away the foreign gods which are among you, and incline your heart to the LORD God of Israel" (24:23 NKJV).

QUOTABLE

> "Have I not commanded you? Be strong and courageous. Do not be afraid; do not be discouraged, for the LORD your God will be with you wherever you go" (1:9 NIV).

UNIQUE AND UNUSUAL

Fearing for their lives, the Gibeonites appeared before Joshua dressed in old clothes, carrying dry, moldy bread, claiming they had come from a faraway land. Joshua and the Israelite leaders "asked not counsel at the mouth of the LORD" (9:14 KJV) and agreed to a peace treaty. When Joshua learned the truth, he honored his agreement with the Gibeonites—but made them slaves.

SO WHAT?

Joshua shows, over and over, how God blesses His people. The promised land was His gift to them, as were the military victories that He engineered.

READ DEUTERONOMY 31:1–8 AND JOSHUA 1.

- ● One-Month Course: your next reading is on page 40.   →
- ● Three-Month Course: your next reading is on page 35.   →
- ● Six-Month Course: your next reading is on page 35.   →

HEART OF THE BOOK

JOSHUA THE MIGHTY WARRIOR

Joshua is one of few major Bible characters who seemed to do everything right—he was a strong leader, completely committed to God, who never fell into recorded sin or disobedience. He is famous for challenging the Israelites, "Choose you this day whom ye will serve. . .as for me and my house, we will serve the LORD" (Joshua 24:15 KJV).

Joshua was a powerful leader who led the Israelites in defeating the Amalekites—a victory depicted in the painting *The Victory of Joshua over the Amalekites* by Nicolas Poussin (1594–1665).

When Joshua was a young man he was Moses' personal assistant. "Joshua son of Nun. . .had been Moses' aide since youth" (Numbers 11:28 NIV). Already in the earliest days, just after leaving Egypt, he was in charge of the army of the Israelites (Exodus 17:9). He was one of the twelve men whom Moses sent to spy out Canaan, and only he and Caleb believed that they could conquer the Canaanites (Numbers 14:6–8). He declared, "Do not be afraid of the people of the land, because. . .their protection is gone, but the LORD is with us" (Numbers 14:9 NIV).

After Moses died, God anointed Joshua to replace him as leader of the Israelites. Besides being a mighty warrior, Joshua was a deeply spiritual man who heard God's instructions clearly. He had the faith to believe what God said, no matter how strange it seemed—such as walking into the flooded Jordan River and expecting the water to part, or marching seven times around Jericho and expecting the walls to fall.

Only one mistake mars Joshua's record: when the Gibeonites (Amorites he should have driven out) came to make a treaty, Joshua failed to pray before agreeing.

READ JOSHUA 9 AND 23.

● Three-Month Course: your next reading is on page 40.   →

● Six-Month Course: your next reading is on page 36.   →

CLOSER LOOK

RAHAB AND JERICHO

Rahab was important in the fall of Jericho and is portrayed in *The Harlot of Jericho and the Two Spies* by James Tissot (1836–1902).

Jericho was a massive, well-fortified city and the gateway to Canaan. After crossing the Jordan River, one immediately faced Jericho. While they were still east of the Jordan, Joshua sent two men to spy out the land, particularly Jericho. However, someone told the king when they saw the spies entering the inn of Rahab the prostitute. But Rahab hid them on her rooftop and helped them escape, in exchange for the promise that the Israelites would spare her and her family when they conquered the city.

When Joshua's armies crossed the river and camped around Jericho, God gave him odd instructions, and following Joshua's lead, the Israelites obeyed implicitly. The priests carried the ark of the covenant—with the army flanking them before and behind—and marched around the city once a day for six days. The priests blew ram's horns the entire time. On the seventh day they marched around the city seven times then blew the ram's horns and everyone shouted.

It took tremendous faith to believe such a tactic would work—but Joshua believed. So they obeyed God's instructions to the letter, and the mighty walls of Jericho came crashing down, falling outward, and the Israelite army charged directly into the undefended city, killing everyone. Only Rahab and her family were spared.

We don't know how God did this miracle. He possibly sent an earthquake at the exact second the army shouted. However He did it, the other Canaanites heard of Jericho's fall and were absolutely terrified.

READ JOSHUA 2 AND 6.

● Six-Month Course: your next reading is on page 37.   →

CLOSER LOOK

Seven Years of Conquest

Because the Gibeonites had made a treaty with Israel, the armies of five Amorite kings besieged them. The Gibeonites begged Israel to come to their defense, and after an all-night march, the Israelites struck the Amorite armies at dawn. The fighting was fierce and lasted all day. God did mighty miracles to help Joshua, and the Amorites finally fled. After the battle of Gibeon, the Israelites continued attacking enemy cities and rapidly conquered much of south Canaan—all in a single campaign (Joshua 10:28–43).

These stunning victories alarmed the Canaanites in the north, and the king of Hazor quickly assembled a coalition of many kings. Soon a vast horde of fighting men and chariots was marshaled at the waters of Merom. Without hesitation, Joshua marched his entire army north and made a preemptive attack, and the Lord gave Israel a tremendous victory. They completely routed their enemies, fighting until no Canaanite soldier remained alive.

It only took Joshua a few weeks to gain control of most of Canaan—pictured here from Mount Nebo—but Joshua continued to fight for seven years in order to conquer the rest of the land.

In just two huge campaigns, in just a few weeks, the Israelites conquered most of northern and southern Canaan. "So Joshua took this entire land: the hill country, all the Negev. . .the western foothills, the Arabah and the mountains of Israel." However, the Bible also informs us that "Joshua waged war. . .for a long time" (Joshua 11:16, 18 NIV). These wars lasted about seven years. "So Joshua took the whole land. . .and Joshua gave it as an inheritance to Israel according to their divisions by their tribes. Then the land rested from war" (Joshua 11:23 NKJV).

READ JOSHUA 10:16–11:23.

● Six-Month Course: your next reading is on page 40.   →

DEFEAT AT AI

Then the Israelites came to Ai. Now, *Ai* means "ruins," and it was little more than Canaanites living inside the ruins of a former town. But when the Israelites attacked, the men of Ai charged. The Israelites fled, and thirty-six were killed. God then told Joshua that Israel had disobeyed and had taken "some of the accursed things" (Joshua 7:11 NKJV). He had warned them not to take any plunder from Jericho, but an Israelite named Achan had taken a wedge of gold and some other treasure. Because of this disobedience God had allowed the entire nation to suffer defeat. After they had dealt with Achan, God told Joshua to attack Ai again. This time the Israelites did things God's way and succeeded.

READ JOSHUA 7:1–8:29.

THE SUN STANDS STILL

When Israel fought the armies of five Amorite kings at Gibeon, the combat lasted all day. It continued to rage even as the sun was setting in the west. Joshua needed to finish the battle, so he prayed, "'Let the sun stand still over Gibeon, and the moon over the valley of Aijalon.' So the sun stood still and the moon stayed in place until the nation of Israel had defeated its enemies" (Joshua 10:12–13 NLT). As the daylight refused to fade, the Amorites finally broke ranks—but the Lord destroyed them with a terrific hailstorm as they ran. The hail killed more men than the Israelites had. These miracles,

When Joshua needed to defeat the Amorites, he prayed for the sun to stay still; time didn't pass until the Israelites secured the victory.

together with the drying up of the Jordan, demonstrated that God Himself was fighting for Israel (Deuteronomy 1:30).

READ JOSHUA 3 AND 10:1–15.

Unconquered Land

Some years later, after old age had forced Joshua to retire, God told him, "You are now very old, and there are still very large areas of land to be taken over" (Joshua 13:1 NIV). Israel had already conquered vast tracts of land, but there still remained much to be conquered. By this time, however, the twelve tribes had settled into their individual regions, so it was up to them to drive the Canaanites from the remaining territory allotted to them. Joshua therefore commissioned the younger generation to rise to the challenge. They began to do this after his death (Judges 1:1–26). God had helped their fathers gain great victories, but the battles weren't all finished. There was still some mopping up to do.

READ JOSHUA 13 AND JUDGES 1.

Serve the Lord

When Joshua knew that he'd soon die, he assembled the Israelite leaders and gave them final instructions. Then, knowing that they could only be

victorious if they obeyed God, he said, "If it is disagreeable in your sight to serve the LORD, choose for yourselves today whom you will serve: whether. . .the gods of the Amorites in whose land you are living; but as for me and my house, we will serve the LORD" (Joshua 24:15 NASB). The people promised to serve God, but Joshua warned them that the same God who had done good for them would fight them if they turned from Him. But the people insisted, "We will serve the LORD our God and we will obey His voice" (Joshua 24:24 NASB).

Joshua reminded the Israelites that God would fight them if they turned from Him and worshipped idols. This statue represents a worshipper of the false god Amurru.

READ JOSHUA 24 AND PSALMS 6 AND 16.

BASIC SURVEY

JUDGES

AUTHOR: Unknown; some suggest the prophet Samuel.

DATE: Written approximately 1050 BC, covering events that occurred as far back as 1375 BC.

IN TEN WORDS OR LESS

Israel goes through cycles of sin, suffering, and salvation.

DETAILS, PLEASE

After Joshua's death, Israel wasn't ruled by kings like other nations, but was a loose-knit confederation of tribes governed by judges. Lesser-known judges include Othniel, Ehud, Shamgar, Tola, Jair, Jephthah, Ibzan, Elon, and Abdon. More familiar figures are Deborah, who led a military victory against the Canaanites; Gideon, who tested God's will with a fleece and defeated the armies of Midian; and Samson, who defeated the Philistines.

QUOTABLE

> They abandoned the LORD, the God of their ancestors, who had brought them out of Egypt. They went after other gods, worshiping the gods of the people around them (2:12 NLT).

UNIQUE AND UNUSUAL

Several judges had unusual families by today's standards: Jair had thirty sons (10:4), Abdon had forty sons (12:14), and Ibzan had thirty sons and thirty daughters (12:9). Jephthah had only one child, a daughter, whom he foolishly vowed to sacrifice to God in exchange for a military victory (11:30–40).

SO WHAT?

The ancient Israelites got into trouble when they "did that which was right in [their] own eyes" (17:6; 21:25 KJV) rather than what God wanted them to do. Don't make the same mistake yourself!

READ JUDGES 10:6–17 AND PSALM 103.

- ● One-Month Course: your next reading is on page 46.   →
- ● Three-Month Course: your next reading is on page 41.   →
- ● Six-Month Course: your next reading is on page 41.   →

HEART OF THE BOOK

CYCLES OF APOSTASY AND REPENTANCE

After Joshua's death, the Israelites constantly walked away from their oath to serve God. As a result, they lost the power to expel the Canaanites from the promised land. "The children of Benjamin did not drive out the Jebusites that inhabited Jerusalem" (Judges 1:21 KJV), and this was characteristic of many tribes, which allowed idol worshippers to stay in their midst—with tragic results. God said to His people, "You have not obeyed My voice. . . . Therefore I also said, 'I will not drive them out before you; but they shall be thorns in your side, and their gods shall be a snare to you'" (Judges 2:2–3 NKJV).

That's exactly what happened, as the Israelites began a cycle of worshipping idols, suffering punishment by attackers, crying to God for help, and receiving God's aid in the form of a human judge (or "deliverer").

"So He delivered them into the hands. . .of their enemies all around, so that they could no longer stand before their enemies. Wherever they went out, the hand of the LORD was against them for calamity. . .and they

After Joshua died, the Israelites repeatedly worshipped other gods—a scene much like the one depicted in *La Fiancée de Bélus* by Henri Motte (1846–1922).

were greatly distressed. Nevertheless, the LORD raised up judges who delivered them out of the hand of those who plundered them. . . . For the LORD was moved to pity by their groaning because of those who oppressed them and harassed them. And it came to pass, when the judge was dead, that they reverted and behaved more corruptly than their fathers" (Judges 2:14–16, 18–19 NKJV).

This pattern would continue for most of Israel's history.

READ JUDGES 2 AND PSALM 106.

- Three-Month Course: your next reading is on page 46. →
- Six-Month Course: your next reading is on page 42. →

CLOSER LOOK

Deborah and Barak

A common complaint the Israelites gave for not driving out the Canaanites was that they had iron chariots. When the men of Ephraim and Manasseh told this to Joshua, he assured them that they could "drive out the Canaanites, though they have iron chariots and are strong" (Joshua 17:18 NKJV). Now, some fifty years after Joshua, a Canaanite king named Jabin reoccupied Hazor, built up an army of nine hundred chariots, then conquered all the Israelites of the north, particularly in the Jezreel Valley where the Kishon River flowed. Jabin oppressed them for twenty years.

Deborah was one of the judges of Israel, and she led the Israelite army to victory over the Canaanites. She is portrayed here in the painting titled *Jael, Deborah and Barak* by Salomon de Bray (1597–1664).

Now, God raised up a woman named Deborah to judge Israel. One day she summoned the warrior Barak and told him that if he assembled an army on Mount Tabor near the Kishon River, God would lure the Canaanites in to fight and would deliver them into his hands. Barak knew that God's presence was with Deborah, so he said, "If you go with me, I will go; but if you don't go with me, I won't go" (Judges 4:8 NIV). So Deborah went.

Apparently, God sent a sudden, heavy downpour, causing the Kishon River to overflow its banks, and most of the nine hundred chariots were swept away (Judges 5:4, 21). Barak then attacked those who had survived. This battle broke the back of the Canaanite army. "And from that time on Israel became stronger and stronger against King Jabin until they finally destroyed him" (Judges 4:24 NLT).

READ JUDGES 4–5.

● Six-Month Course: your next reading is on page 43.   →

GIDEON AND THE MIDIANITES

For seven years, whenever it was harvesttime in Israel, hordes of Midianites on camels swept in from the southeastern deserts, and their vast flocks and herds completely devoured the Israelites' crops. The Israelites cried out to God for deliverance, and one day an angel appeared to a man named Gideon. He announced, "Mighty hero, the LORD is with you!" Gideon re-

plied, "Sir. . .if the LORD is with us. . . where are all the miracles our ancestors told us about?" (Judges 6:12–13 NLT). Gideon would *get* his answer.

Gideon had faltering faith and had to be reassured repeatedly. He is famous for setting fleeces (sheepskins) out before the Lord and requesting miraculous signs as proof that God *was* with him. But in the end, he had the faith to obey and gathered an army of thirty-two thousand men. Then God

Nicolas Poussin (1594–1665) depicted Gideon's victory over the Midianites in *Battle of Gideon against the Midianites*.

really tested Gideon's faith by saying, "The people who are with you are too many for Me to give Midian into their hands, for Israel would become boastful, saying, 'My own power has delivered me'" (Judges 7:2 NASB). So He had Gideon send everyone home except for three hundred men.

God had Gideon position these men on the hills around the enemy camp by night. Then every man smashed a clay pot, held up a torch, and blew on a trumpet. The Midianites panicked, began killing one another, and fled. Then all Israel rallied and helped defeat them. God often uses our strength and skills, but there are times when He wants to defy logic and do a miracle.

READ JUDGES 6–7.

 Six-Month Course: your next reading is on page 46. →

OTHNIEL RISES UP

During Joshua's initial wars of conquest, Caleb promised, "I will give my daughter Aksah in marriage to the man who attacks and captures Kiriath Sepher" (Joshua 15:16 NIV). Othniel led an army to conquer this city then married Aksah. Then he enjoyed many years of farming, loving his wife, and raising a family. But when he was old, a foreign king, Cushan-Rishathaim, oppressed Israel for eight years. Then "the Spirit of the LORD came on [Othniel], so that he became Israel's judge and went to war" (Judges 3:10 NIV). He rallied the Israelites and drove out the invaders. Then he judged Israel for forty years. God obviously wasn't through with Othniel just because he had become old (see Psalm 71:9).

READ JOSHUA 15:13–19; JUDGES 3:7–11; AND PSALM 71.

EHUD THE LEFT-HANDED JUDGE

Ehud Kills Eglon by Ford Madox Brown (1821–1893) shows how Ehud used his left hand to slay the king of Moab.

Now, the Israelites sinned against God, so "the LORD strengthened Eglon the king of Moab against Israel" (Judges 3:12 NASB). Eglon made Israel pay tribute for eighteen years. A left-handed Israelite named Ehud normally delivered their payments, and God gave him a daring plan. Ehud fastened a dagger beneath his robe on the right side. The guards suspected nothing, because in a nation of right-handed warriors, a weapon was invariably fastened on the left side. After Ehud delivered the tribute, he told Eglon, "I have a secret message for you, O king." Eglon ordered, "Keep silence!" He sent his attendants from the room and closed the doors (Judges 3:19 NKJV). Ehud then slew the despot, escaped by the porch, rallied the Israelites, and drove out the Moabites.

READ JUDGES 3:12–30 AND PSALM 18.

SAMSON THE STRONGMAN

About 1150 BC the Philistines overran Israel. Now, an Israelite named Samson fell in love with a Philistine woman. When he was going to visit her, a lion attacked him, but "the Spirit of the LORD came powerfully upon him so that he tore the lion apart with his bare hands" (Judges 14:6 NIV). At his marriage, he told a riddle about this. The Philistines, however, forced Samson's wife to tell the answer, so he went out and killed thirty Philistines. Afterward, Samson caught foxes, tied torches to their tails, and set them loose in the grain fields. Then the Spirit of the Lord came mightily on Samson, and "finding a fresh jawbone of a donkey, he grabbed it and struck down a thousand men" (Judges 15:15 NIV).

Lucas Cranach (1472–1553) portrayed Samson's incredible strength in his painting *Samson's Fight with the Lion.*

READ JUDGES 13–14.

SAMSON'S DOWNFALL

Despite his incredible strength, Samson had a weakness for women, and it brought about his downfall. Several years later, he fell in love with a woman named Delilah. The Philistines offered her great rewards if she discovered the secret to Samson's strength, so Delilah "tormented him with her nagging day after day until he was sick to death of it" (Judges 16:16 NLT). Samson finally revealed that his strength was due to his long hair, so while he slept, Delilah cut it off. Samson's strength immediately departed, and the Philistines

captured and blinded him. One day they brought Samson out to mock him. But his hair had grown back, and in one final, mighty act, he pushed apart the two main pillars supporting the temple roof. The entire building collapsed— killing thousands of leading Philistines and setting his people free.

Samson's love for Delilah was his downfall and is depicted in *Samson and Delilah* by Matthias Stom (c. 1600–1650).

READ JUDGES 15–16.

BASIC SURVEY

RUTH

AUTHOR: Not stated; some suggest Samuel.

DATE: Ruth, as great-grandmother of King David (who reigned approximately 1010–970 BC), probably lived around 1100 BC.

IN TEN WORDS OR LESS

Loyal daughter-in-law pictures God's faithfulness, love, and care.

DETAILS, PLEASE

Ruth, a Gentile woman, marries into a Jewish family. When all the men of the family die, Ruth shows loyalty to her mother-in-law, Naomi, staying with her and scavenging food to keep them alive. As Ruth gleans barley in a field of the wealthy Boaz, he takes an interest in her and orders his workers to watch over her. Naomi recognizes Boaz as her late husband's relative and encourages Ruth to pursue him as a "kinsman redeemer," one who weds a relative's widow to continue a family line. Boaz marries Ruth, starting a prominent family.

QUOTABLE

> "For wherever you go, I will go; and wherever you lodge, I will lodge; your people shall be my people, and your God, my God" (1:16 NKJV).

UNIQUE AND UNUSUAL

Ruth, from the pagan land of Moab, married a Jewish man and became the great-grandmother of Israel's greatest king, David—and an ancestor of Jesus Christ.

SO WHAT?

We can trust God to provide what we need, when we need it—and to work out our lives in ways that are better than we ever imagined.

READ PSALM 68 AND PROVERBS 16.

● One-Month Course: your next reading is on page 49. →

● Three-Month Course: your next reading is on page 49. →

● Six-Month Course: your next reading is on page 47. →

CLOSER LOOK

NAOMI'S TROUBLES

As Naomi was grieving the loss of her husband and sons, she decided to move back to Israel. She is shown with her daughters-in-law in this painting by William Blake (1757–1827) titled *Naomi Entreating Ruth and Orpah to Return to the Land of Moab.*

In the days of the judges there was a long famine in Israel, so Naomi, her husband, and their two sons sold their land, uprooted from Bethlehem, and immigrated to Moab. Their sons married Moabite women; but just when they'd found a little relief and happiness, tragedy struck again: Naomi's husband and both sons died.

Naomi was overwhelmed with grief and financially destitute. Unable to make any sense of her life, she decided to return to Israel. As she was saying good-bye to her daughters-in-law, she lamented, "Things are far more bitter for me than for you, because the LORD himself has raised his fist against me" (Ruth 1:13 NLT).

Naomi returned to Bethlehem and her old neighbors exclaimed, "Isn't this Naomi?" In despair, she answered, "Don't call me Naomi [pleasant]. . . . Call me Mara [bitter], because the Almighty has made my life very bitter. I went away full, but the LORD has brought me back empty. Why call me Naomi? The LORD has afflicted me; the Almighty has brought misfortune upon me" (Ruth 1:20–21 NIV).

But we know the end of her story: Naomi's daughter-in-law, Ruth, who had returned with her, married a wealthy landowner and Naomi was once again happy and provided for. She finally understood that through it all, God had been working out His purposes. Not only did Naomi understand the reason for her suffering, but the best part was that Ruth gave birth to a son who became the ancestor of David, Israel's greatest king.

READ RUTH 1 AND PSALM 113.

● Six-Month Course: your next reading is on page 49.   →

RUTH AND THE MOABITES

Ruth left her home in Moab and joined Naomi in traveling to Israel. *Ruth and Boaz* by Gerbrand van den Eeckhout (1621–1674) portrays Boaz as he blesses Ruth for her dedication and loyalty.

The land of Moab bordered Israel, lying to the east of the Dead Sea. The Moabites were also Hebrews; they were descended from Lot, Abraham's nephew (Genesis 19:30–37). The Moabites worshipped a god called Chemosh and throughout their history were sometimes friends and sometimes enemies of God's people. But Ruth, who married Naomi's son, converted to faith in the true God. When Naomi returned to Israel, Ruth went with her, saying, "Wherever you go, I will go; wherever you live, I will live. Your people will be my people, and your God will be my God" (Ruth 1:16 NLT). And Boaz blessed her, saying, "May the LORD, the God of Israel, under whose wings you have come to take refuge, reward you fully" (Ruth 2:12 NLT).

READ RUTH 2–3.

THE KINSMAN-REDEEMER

When a poor Israelite was forced to sell his land outside his extended family, a near relative (kinsman) had the obligation to buy back (redeem) that land (Leviticus 25:25–28). Kinsmen were also responsible to marry the widow of a deceased brother and produce an heir for him (Deuteronomy 25:5–10). Since Boaz was a near kinsman of Naomi, he was obliged to redeem her land. He also had the right and duty to marry Ruth, the widow of Naomi's son. Boaz was more than happy to do both. Just like Boaz, Jesus is our kinsman who redeemed us; He did this by paying the price for our sin: "For You [Jesus] were slain, and have redeemed us to God by Your blood" (Revelation 5:9 NKJV).

READ RUTH 4 AND PSALM 146.

Nicolas Poussin (1594–1665) painted *Summer (Ruth and Boaz)*, which illustrates how Boaz redeemed and rescued Ruth.

BASIC SURVEY

1 SAMUEL

AUTHOR: Not stated. Samuel himself was likely involved, though some of the history of 1 Samuel occurs after the prophet's death.

DATE: Approximately 1100–1000 BC.

IN TEN WORDS OR LESS

Israel's twelve tribes unite under a king.

DETAILS, PLEASE

The prophet Samuel is the last of Israel's judges; then the people demand a king to rule over them like all other nations. So God tells Samuel to anoint Saul as Israel's first king. Saul starts his reign well but then makes a series of colossally bad choices, so Samuel tells Saul that he will be replaced. Saul's successor will be a shepherd named David. The jealous king seeks to kill David, who runs for his life. David rejects opportunities to kill Saul himself, saying, "The LORD forbid that I should stretch forth mine hand against the LORD's anointed" (26:11 KJV). At the end of 1 Samuel, Saul dies battling the Philistines, making way for David to become king.

QUOTABLE

> "To obey is better than sacrifice, and to heed is better than the fat of rams" (15:22 NIV).

UNIQUE AND UNUSUAL

The future King Saul is a donkey herder (9:5) who tries to hide from his own coronation (10:21–22). As king, Saul breaks his own law by asking a medium to call up the spirit of the dead Samuel (chapter 28).

SO WHAT?

Selfish choices—such as the Israelites' request for a king and Saul's decision to offer a sacrifice he had no business making—can have heavy, even tragic, consequences.

READ 1 SAMUEL 8 AND 13.

● One-Month Course: your next reading is on page 54.   →

● Three-Month Course: your next reading is on page 50.   →

● Six-Month Course: your next reading is on page 50.   →

HEART OF THE BOOK

THE PROPHET SAMUEL

Hannah dedicated her son, Samuel, to the Lord, which is depicted in *Hannah Giving Her Son Samuel to the Priest* by Jan Victors (1619–1676).

The prophet Samuel was the last of Israel's judges. A barren woman, Hannah, begged God for a son, promising to dedicate him to the Lord. So after Samuel was born, she took him to the temple when he was still a child to be with the aging priest Eli and serve in the temple. When Samuel was still a youth, he heard the Lord call his name three times in the middle of the night (1 Samuel 3). After that, God continued speaking to him, and "all Israel. . . knew that Samuel had been established as a prophet of the LORD" (1 Samuel 3:20 NKJV).

When Samuel was a young man, Eli's sinful sons died in battle, and Eli, hearing the news, collapsed and died. After this, Samuel became judge of Israel. He also was a military leader, helping subdue the nation's fearsome enemies, the Philistines (1 Samuel 7:3–14). Samuel was counted the greatest, most righteous man of God since Moses (Jeremiah 15:1).

Samuel's sons, however, didn't follow in his footsteps, and as he aged, Israel's tribal leaders rejected them as judges and asked for a king. So God directed Samuel to anoint Saul as Israel's first regent. However, years later, after Saul had continually disobeyed the Lord, God sent Samuel to Bethlehem to secretly anoint David as king instead. Samuel died at a good old age and was mourned by all Israel (1 Samuel 28:3). Sometime after his death, Samuel's spirit appeared to warn Saul of his doom (1 Samuel 28:4–19).

READ 1 SAMUEL 3 AND 7.

● Three-Month Course: your next reading is on page 51.   →

● Six-Month Course: your next reading is on page 51.   →

HEART OF THE BOOK

SAUL—A TRAGIC STORY

One day the Israelites demanded that Samuel give them a king. Samuel warned that a king would tax the people and force them into his service, but the people still insisted, so God told Samuel to anoint tall, good-looking Saul as ruler. Saul started very well. When the city of Jabesh Gilead was under attack, the Spirit of God came upon Saul in great power and he led the Israelites to a dramatic victory over the enemy. He later "fought against all his enemies on every side," and God gave him victory "wherever he turned" (1 Samuel 14:47 NKJV).

But fear, a lust for power, and man-pleasing began causing him to make repeated poor choices—and when he disobediently offered a sacrifice to God, Samuel told Saul that he would be replaced. Saul went on to further disobey God's specific commands concerning the Amalekites. Then "the Spirit of the LORD had departed from Saul, and an evil spirit from the LORD tormented him" (1 Samuel 16:14 NIV).

King Saul eventually turned from the Lord and was killed in a battle with the Philistines. Elie Marcuse (1817–1902) painted this tragic ending in *Death of King Saul.*

At first, Saul loved David, and the music David played brought peace to the troubled king, but after a while fits of jealous rage seized Saul and he sought to kill David, who ran for his life. But Saul was still king, so David rejected two opportunities to kill him, saying, "The LORD forbid that I should stretch forth mine hand against the LORD's anointed" (1 Samuel 26:11 KJV). At the end of 1 Samuel, Saul died in battle against the Philistines. After that, David became king.

READ 1 SAMUEL 11 AND 15.

● Three-Month Course: your next reading is on page 54.   →
● Six-Month Course: your next reading is on page 54.   →

PRINCE JONATHAN

Jonathan was King Saul's son and was very courageous. Once when Saul and his army feared to face the Philistines, just Jonathan and his armor bearer attacked a garrison. Jonathan stated, "Perhaps the LORD will help us, for. . . he can win a battle whether he has many warriors or only a few!" (1 Samuel 14:6 NLT). And he gained a tremendous victory. Later, after David killed Goliath, "the soul of Jonathan was knit to the soul of David, and Jonathan loved him as himself" (1 Samuel 18:1 NASB). Jonathan was very generous. He gave up his claim to the throne and vowed to support David as king (1 Samuel 23:16–18). When Jonathan died in battle, David greatly mourned him (2 Samuel 1:17–27).

READ 1 SAMUEL 14:1–23 AND 20.

DAVID AND GOLIATH

One day the Philistines were arrayed in battle against the Israelites, and a giant named Goliath shouted out a challenge. He dared any Israelite soldier to face him in single combat. Whichever champion lost, his people would become slaves. For forty days, Goliath repeated his words, but no Israelite dared fight him. Then David stepped up and accepted the challenge. As he rushed forward, he cried, "You come against me with sword and spear and javelin, but I come against you in the name of the LORD Almighty" (1 Samuel 17:45 NIV). David swung his sling, sent a stone slamming into the giant's forehead, and Goliath dropped. The Philistine army fled, and God gave the Israelites a great victory. David became Israel's hero.

READ 1 SAMUEL 17 AND PSALM 35.

David's victory over Goliath that led the Israelites to defeat the Philistines is shown in *David and Goliath* by Michelangelo (1475–1564).

DAVID'S DEEP DISCOURAGEMENT

Saul became jealous of David and twice tried to kill him. David fled, and Saul repeatedly led his army out, obsessed with trying to kill him (1 Samuel 23:7–8, 14). After years of barely escaping Saul, David began to doubt that God would protect him, let alone fulfill His promises to make him king. "David kept thinking to himself, 'Someday Saul is going to get me. The best thing I can do is escape to the Philistines. Then. . .I will finally be safe'" (1 Samuel 27:1 NLT). There's no indication that David prayed about this decision, but the next thing we hear, he and his six hundred men and their families had gone to Gath (1 Samuel 27:2–3). This ended up causing him great trouble.

READ PSALMS 7 AND 94.

TRIUMPH OVER DISASTER

David's men were away from Ziklag for a few days, and when they returned, they found their town burned and all their wives and children gone. David and his men "wept until there was no strength in them to weep" (1 Samuel 30:4 NASB). He was in deep despair, but instead of giving up, "David encouraged himself in the LORD his God" (1 Samuel 30:6 KJV). He then asked God if they could possibly find or overtake the raiders at this late date. God answered that they would not only overtake them, but recover everyone. Sure enough, after several days, they found the enemy camp, attacked it, fought furiously, and rescued everyone. When David was at his wit's end, he looked to God.

When David was troubled or sad, he turned to God and played music for comfort. This is depicted in *King David Playing the Harp* by Gerard van Honthorst (1592–1656).

READ 1 SAMUEL 30 AND PSALM 37.

BASIC SURVEY

2 SAMUEL

AUTHOR: Unknown, but not Samuel—since the events of the book take place after his death. Some suggest Abiathar the priest (15:35).

DATE: Approximately 1010–970 BC, the reign of King David.

IN TEN WORDS OR LESS

David becomes Israel's greatest king—but with major flaws.

DETAILS, PLEASE

When King Saul dies, David is made king by the southern tribe of Judah. After the death of Saul's son Ish-bosheth, king of the northern tribes, David becomes ruler of all Israel. God promises David, "Your throne will be established forever" (7:16 NIV). Military victories make Israel strong, but David commits adultery with a beautiful neighbor, Bathsheba, then has her husband, Uriah, murdered. David repents and God forgives his sins, but their consequences will affect David powerfully. David's family begins to splinter apart. David's son, Amnon, rapes his half sister, and a second son, Absalom—full brother to the violated girl—kills Amnon. Absalom later pulls a military coup, causing his father to flee for his life. Ultimately, David returns to Jerusalem to reassert his kingship.

QUOTABLE

> "Who am I, O Lord GOD? And what is my house, that You have brought me this far?" (7:18 NKJV).

UNIQUE AND UNUSUAL

David's nephew killed a Philistine, "a huge man with six fingers on each hand and six toes on each foot, twenty-four in all" (21:20 NLT). David's top soldier, Adino, once killed eight hundred men single-handedly (23:8).

SO WHAT?

King David's story highlights the vital importance of the choices we make. Who would have guessed that such a great man could fall into such terrible sin?

READ 2 SAMUEL 5 AND PSALM 17.

● One-Month Course: your next reading is on page 61. →

● Three-Month Course: your next reading is on page 55. →

● Six-Month Course: your next reading is on page 55. →

HEART OF THE BOOK

DAVID—A GODLY KING

When Saul continually disobeyed
God, Samuel informed him that God
had chosen "a man after His own
heart" as king (1 Samuel 13:14 NKJV)
who would do things God's way. The
apostle Peter underlined this, saying:
"I have found David the son of Jesse, a
man after My heart, who will do all My
will" (Acts 13:22 NASB). David not only
loved God passionately, but proved it
by obeying Him. "David did what was

King David was chosen by God for his righteousness and love for the Lord.

right in the eyes of the LORD, and had not turned aside from anything that
He commanded him all the days of his life, except in the matter of Uriah the
Hittite" (1 Kings 15:5 NKJV).

David felt guilty living in a palace of costly stones, cedar, and gold, whereas
the ark of the covenant symbolizing the presence of God resided in a mere
tent. He wanted to build God a house, but instead God promised to build
David's house: "Your house and your kingdom will endure forever before me;
your throne will be established forever" (2 Samuel 7:16 NIV). This prophecy
was ultimately fulfilled in Jesus Christ, of whom the angel said, "The Lord
God will give him the throne of his father David, and. . .his kingdom will
never end" (Luke 1:32–33 NIV).

David was also an anointed musician who wrote many psalms of praise
to God. His music even had the power to soothe King Saul's troubled mind
(1 Samuel 16:23). David organized the temple singers and even invented
new musical instruments (Amos 6:5 NKJV).

READ 2 SAMUEL 7 AND PSALM 55.

● Three-Month Course: your next reading is on page 61.   →

● Six-Month Course: your next reading is on page 56.   →

CLOSER LOOK

DAVID BUILDS AN EMPIRE

For seven years after the Philistines had defeated Israel and killed King Saul, the Israelites were engaged in a civil war. When David was proclaimed king of all Israel, the Philistines became alarmed and decided to crush Is-

rael once again. But when they massed their armies south of Jerusalem, David attacked and defeated them. When the Philistines advanced again, God gave David specific battle instructions. "So David did as God commanded him, and they drove back the army of the Philistines." He "attacked the Philistines and subdued them" (1 Chronicles 14:16; 2 Samuel 8:1 NKJV).

King David followed God and helped build Israel into a powerful empire.

After these victories, "the LORD brought the fear of him on all the nations" (1 Chronicles 14:17 NASB). David then defeated Moab. "So the Moabites became subject to David and brought him tribute" (2 Samuel 8:2 NIV). At this time, the Aramean kingdoms to the far north were battling each other, so David chose this strategic moment to launch an attack far beyond his borders—and defeated much greater armies. With this victory, he fulfilled an ancient prophecy that God would give the Israelites not just Canaan, but all lands from the Red Sea to the Euphrates River (Exodus 23:31). Even Joshua hadn't fulfilled this.

David went from being a persecuted fugitive to king of an empire stretching from Egypt to the Euphrates. He and his son Solomon ruled over this far-reaching empire for nearly seventy years. Even the Persians, some five hundred years later, would hear of its fame (Ezra 4:20).

READ 2 SAMUEL 8 AND PSALM 20.

● Six-Month Course: your next reading is on page 57.   →

CLOSER LOOK

DAVID AND BATHSHEBA

One evening when David was on his palace roof, he glanced down into a neighboring courtyard and saw a beautiful woman named Bathsheba bathing. She was the wife of Uriah, one of David's soldiers, who was presently out with the army. David immediately had Bathsheba brought to him and committed adultery with her. When she became pregnant, David summoned her husband home from the war, hoping that he'd sleep with her and think that the child was his. When Uriah didn't do that, David had him placed in the heaviest fighting, then had the army withdraw from him, leaving him to die. David then took Bathsheba as his own wife.

The prophet Nathan confronted David by telling him the story of a rich man who had many flocks, but who mercilessly butchered a poor man's only ewe lamb. When David heard the account, he was furious and declared, "As the LORD lives, surely the man who has done this deserves to die." Then Nathan announced, "You are the man!" (2 Samuel 12:5, 7 NASB). David then repented and poured out a confession to God (see Psalm 51).

God forgave him, but there were still consequences: the baby conceived in the tryst died. "Then David comforted his wife Bathsheba, and went in to her and lay with her; and she gave birth to a son, and he named him Solomon. Now the LORD loved him and sent word through Nathan the prophet, and he named him Jedidiah [Beloved of the LORD]" (2 Samuel 12:24–25 NASB).

READ 2 SAMUEL 11:1–12:15, AND PSALM 51.

 Six-Month Course: your next reading is on page 58. →

CLOSER LOOK

ABSALOM'S REBELLION

Nathan had told David, "You have struck down Uriah the Hittite with the sword. . . . Now therefore, the sword shall never depart from your house. . . . Thus says the LORD, 'Behold, I will raise up evil against you from your own household'" (2 Samuel 12:9–11 NASB).

This is how that trouble came about: David's eldest son, Amnon, who was first in line for the throne, raped his half sister, Tamar. A second son, Absalom—full brother to the violated girl—then killed Amnon in revenge. Absalom fled and lived in exile for three years, but eventually David was persuaded to forgive him and invited him back to Jerusalem.

Absalom was a strikingly handsome man (2 Samuel 14:25–26), and considering that he had exacted "justice" when his father hadn't, began to think that he'd make a better king. So he conspired to steal the kingdom from his father, and day after day he wooed the Israelites who came to Jerusalem seeking audiences with King David. He would tell them that David hadn't appointed anyone to hear their case, then say that he wished someone would appoint *him* judge so that he could administer justice. "So Absalom stole the hearts of the men of Israel" (2 Samuel 15:6 NKJV).

When he had won much of the nation over, Absalom then gathered an army and marched on Jerusalem. David barely heard about it in time, fled Jerusalem, and crossed the Jordan River, where he gathered his armies. After Absalom died in battle with David's men, David returned to Jerusalem to reassert his kingship.

READ 2 SAMUEL 15 AND 18.

● Six-Month Course: your next reading is on page 61.

CIVIL WAR IN ISRAEL

After Saul's death, his general Abner declared Saul's son Ish-Bosheth king of Israel, who then reigned in the north. However, it was clearly God's will that *David* become king. Even Saul's firstborn, Jonathan, had conceded that (1 Samuel 23:16–18). So the southern tribes followed David. "Now there was a long war between the house of Saul and the house of David. But David grew stronger and stronger, and the house of Saul grew weaker and weaker"

(2 Samuel 3:1 NKJV). David could have mounted a full-scale invasion of the north, but that wasn't God's will, so he patiently waited on God. After the death of Abner, Ish-Bosheth was greatly weakened, and soon was assassinated by his own servants. Then all Israel accepted David as king (2 Samuel 5:1–5).

A famous battle between their armies is depicted in *Combat between Soldiers of Ish-Bosheth and David* by Gustave Doré (1832–1883). After Ish-Bosheth was killed, David became king of all Israel.

READ 2 SAMUEL 2:1–11 AND 3:1–21.

DAVID CONQUERS JERUSALEM

When David became king of all Israel, he needed a more central capital, so he chose the Canaanite stronghold of Jebus, formerly called Jerusalem. Jebus had high walls, but David had grown up nearby and knew that their water supply was just outside the walls, and a small opening led under the city—and

from there a water shaft went up. David sent men through the opening and they scaled the water shaft (2 Samuel 5:6–8; 1 Chronicles 11:4–6). Once inside, they opened the gate for the army. David then renamed it Jerusalem, and it became known as the City of David, "the city which the LORD had chosen out of all the tribes of Israel, to put His name there" (2 Chronicles 12:13 NKJV).

David's knowledge of the city's walls allowed him to enter and conquer the city of Jebus. He then renamed it Jerusalem—also called the City of David.

READ PSALMS 48 AND 87.

BRINGING THE ARK TO JERUSALEM

One day David decided to bring the ark of God to Jerusalem. But he failed to read the scriptures that specified *how* to transport it (Exodus 25:10–14; Numbers 4:5–6, 15). So they placed it on an oxcart and headed down the road. Suddenly the oxen stumbled. A man steadied the ark to keep it from falling and was struck dead, so David was afraid to bring it into Jerusalem. Years passed before he attempted to move it again. By now, however, he had learned that the Levites were to carry it. Once again David gathered priests and Levites, and once again they moved the ark. This time they did it the *right* way and brought it safely into Jerusalem.

David moved the ark of the covenant to Jerusalem. The celebratory scene is shown in this image titled *David Dancing before the Ark.*

READ 2 SAMUEL 6 AND PSALM 80.

THE PLAGUE AND THE TEMPLE

God can get great good out of people's serious mistakes. One day David decided to number all the fighting men of Israel to know how strong he was. "God was very displeased with the census, and he punished Israel for it" (1 Chronicles 21:7 NLT). He sent an angel to bring a plague, and seventy thousand people died. When the angel arrived at Jerusalem, David prayed for God to spare the people, so God stopped the angel on Mount Moriah and instructed David to build an altar there. Then David realized, "This is the house of the LORD God, and this is the altar of burnt offering for Israel" (1 Chronicles 22:1 NKJV). And the temple of God was built there (2 Chronicles 3:1).

READ 2 SAMUEL 24 AND PSALM 28.

BASIC SURVEY

1 KINGS

AUTHOR: Not stated and unknown; one early tradition claimed Jeremiah wrote 1 and 2 Kings.

DATE: Covering events from about 970–850 BC, 1 Kings was probably written sometime after the Babylonian destruction of Jerusalem in 586 BC.

IN TEN WORDS OR LESS

Israel divides into rival northern and southern nations.

DETAILS, PLEASE

After David's death, Solomon becomes king and builds God a temple in Jerusalem. God gives Solomon great wisdom, power, and wealth. Sadly, Solomon's wisdom fails him and he marries seven hundred wives, many of whom are foreign women who turn his heart to idols. When he dies, only the southern tribes follow his son Rehoboam in a nation called Judah. A former royal official named Jeroboam becomes king of the ten northern tribes; he initiates idol worship and many wicked rulers follow. Later, the prophet Elijah confronts evil King Ahab (and his wife, Jezebel) of Israel over their worship of the false god Baal.

QUOTABLE

> "Answer me, LORD, answer me, so these people will know that you, LORD, are God, and that you are turning their hearts back again" (18:37 NIV).

UNIQUE AND UNUSUAL

Scholars say 1 and 2 Kings were originally a single volume—and were split in half to allow for copying onto normal-sized scrolls.

SO WHAT?

Solomon's example provides a strong warning: even the most blessed person can drift from God and make big mistakes.

READ PSALM 72 AND PROVERBS 19.

● One-Month Course: your next reading is on page 68.   →

● Three-Month Course: your next reading is on page 62.   →

● Six-Month Course: your next reading is on page 62.   →

HEART OF THE BOOK

SOLOMON'S RISE AND FALL

King David, in declining health, named Solomon (his son with Bathsheba) as his successor. After David's death, God spoke to Solomon in a dream, offering him anything he wanted—and Solomon chose wisdom. He requested, "Give therefore thy servant an understanding heart to judge thy people, that I may discern between good and bad: for who is able to judge this thy so great a people?" (1 Kings 3:9 KJV). God was so pleased with Solomon's request that in addition to giving him great wisdom, He gave him tremendous power and wealth.

Solomon soon built God a permanent temple in Jerusalem, and the Lord visited him again to promise blessings for obedience and trouble for disobedience (1 Kings 9:1–9). If His people disobeyed Him, God would

Solomon was named king when David, his father, died.

even abandon this temple Solomon had built. For most of his life Solomon *was* faithful, so God fulfilled His promise to make him wealthier, wiser, and more glorious than all other kings on earth.

Sadly, as Solomon grew old, his wisdom failed him; he married seven hundred women, many of them foreigners. Solomon compromised to please his pagan wives, and as a result, the Spirit of God lifted from his life and his wisdom departed. Worst of all, Solomon led all Israel into great sin. Therefore, God determined to remove most of his kingdom, leaving only Judah to David's line.

Nehemiah said, "Among many nations there was no king like him, who was beloved of his God; and God made him king over all Israel. Nevertheless pagan women caused even him to sin" (Nehemiah 13:26 NKJV).

READ 1 KINGS 3 AND 9.

● Three-Month Course: your next reading is on page 68.   →

● Six-Month Course: your next reading is on page 63.   →

SOLOMON BUILDS GOD'S TEMPLE

David had made extensive preparations for building the temple, and once Solomon became king, he requested King Hiram of Tyre to send the final cedar logs. Then, in the fourth year of his reign, Solomon began building, and Hiram sent skilled architects and stonemasons to help him. He also needed artisans to create pillars, statues of oxen, carts, a great basin, and other articles of bronze—as well as many smaller bowls, cups, and objects of gold and silver. A skilled bronze-worker named Huram (an Israelite) was living in Tyre, so King Hiram sent him as well.

It took seven years for King Solomon to build the temple. This lithograph shows Solomon discussing his plans.

This work took a tremendous amount of manpower, and though many Israelites helped, the main labor force were descendants of the Canaanites who remained in Israel. David organized them into labor gangs and set them to work (1 Chronicles 22:1–2). In addition, Solomon conscripted tens of thousands of Israelites to chop down cedars in Lebanon, quarry stones, and oversee the labor (1 Kings 5:13–16).

It took Solomon only seven years to do all the construction. Then the temple was complete, paneled inside with cedar boards and covered with gold. And all the articles for the temple were finished. The priests placed the ark of God in the Holy Place inside the temple. Then Solomon dedicated God's house. When he finished praying, fire fell from heaven and consumed the sacrifices, and the cloud of the Lord's presence completely filled the temple (1 Kings 8:1–11; 2 Chronicles 7:1–3).

READ 1 KINGS 6 AND 2 CHRONICLES 6.

● Six-Month Course: your next reading is on page 64.   →

CLOSER LOOK

REHOBOAM AND JEROBOAM

Jeroboam led the Israelites away from God when he set up two golden calves to worship.

Because of Solomon's sins, God had vowed to tear most of the kingdom away from David's descendants, so while Solomon was still king, God sent the prophet Ahijah to anoint Jeroboam (one of Solomon's officers) king over the northern ten tribes.

After Solomon died, all Israel gathered to make his son Rehoboam king. But first they complained that his father had imposed heavy taxes and labor requirements on them; if he'd lighten their load, they would serve him faithfully. Rehoboam checked with the older counselors and they advised him to listen to the people. But Rehoboam's young companions convinced him to "show them who was boss" by declaring that he'd make their load even heavier. When the northern tribes heard this answer, they revolted. Then Jeroboam became their king.

God promised Jeroboam: "If you do whatever I command you and walk in obedience to me. . .I will be with you. I will build you a dynasty as enduring as the one I built for David" (1 Kings 11:38 NIV). But when Jeroboam realized that his people would continue going to Jerusalem to worship God, he worried that they'd eventually give their allegiance to Rehoboam. Therefore, "on the advice of his counselors," Jeroboam set up golden calves in the northern kingdom to worship, so his people wouldn't go to Judah (1 Kings 12:28 NLT). This led the Israelites into idolatry, and God warned that He'd judge Jeroboam and his entire kingdom as a result.

READ 1 KINGS 11–12.

● Six-Month Course: your next reading is on page 65.   →

Ahab, Jezebel, and Elijah

In northern Israel, Ahab son of Omri became king, and he "did more evil in the eyes of the Lord than any of those before him" (1 Kings 16:30 niv). He not only worshipped the golden calves, but he married Jezebel, a Canaanite princess from Sidon, and began to worship her gods. Ahab built a temple for Baal in Samaria, and soon 450 prophets of Baal and 400 prophets of Asherah ate daily at Jezebel's table and promoted idol worship in Israel. Jezebel then launched a campaign to massacre every prophet of God (1 Kings 18:13, 19).

God raised up a powerful, miracle-working prophet named Elijah to withstand them. He called for a devastating drought on the land to punish Ahab and all Israel for their idolatry. Later, he challenged the priests of Baal on top of Mount Carmel to prove that their god was real by praying for him

to send down fire from heaven to devour their sacrifice. Baal failed to respond, and only the true God sent fire.

One day, Ahab coveted the vineyard of an Israelite named Naboth, and when Naboth declined to sell it, Jezebel had false witnesses testify that he had "blasphemed God" (1 Kings 21:10 nkjv). Innocent Naboth was then stoned for blasphemy, and Ahab—the *real* blasphemer—took his vineyard.

Ahab did evil in the eyes of the Lord, such as when he blasphemed to get Naboth's vineyard. This painting by Sir Frank Dicksee (1853–1928) is titled *Jezebel and Ahab Meeting Elijah in Naboth's Vineyard*.

Elijah declared, "There was never anyone like Ahab, who sold himself to do evil in the eyes of the Lord, urged on by Jezebel his wife" (1 Kings 21:25 niv).

READ 1 KINGS 16:29–17:7 AND 21.

 Six-Month Course: your next reading is on page 68. →

THE TWO PROPHETS

Soon after Jeroboam set up the calf idol and an altar in Bethel, a prophet of God arrived from Judah and prophesied against the altar. Immediately it split apart and ashes flowed out. God had commanded the prophet not to eat or drink anything in Bethel, but to return straight to Judah, so he set out down the road. But an old prophet rode after him and lied that an angel had told him to bring him back to eat and drink. When they had eaten, the old prophet announced that the young prophet had disobeyed God, and on his way south, a lion killed him. God dealt so severely with the young prophet because He'd done outstanding miracles through him and had spoken clearly to him—yet he disobeyed.

READ 1 KINGS 13 AND PROVERBS 14.

THE WIDOW OF ZAREPHATH

After delivering his warning of a coming drought, Elijah hid in the Cherith ravine. Later, God sent him north to Zarephath, in Phoenicia. There, Elijah asked a widow for bread. She answered that she had only a handful of flour and a little oil. Elijah told her not to fear and promised that if she shared the last of her food with him, God would make her tiny supply of flour and oil last for *years*. The widow believed him and "she and he and her household ate for many days. The bin of flour was

The painting *Elijah and the Widow of Zarephath* by Jan Victors (1619–1676) portrays the woman who was rewarded for feeding the prophet.

not used up, nor did the jar of oil run dry" (1 Kings 17:15–16 NKJV). Jesus Himself spoke of God's tender care for this Canaanite woman (Luke 4:25–26).

READ 1 KINGS 17 AND MATTHEW 15.

GOD VERSUS BAAL

The Baal prophets could not perform the feats that Elijah did in God's name. This image by Gustave Doré (1832–1883) is titled *Slaughter of the Baal Prophets.*

Elijah sent a message to Ahab, telling him to assemble the prophets of Baal on Mount Carmel. Both Elijah and the false prophets built altars, piled wood on them, and put a sacrifice on that. Then Elijah stated, "The God who answers by fire, He is God" (1 Kings 18:24 NASB). The prophets of Baal agreed. But though they prayed all day, there was no answer. Finally they gave up. Then Elijah soaked the wood of his altar with water and prayed to God. Immediately fire blazed down and burned up the sacrifice, the wood, the stones, and the dust. It even vaporized the water in the ditches around the altar. Then all the people cried, "The LORD—he is God!" (1 Kings 18:39 NLT).

READ 1 KINGS 18 AND 2 KINGS 1.

GOD ENCOURAGES ELIJAH

After God sent fire on Mount Carmel, Elijah prayed for rain, and God sent a heavy rainstorm. The drought was over! Many Israelites were convinced that the Lord was God, but the miracles didn't cause a nationwide revival. So when Jezebel threatened to have Elijah killed, and no one stood with him, he became depressed. He fled south and prayed, "It is enough! Now, LORD, take my life" (1 Kings 19:4 NKJV). Instead, God sent an angel to strengthen him. Eventually Elijah arrived at Mount Sinai. God sent a great wind, then an earthquake; then fire swept across the mountain. But the Lord wasn't in these things. Then God spoke to Elijah in "a still small voice" (1 Kings 19:12 KJV) and mightily encouraged him to continue.

READ 1 KINGS 19 AND PSALM 56.

BASIC SURVEY

2 KINGS

AUTHOR: Not stated and unknown; one early tradition claimed Jeremiah wrote 1 and 2 Kings.

DATE: Covering about three hundred years from the 800s BC on, 2 Kings was probably written sometime after the Babylonian destruction of Jerusalem in 586 BC.

IN TEN WORDS OR LESS

Both Jewish nations are destroyed for their disobedience to God.

DETAILS, PLEASE

The story of 1 Kings continues, with more bad rulers, a handful of good ones, and the loss of the two Jewish nations. Early in 2 Kings, Elijah's successor, Elisha, performs many miracles. The northern kingdom's rulers are entirely wicked, and Israel is "carried. . .away into Assyria" (17:6 KJV) in 722 BC. Judah, with occasional good kings such as Hezekiah and Josiah, lasts longer—but in 586 BC, the southern kingdom's capital of Jerusalem falls to Babylonian armies. The Babylonians burn and destroy the temple Solomon had built and break down all the walls of Jerusalem to prevent the Jews from ever rebelling against them again.

QUOTABLE

> The LORD rejected all the descendants of Israel and afflicted them and gave them into the hand of plunderers, until He had cast them out of His sight (17:20 NASB).

UNIQUE AND UNUSUAL

Elijah was the second man (after Enoch in Genesis 5:24) to go straight to heaven without dying. One of Judah's best kings, Josiah, was only eight years old when he took the throne (22:1).

SO WHAT?

Both Israel and Judah found that there were terrible consequences to sin. Even bad examples can be helpful, if we decide not to do the things that bring us trouble.

READ 2 KINGS 2 AND PSALM 41.

● One-Month Course: your next reading is on page 74.   →

● Three-Month Course: your next reading is on page 69.   →

● Six-Month Course: your next reading is on page 69.   →

HEART OF THE BOOK

Elisha the Miracle Worker

Directed by God, the prophet Elijah chose a successor, a man named Elisha. For years, Elisha learned from Elijah—even humbly pouring water as Elijah washed his hands (2 Kings 3:11). Then the Lord decided to take Elijah.

When asked what his final request was, Elisha asked, "Let a double portion of your spirit be upon me" (2 Kings 2:9 NASB). He and Elisha were walking along when "suddenly a chariot of fire and horses of fire appeared and separated the two of them, and Elijah went up to heaven in a whirlwind" (2 Kings 2:11 NIV). Elisha caught his mantle (cloak) as it fell, and the power of Elijah rested on him. Elisha did twice as many miracles as Elijah had done!

Elisha parted the Jordan River, purified a spring of water, called wild bears to protect himself, believed for water for a thirsty army, miraculously increased a widow's oil, raised a boy from the dead, made poisonous stew edible, multiplied barely loaves, healed a leper, made an iron ax head float, blinded an entire enemy army, foresaw that God would supply food for a starving city—and raised a dead man to life after *he himself* was dead!

Elisha performed many miracles, including raising a boy from the dead. This miracle is depicted in the image *Elisha Raising the Shunammite's Son.*

Elisha lived during a very difficult time in northern Israel's history. A powerful northern kingdom called Aram was constantly seeking to conquer them. Wicked King Ahab had died, but his sons ruled. They destroyed idols of Baal, but worshipped the golden calves and vacillated between heeding the prophet and seeking to kill him (2 Kings 6:8–10, 31).

READ 2 KINGS 4–5.

● **Three-Month Course: your next reading is on page 74.** →

● **Six-Month Course: your next reading is on page 70.** →

CLOSER LOOK

BATTLING THE ARAMEANS

The Arameans (called Syrians in the KJV) lived in what is now modern Syria, to the north of Israel. Already in 1000 BC, King David repeatedly battled Aramean kingdoms (2 Samuel 8:3–6). He finally subjugated them, and he and Solomon ruled over them for several decades. But toward the end of Solomon's reign, the Arameans threw off the Israelite yoke and regained their independence.

By the days of Ahab, king of Israel, the Arameans were united in one powerful kingdom and were constantly seeking to conquer Israel. Even though Ahab was a wicked king, there were times when he acknowledged God and followed the advice of His prophets—so God allowed him to defeat the Arameans twice. However, when he had a chance to completely crush them, Ahab foolishly made a peace pact. Later, Ahab waged war with Aram again, but died in battle (1 Kings 20:1–43; 22:1–4, 29–37).

The Arameans continued to oppress Israel during the days of Ahab's sons, Ahaziah and Joram—and during the reigns of later kings such as Jehu, Jehoahaz, and Jehoash. But north of Aram an even more powerful empire was rising—the Assyrians—and the kings of Judah and Israel alternated between alliances with Assyria and Aram, to offset each one's power. About 780 to 770 BC, Jeroboam II of Israel reconquered lands that Aram had taken. Then, in 732 BC, the Assyrians utterly conquered Aram and deported their people. From then on, Assyria was the greatest threat to Israel and Judah.

READ 1 KINGS 20 AND 2 KINGS 6:8–23.

● Six-Month Course: your next reading is on page 71.

CLOSER LOOK

THE NORTHERN KINGDOM

Tiglath-Pileser, who is featured in this stone artwork, led the Assyrians to attack Israel.

About 915 BC, during the reign of Israel's first king, Ahijah prophesied that because Jeroboam had led the northern kingdom into worshipping the golden calves, "the LORD will strike Israel. . . . He will uproot Israel from this good land which He gave to their fathers, and will scatter them beyond the [Euphrates] River" (1 Kings 14:15 NKJV).

Nearly two hundred years passed and they never repented—even though God mercifully sent them prophets like Elijah and Elisha to do miracles and to repeatedly deliver them from their enemies, the Arameans. Finally the prophet Oded declared that "the fierce wrath of the LORD is upon you" (2 Chronicles 28:11 NKJV). It had come time to pay for two centuries of sins and idol worship.

During King Pekah's reign, Tiglath-Pileser of Assyria attacked Israel and sacked many cities. He also conquered the regions of Gilead, Galilee, and the north, and took many captives. After Hoshea became king of Israel, the Assyrians returned—this time to stay—and Hoshea was forced to pay heavy tribute for several years. Then Hoshea tried to get Egypt's help to break free. The Assyrians discovered his plot, invaded the entire country, and after a three-year siege, Samaria fell. Then the Assyrians took all Israel captive. . .and that was the *end* of the northern kingdom.

"This disaster came upon the people of Israel because they. . .had done many evil things, arousing the LORD's anger. Yes, they worshiped idols, despite the LORD's specific and repeated warnings" (2 Kings 17:7, 11–12 NLT).

READ 2 KINGS 15:8–31 AND 17:1–23.

● Six-Month Course: your next reading is on page 74.   →

NAAMAN THE LEPER IS HEALED

Naaman, commander of the Aramean army, was a leper. One day his wife's Hebrew slave girl said, "I wish my master would go to see the prophet in Samaria. He would heal him." Soon Naaman and his servants were standing outside Elisha's door. Elisha sent a servant out saying, "Go and wash yourself seven times in the

Naaman was healed when he washed himself in the Jordan River.

Jordan River. Then. . .you will be healed of your leprosy" (2 Kings 5:3, 10 NLT). Naaman was offended. He complained that the rivers of Damascus were much cleaner than the Jordan. He was about to leave, but his servants pointed out that he'd been told to do something quite simple. It was at least worth trying. So Naaman humbled himself and washed. . .and was healed!

READ 2 KINGS 5 AND LUKE 4:14–30.

THE SIEGE OF SAMARIA

One time the Aramean army besieged Samaria, the capital of Israel, and there was a severe famine in the city. People ate disgusting things to survive. Finally, the king of Israel was ready to give up. However, Elisha told him that by tomorrow morning the siege would be over and there would be more than enough food for everyone. One of the king's officers mocked, "Look, if the LORD would make windows in heaven, could this thing be?" (2 Kings 7:2 NKJV). That night, however, God caused the Arameans to hear the noise of many chariots and horses. Thinking that it was the Egyptian army, the Arameans fled, leaving all their tents and food behind. The next morning the people had plenty of food again.

READ 2 KINGS 6:24–7:29 AND PSALM 104.

RUTHLESS KING JEHU

Elisha sent a prophet to tell Jehu, the fierce army commander, that God had anointed him king of Israel and that he was to wipe out Ahab's wicked house. Jehu immediately raced to Jezreel and slew King Joram (Ahab's son)

and Ahaziah king of Judah (Ahab's relative). Jehu commanded Jezebel's servants to push her out a tower window, and they did. Jehu then besieged the city where Ahab's seventy sons were and persuaded the elders to kill them. Jehu then had all the priests of Baal slain, eliminating Baal worship from Israel. Jehu was a ruthless man, so he gladly did these violent deeds. . .but he didn't truly love God. For example, he refused to get rid of the golden calves—and this doomed the nation.

Jehu was a violent leader and ordered Jezebel's servants to throw her out a window. This scene is depicted in *The Death of Jezebel* by Gustave Doré (1832–1883).

READ 2 KINGS 9– 10.

ELISHA'S FINAL PROPHECY

The Arameans bitterly oppressed Israel, so God had mercy. Forty years had passed since Elisha's last prophecy or miracle, but when he was old and sick, he summoned King Jehoash. First, Elisha had the king shoot an "arrow of deliverance" out the window. Then Elisha told him to seize a bundle of arrows and strike the floor. Jehoash struck three times and stopped. Elisha was angry, saying that he should have struck five or six times; then he would have utterly defeated the Arameans. Sure enough, Jehoram defeated Aram only three times. After he died, Jeroboam II became king. The prophet Jonah declared that Jeroboam would restore the size of the kingdom—and he *did* (2 Kings 14:23–26). Jeroboam did what Jehoash had failed to do.

King Jehoash only struck the floor three times with arrows, and he only defeated the Arameans three times.

READ 2 KINGS 13 AND PSALM 118.

BASIC SURVEY

1 CHRONICLES

AUTHOR: Not stated, but traditionally Ezra the priest.

DATE: Covers the history of Israel, from around 1010 BC (the death of King Saul) to about 970 BC (the death of King David).

IN TEN WORDS OR LESS

King David's reign is detailed and analyzed.

DETAILS, PLEASE

First Chronicles provides a history of Israel, going as far back as Adam. By the eleventh chapter, the story turns to Israel's greatest king, David, with special emphasis on his leadership of national worship. Another important focus is on God's promise that David would have an eternal kingly line through his descendant Jesus Christ.

QUOTABLE

> "And I will establish him in My house and in My kingdom forever; and his throne shall be established forever" (17:14 NKJV).

UNIQUE AND UNUSUAL

First Chronicles covers much of the same information as 2 Samuel does, but without some of the seedier aspects of David's life—such as his adultery with Bathsheba and the engineered killing of her husband, Uriah.

SO WHAT?

The positive focus of 1 Chronicles is designed to remind the Jews that, despite their punishment for sin, they were still God's special people. When God makes a promise, He keeps it.

READ 1 CHRONICLES 16 AND PROVERBS 2.

● One-Month Course: your next reading is on page 77.   →

● Three-Month Course: your next reading is on page 77.   →

● Six-Month Course: your next reading is on page 77.   →

DAVID'S MIGHTY MEN

While David was hiding in the wilderness, God raised up mighty men—fighters of almost superhuman strength and ability—to help him. For example, Gad's greatest warriors joined him. "These Gadites were army commanders; the least was a match for a hundred, and the greatest for a thousand" (1 Chronicles 12:14 NIV). Adino the Eznite, chief among David's captains, "killed eight hundred men at one time" (2 Samuel 23:8 NKJV). Then there

was Shammah. The Philistines had gathered together into a troop. Shammah's men were frightened and fled, but he took a stand alone in the middle of that field and killed all the Philistines who attacked. God gave these men extraordinary strength and skill to establish David as king and to help him build his kingdom.

God strengthened King David's men so that David could build his kingdom. This woodcut of King David was created by Julius Schnorr von Carolsfeld (1794–1872).

READ 1 CHRONICLES 11:10–25 AND 12:1–22.

AMMONITES AND ARAMEANS DEFEATED

One time Hanun, king of Ammon, deliberately offended David. Then, realizing the seriousness of his mistake, he hired two Aramean kingdoms to fight for him. Joab arrived with a medium-sized army and found himself surrounded by over 32,000 soldiers. So he put half the army under the command of his brother. He then said, "If the Arameans are too strong for

me, then come over and help me. . . . And if the Ammonites are too strong for you, I will help you. Be courageous! Let us fight bravely. . . . May the LORD's will be done" (1 Chronicles 19:12–13 NLT). The men of Israel fought so fiercely that the enemy fled from them. They won against superior forces because they fought courageously and well, and had one another's backs.

Although David was not allowed to build the temple, he had an active role in the preparations. Jean Fouquet (c. 1420–1480) painted this image titled *Construction of the Temple of Jerusalem.*

READ 1 CHRONICLES 19 AND PSALM 144.

HIDDEN TREASURE

DAVID PREPARES TO BUILD

David had wanted to build a temple for God, but God told him that he had shed too much blood, so his son would build it. Nevertheless, David had a part to play. As he said, "My son Solomon is still young and inexperienced. And since the Temple to be built for the LORD must be a magnificent structure, famous and glorious throughout the world, I will begin making preparations for it now" (1 Chronicles 22:5 NLT). So David gathered abundant amounts of gold, silver, cedar, and other materials. He had labor gangs quarry stones. He also designed the temple and gave Solomon the blueprints. Because of David's many preparations, it took Solomon only seven years to do the construction (1 Kings 6:37–38).

READ 1 CHRONICLES 28–29.

HIDDEN TREASURE

DAVID ORGANIZES THE LEVITES

About 1445 BC, Moses organized the Levites and assigned them their duties (Numbers 3:14–38), but this was when God's house was a mobile tent (tabernacle) and their duties consisted of constantly dismantling and setting it up. By David's day, the tabernacle had been stationary for centuries, and the Levites no longer had assigned duties. When David was still young, he and Samuel began to organize the Levites by assigning the gatekeepers their

positions (1 Chronicles 9:22). Around 1000 BC, David appointed singers to worship God (1 Chronicles 6:31–43). Around 980 to 970 BC, when he was making preparations for building a stone temple, God inspired him to assign new duties to the remaining divisions of Levites (1 Chronicles 23:1–32).

Once the tabernacle was stationary, David assigned duties to the Levites, who were the priests and caretakers of the tabernacle.

READ 1 CHRONICLES 23 AND PSALM 147.

BASIC SURVEY

2 CHRONICLES

AUTHOR: Not stated, but traditionally Ezra the priest.

DATE: Covers Israelite history from around 970 BC (the accession of King Solomon) to the 500s BC (when exiled Jews return to Jerusalem).

IN TEN WORDS OR LESS

The history of Israel, from Solomon, through division, to destruction.

DETAILS, PLEASE

David's son Solomon is made king, builds the temple, and becomes one of the most prominent rulers ever. But when he dies, the Jewish nation divides. In the remainder of 2 Chronicles, the various kings of the relatively godlier southern nation of Judah are profiled, through the destruction of Jerusalem by the Babylonians. The book ends with the Persian King Cyrus allowing the Jews to rebuild the devastated temple.

QUOTABLE

> "O LORD, God of Israel, there is no God like you in all of heaven and earth. You keep your covenant and show unfailing love to all who walk before you in wholehearted devotion" (6:14 NLT).

UNIQUE AND UNUSUAL

Continuing the positive approach of 1 Chronicles (the two books were originally one), 2 Chronicles ends with two verses that exactly repeat the first three verses of Ezra.

SO WHAT?

God's punishment isn't intended to hurt people but to bring them back to Him.

READ PSALMS 74 AND 105.

● One-Month Course: your next reading is on page 83.   →

● Three-Month Course: your next reading is on page 83.   →

● Six-Month Course: your next reading is on page 78.   →

CLOSER LOOK

A GOOD KING'S MISTAKES

Jehoshaphat was a good king. "The LORD was with Jehoshaphat, because he. . .walked in His commandments and not according to the acts of Israel. Therefore the LORD established the kingdom in his hand. . .and he had riches and honor in abundance. And his heart took delight in the ways of the LORD" (2 Chronicles 17:3–6 NKJV).

But "he made an alliance with Ahab of Israel by having his son marry Ahab's daughter" (2 Chronicles 18:1 NLT). So although he knew that God wanted to destroy evil Ahab (1 Kings 22:20–23), he helped Ahab fight the Arameans. After the battle, a prophet said, "Should you help the wicked and love those who hate the LORD? Therefore the wrath of the LORD is upon you" (2 Chronicles 19:2 NKJV).

"After this Jehoshaphat. . .allied himself with Ahaziah [Ahab's son] king of Israel. He acted wickedly in so doing." They made a fleet of trading ships. Another prophet declared, "Because you have allied yourself with Ahaziah, the LORD has destroyed your works" (2 Chronicles 20:35, 37 NASB). And all his ships were wrecked. After *this*, Jehoshaphat joined Ahab's other son Jehoram in battle against Moab (2 Kings 3:1–14). Although God gave them an initial victory, they failed to conquer Moab.

Nevertheless, Jehoshaphat loved God and trusted Him completely. When the armies of three kings were invading, he prayed, "Our God. . .we have no power to face this vast army that is attacking us. We do not know what to do, but our eyes are on you" (2 Chronicles 20:12 NIV). As a result, God gave him a miraculous victory.

READ 2 CHRONICLES 17 AND 20.

● Six-Month Course: your next reading is on page 79.   →

CLOSER LOOK

HEZEKIAH AND THE ASSYRIANS

King Hezekiah was faithful to God and refused to pay tribute to the Assyrians.

Hezekiah became king of Judah, revolted against Assyria, and refused to pay tribute. He trusted God and was "faithful to the LORD in everything. . . . So the LORD was with him, and Hezekiah was successful in everything he did" (2 Kings 18:6–7 NLT). He became so strong that he even conquered the Philistines.

Years later, however, Sennacherib invaded Judah. Only Jerusalem withstood. Hezekiah sent this message: "I will pay whatever tribute money you demand if you will only withdraw" (2 Kings 18:14 NLT). Sennacherib demanded eleven tons of silver and a ton of gold—so Hezekiah handed over all the silver and gold in his palace and the temple. But after Sennacherib received it, he reneged. He sent an army commander to Jerusalem demanding its surrender, saying that he'd deport everyone to a distant land.

Hezekiah encouraged his people, "With him is only the arm of flesh, but with us is the LORD our God to help us and to fight our battles" (2 Chronicles 32:8 NIV). The commander laughed. "Don't let him fool you into trusting in the LORD. . . . What makes you think that the LORD can rescue Jerusalem from me?" (2 Kings 18:30, 35 NLT).

Hezekiah went into the temple and prayed desperately. A few nights later, God sent an angel into the Assyrian camp and wiped out 185,000 soldiers. After that, Hezekiah "was exalted in the sight of all nations" and many foreigners brought offerings for God (2 Chronicles 32:23 NASB). God not only honored Hezekiah, but restored riches to him.

READ 2 CHRONICLES 31:1–32:23.

● Six-Month Course: your next reading is on page 80.   →

CLOSER LOOK

JOSIAH DESTROYS IDOL WORSHIP

God's temple had been neglected for decades, and King Josiah had workmen repair it. Then the high priest found the lost Law of Moses. A scribe took it to Josiah and read it, and when he heard its warnings for disobedience, Josiah became afraid that judgment was imminent. However, a prophetess named Huldah said that because of Josiah's tender heart, the disaster wouldn't happen in his day.

Josiah now knew just how abhorrent idol worship was to God, so he gathered his people and reaffirmed their commitment to the Lord. He then threw the idols and pagan altars out of the temple of God and got rid of the idolatrous priests throughout Judea. "Neither before nor after Josiah was there a king like him who turned to the LORD as he did—with all his heart and with all his soul and with all his strength" (2 Kings 23:25 NIV). So "Josiah removed all detestable idols from the entire land of Israel" (2 Chronicles 34:33 NLT).

Josiah died while trying to intervene when Pharaoh Necho (seen here as a statue) fought Babylon.

King Josiah committed his life to the Lord, and God richly rewarded him. In 628 BC, the Assyrian king died, and with his once-mighty empire in decline, the Assyrians were forced to abandon northern Israel. With them gone, Josiah expanded his kingdom. The first thing he did was to abolish idols throughout the north.

Then in 609 BC, Pharaoh Neco led an army out of Egypt to help the Assyrians fight the Babylonians. Josiah tried to intervene but died in that battle.

READ 2 CHRONICLES 34–35.

● Six-Month Course: your next reading is on page 83.   →

HIDDEN TREASURE

THE PRIEST AND THE PRINCE

When King Ahaziah died, his mother, Athaliah, sent soldiers to murder all her grandsons. But Princess Jehosheba grabbed her nephew, baby Joash, and hid him in another bedroom. She was the wife of the high priest, Jehoiada, so she smuggled the baby into the temple. For six years Athaliah ruled Judah and enforced Baal worship. Then Jehoiada called the commanders of the temple guards, showed them Prince Joash, and had them swear loyalty. Next he informed all the priests and rulers. Then Jehoiada gathered all of the temple guards, crowned Joash, and shouted, "Long live the king!" (2 Chronicles 23:11 NKJV). The temple guards executed Athaliah; then seven-year-old Joash sat on the throne with Jehoiada to advise him.

READ 2 CHRONICLES 22–23.

HIDDEN TREASURE

AMAZIAH'S FOLLY

When he became king of Judah, Amaziah worshipped the Lord. Therefore, God gave him a great victory over the Edomites. Then, astonishingly, he brought back the idols of Edom and worshipped them. A prophet rebuked the king for worshipping idols that hadn't even been able to save people from *him*. But Amaziah didn't listen. He then challenged Jehoash, king of Israel: "Come, let us face each other in battle." Jehoash answered, "Why should you meddle with trouble so that you fall—you and Judah with you?" (2 Kings 14:10 NKJV). But Amaziah again refused to listen, and in the battle that followed, Judah was defeated. Amaziah was imprisoned in Samaria for ten years. After Jehoash's death, he was released and returned to Judah.

READ 2 CHRONICLES 25 AND PSALM 107.

HEZEKIAH'S SICKNESS

One day King Hezekiah became deathly sick from a boil. God sent Isaiah to tell him to put his house in order, for he would surely die. After Isaiah left his bedchamber, Hezekiah wept bitterly and prayed, reminding God that he had served Him faithfully. God stopped Isaiah before he reached the middle court and sent him back with this message: "I have heard your prayer, I have seen your tears; surely I will heal you. . . . And I will add to your days fifteen years" (2 Kings 20:5–6 NKJV). Despite his miraculous healing, however, "Hezekiah did not repay according to the favor shown him, for his heart was lifted up." But again "Hezekiah humbled himself," and *again* God held back His judgment (2 Chronicles 32:25–26 NKJV).

READ 2 CHRONICLES 32:24-33 AND PSALMS 93-94.

MANASSEH'S EVIL AND REPENTANCE

When Manasseh became king, he became a vassal of the Assyrians. He worshipped Baal and other pagan gods, built them altars in God's temple, practiced witchcraft, consulted mediums, and killed many innocent people. Then the Assyrians suspected Manasseh of plotting against them, so they imprisoned him in Babylon. "In his distress he sought the favor of the LORD his God and humbled himself greatly." God heard him and restored him to his throne. "Then Manasseh knew that the LORD is God" (2 Chronicles 33:12–13 NIV). Manasseh removed the idol altar from God's temple. He tore down all the pagan altars he had built in Jerusalem. Then he restored the altar of the Lord and commanded all Judah to serve the Lord.

READ 2 CHRONICLES 33 AND PSALM 83.

Manasseh originally worshipped other gods—including Baal, as seen in this image. However, he turned to God when he was captured and imprisoned.

BASIC SURVEY

EZRA

AUTHOR: Not stated, but traditionally Ezra, a priest (7:11).
DATE: Approximately 539 BC to the mid-400s BC.

IN TEN WORDS OR LESS

Spiritual renewal begins after the Jews return from exile.

DETAILS, PLEASE

About a half century after the Babylonians sacked Jerusalem and carried the Jews into captivity, Persia is the new world power. King Cyrus allows a group of exiles to return to Judah to rebuild the temple. Some 42,000 people return and resettle the land. Around seventy years later, Ezra is part of a smaller group that also returns. He teaches the Law to the people, who have fallen away from God to the point of intermarrying with nearby pagan nations, something that was strictly forbidden by Moses (7:1–3).

QUOTABLE

> Ezra had prepared his heart to seek the law of the LORD, and to do it, and to teach in Israel statutes and judgments (7:10 KJV).

UNIQUE AND UNUSUAL

Though God has said, "I hate divorce" (Malachi 2:16 NASB), Ezra urged Jewish men to separate from their foreign wives.

SO WHAT?

In Ezra, God shows His willingness to offer a second chance—allowing a nation that had been punished for disobedience to have a fresh start. Guess what? He's still in the second-chance business.

READ EZRA 1–2.

● One-Month Course: your next reading is on page 87.   →
● Three-Month Course: your next reading is on page 87.   →
● Six-Month Course: your next reading is on page 84.   →

REBUILDING GOD'S TEMPLE

In 586 BC, the Babylonians destroyed Jerusalem, tore down the temple Solomon had built, and exiled the Jews to Babylon. Then in 539 BC, the

Persian king Cyrus allowed the Jews to return to Judah and rebuild their temple. In 536 BC, three years later, Zerubbabel led the priests and Levites in laying the foundation of the new temple.

Now, Samaritans were living in the land, and their faith was a mixture of Jewish worship and pagan idolatry. They offered to help rebuild, but when the Jews declined, the Samaritans "set out to discourage the people of Judah and make them afraid to go on building" (Ezra 4:4 NIV).

Cyrus was the king of Persia and allowed the Jews to return to Judah. He is depicted in this painting by Jean Fouquet (c. 1420–1480) titled *Emperor Cyrus the Great of Persia.*

They sent a letter to the new Persian king, Artaxerxes, complaining that this building threatened the peace of his kingdom. Artaxerxes believed them and commanded the Jews to stop. For the next ten years, 530–520 BC, construction on the temple was abandoned.

Cyrus had written an edict permitting the Jews to rebuild, and no law of the Persians could be changed, so they had a *right* to build. But since the present king had ruled against them, the Jews decided to postpone things. They knew that they should build, but reasoned, "The time has not yet come to rebuild the LORD's house" (Haggai 1:2 NIV).

Then God raised up two prophets, Haggai and Zechariah, who encouraged the leaders to finish the work. The Jews began building once again, and in four years, from 520 to 516 BC, they finished all the work and dedicated the new temple (Ezra 6:13–15).

READ EZRA 3–4.

● Six-Month Course: your next reading is on page 85.   →

CLOSER LOOK

Ezra the Scribe

Despite Cyrus's edict allowing the Jews to return to Judea, many of them had continued living in Babylon, and it became a major center of Jewish learning. Ezra was the foremost Jewish scholar during the reign of King Artaxerxes. "Ezra was a scribe who was well versed in the Law of Moses," and he "had determined to study and obey the Law of the Lord and to teach those decrees and regulations to the people of Israel" (Ezra 7:6, 10 nlt).

Besides being a top scholar and teacher, Ezra was a man of great personal faith in God. The priests traveling with him were all carrying valuable treasures of silver and gold for the temple, but Ezra didn't ask the king for armed guards to protect them and the treasure from bandits. He trusted God to protect them on their long journey—and He did!

When Ezra traveled to Israel to teach God's Word, "the king gave him everything he asked for, because the gracious hand of the Lord his God was on him" (Ezra 7:6 nlt). Artaxerxes

Ezra was a scribe who was dedicated to teaching others about God.

sent a letter to his treasurers in the western provinces commanding them to give Ezra whatever he needed. He also sent a letter giving Ezra great judicial and civil authority.

King Artaxerxes wanted to ensure that he had the favor of Israel's God. He needed it. Egypt, right next to Judah, had just revolted and driven out the Persians. The year of Ezra's trip, 458 BC, Artaxerxes was just starting to re-subdue Egypt.

READ EZRA 7–8.

● **Six-Month Course: your next reading is on page 87.**   →

SEARCH FOR A DOCUMENT

The Persian king Artaxerxes told the Jews to stop rebuilding Jerusalem and their temple—but they had received permission from King Cyrus, so they continued working. When Tattenai, the governor, asked them, "Who authorized you to rebuild this temple and to finish it?" (Ezra 5:3 NIV), they replied that Cyrus had. Tattenai then wrote to the Persian king: "Let a search be made in the royal archives of Babylon to see if King Cyrus did in fact issue a decree to rebuild this house of God in Jerusalem" (Ezra 5:17 NIV). A search in the archives of Babylon turned up nothing. But the officials kept looking—and eventually the edict was found in the distant city of Ecbatana. The king then told the Jews to continue rebuilding.

READ EZRA 5-6.

SEPARATING FROM PAGAN WIVES

When Ezra arrived in Judah, he learned that many Jews there were seriously compromising. In disobedience to the Law of Moses, they had been marrying the pagans who lived there (Exodus 34:15–16). It wouldn't be long before they began worshipping their gods and falling into idolatry all over again. They had just survived judgment and exile in Babylon, and God had graciously allowed a remnant to survive and return to their land. But now *this*! Had the pagan women embraced faith in the true God—as Ruth and others had (Ruth 1:16; 2:12; Esther 8:17)—their marriages would have been blessed. But they weren't willing. Thus, painful as it was, Ezra commanded those who had married pagan women to separate from them. And they did.

READ EZRA 9-10.

BASIC SURVEY

NEHEMIAH

AUTHOR: "The words of Nehemiah" (1:1), though Jewish tradition says those words were put on paper by Ezra.

DATE: Approximately 445 BC.

IN TEN WORDS OR LESS

Returning Jewish exiles rebuild the broken walls of Jerusalem.

DETAILS, PLEASE

Nehemiah serves as "the king's cupbearer" (1:11 KJV) in Shushan (Susa), Persia. As a Jew, he's disturbed to learn that even though exiles have been back in Judah for nearly a hundred years, they have not rebuilt the city's walls, devastated by the Babylonians in 586 BC. Nehemiah asks and receives the king's permission to return to Jerusalem, where he leads a team of builders—against much pagan opposition—in reconstructing the walls in only fifty-two days. The quick work on the project shocks the Jews' enemies, who "realized that this work had been done with the help of our God" (6:16 NIV).

QUOTABLE

> Think upon me, my God, for good, according to all that I have done for this people (5:19 KJV).

UNIQUE AND UNUSUAL

Indignant over some fellow Jews' intermarriage with pagans, Nehemiah "cursed them and struck some of them and pulled out their hair" (13:25 NASB).

SO WHAT?

Nehemiah's success in rebuilding Jerusalem's walls provides many leadership principles today—especially his consistent focus on prayer.

READ NEHEMIAH 1 AND 9.

● One-Month Course: your next reading is on page 90. →

● Three-Month Course: your next reading is on page 90. →

● Six-Month Course: your next reading is on page 88. →

CLOSER LOOK

Nehemiah Builds the Wall

During Artaxerxes's reign, a Jew named Nehemiah was the king's cupbearer, a highly trusted servant. Then one of Nehemiah's relatives arrived from Judah with news about the Jews who lived there: "The survivors. . .are there in great distress and reproach. The wall of Jerusalem is also broken down, and its gates are burned with fire" (Nehemiah 1:3 NKJV). Although the temple had been rebuilt, most of the city was still in ruins (Nehemiah 2:17; 7:4). And because it had no walls, the Jews were defenseless against their enemies.

So Nehemiah requested a leave of absence to rebuild Jerusalem, especially the walls. Artaxerxes not only sent Nehemiah there, but appointed him governor of Judah, giving him real authority (Nehemiah 5:14).

After arriving at Jerusalem, Nehemiah inspected the walls then gathered all the Jews and told them his vision. So they began to work. They had nothing to build with other than burned stones buried under tons of rubble. So they dug them out and began setting them in place. It didn't look fancy, but it was a wall.

When the laborers nearly gave up because there was too much rubble, Nehemiah urged them on—and they kept working. "So we rebuilt the wall . . .for the people worked with all their heart." Day after day, they "continued

Nehemiah rebuilt the wall of Jerusalem so that the city was protected.

the work. . .from the first light of dawn till the stars came out" (Nehemiah 4:6, 21 NIV). Finally, the wall was completed, giving the Jews not only real security but tremendous joy.

READ NEHEMIAH 2–3.

● Six-Month Course: your next reading is on page 90.   →

STANDING UP TO THREATS

When Nehemiah and the people began rebuilding the wall around Jerusalem, their enemies were "furious and very indignant, and mocked the Jews" (Nehemiah 4:1 NKJV). They then sent other Jews ten times to warn Nehemiah that an attack was imminent. Nehemiah responded to these threats by posting armed men along the wall in the openings. His enemies tried to trick him into meeting with them, but Nehemiah refused to go. Next, they threatened to report him to the king. Finally, a man warned him that they were coming to kill him in the night and urged him to hide in the temple. But no matter how they threatened him or tried to strike fear into his heart, Nehemiah refused to give up and kept building.

READ NEHEMIAH 4 AND 6.

COMPROMISING WITH THE ENEMY

Unfortunately, many of the Jewish nobles of Judah had pledged their loyalty to Tobiah the Ammonite official, constantly stood up for him, and informed him of everything Nehemiah said (Nehemiah 2:10; 6:17–19). After a few years as governor, Nehemiah returned to the Persian capital to report to the king. When he returned to Jerusalem, he learned that Eliashib the priest, who had authority over the temple storerooms, was allied with Tobiah. There

Tobiah used the temple storeroom for his personal goods until Nehemiah cleaned and rededicated the space.

was a large storeroom in the temple where tithes of grain, wine, and oil were kept, and Eliashib had given this room to Tobiah. Nehemiah angrily tossed all Tobiah's household goods out of the room. Then he ordered it cleansed and rededicated to God's purposes. (See also Ephesians 4:27.)

READ NEHEMIAH 8 AND 13.

BASIC SURVEY

ESTHER

AUTHOR: Not stated, but perhaps Ezra or Nehemiah.

DATE: Approximately 486–465 BC, during the reign of King Ahasuerus (also known as Xerxes) of Persia. Esther became queen around 479 BC.

IN TEN WORDS OR LESS

Beautiful Jewish girl becomes queen, saves fellow Jews from slaughter.

DETAILS, PLEASE

In a nationwide beauty contest, young Esther becomes queen of Persia without revealing her Jewish heritage. When a royal official plots to kill every Jew in the country, Esther risks her own life to request the king's protection. The king, pleased with Esther, is shocked by his official's plan and has the man hanged—while decreeing that the Jews should defend themselves against the planned slaughter. Esther's people prevail and commemorate the event with a holiday called Purim.

QUOTABLE

> Esther obtained favor in the sight of all who saw her (2:15 NKJV).

> "Who knows whether you have come to the kingdom
> for such a time as this?" (4:14 NKJV).

UNIQUE AND UNUSUAL

God's name is never mentioned in the book of Esther. Neither is prayer, though Esther asks her fellow Jews to fast for her before she approaches the king (4:16).

SO WHAT?

When we find ourselves in bad situations, it may be for the same reason Esther did—to accomplish something good.

READ ESTHER 1–2.

● One-Month Course: your next reading is on page 93.   →

● Three-Month Course: your next reading is on page 93.   →

● Six-Month Course: your next reading is on page 91.   →

CLOSER LOOK

Esther and Mordecai

One evening King Xerxes of Persia commanded Queen Vashti to appear before his guests to display her beauty, but Vashti refused. As a result, she was deposed and Xerxes sought a new queen. Now, in the capital lived a Jew named Mordecai. He had a beautiful young cousin named Hadassah (Esther), and when her parents died, he'd taken her in as his own daughter. Esther was brought to Xerxes's palace and "the king was attracted to Esther" and "made her queen" (Esther 2:17 NIV).

After some time, Xerxes appointed Haman the Agagite as his right-hand man, and Haman became angry at Mordecai because he refused to bow to him. Haman plotted not only to kill Mordecai, but to exterminate all

Jews in the Persian Empire. He persuaded King Xerxes to agree to this. When Mordecai found out, he asked Esther to intercede for her people. Esther replied that anyone who went into the inner court to the king uninvited was put to death. The person's life was spared only if the king held out his golden scepter.

Nevertheless, Esther went in, and Xerxes held out the golden scepter. Esther then pled for her life and the

Esther was made queen and saved the Jews from being massacred. She is depicted here in the painting *Esther* by Edwin Long (1829–1891).

lives of her people. When the king demanded to know what man had dared plot such a massacre, Esther revealed that it was evil Haman. The king commanded Haman to be executed and gave Haman's position and ring of authority to Mordecai. And this day of the Jews' deliverance was established as a new feast day called Purim.

READ ESTHER 3–4.

● Six-Month Course: your next reading is on page 93. →

HAMAN THE AGAGITE

Persian officials had plotted against Daniel (Daniel 6:1–9), so wary of anti-Semitism, Mordecai had advised Esther not to reveal her nationality (Esther 2:10). Mordecai's fears were well founded.

Xerxes appointed Haman, an Agagite, as his right-hand man. The Agagites were descendants of Agag, the Amalekite king, and were age-old, bitter enemies of God's people (Exodus 17:8–14; 1 Samuel 15:7–8). Saul had been ordered to wipe out the Amalekites, but had failed, as they still existed in David's day and

Haman plotted to kill the Jews, but he was stopped by Esther. They are seen in this painting titled *Esther, Ahasuerus, and Haman* by Jan Steen (c.1626–1679).

Hezekiah's day (1 Samuel 27:8; 1 Chronicles 4:41–43). This is why Mordecai refused to bow down to Haman. He wasn't merely being stubborn. The situation turned dangerous, however, when Haman learned that Mordecai was Jewish. But God protected the Jews from Haman's plot.

READ ESTHER 5–7.

PERSIA'S IRREVERSIBLE LAWS

When Esther asked Xerxes to countermand Haman's edict (to destroy the Jews), he stated that no Persian law could be changed (Esther 8:3–8). But he sent out a *new* edict, allowing the Jews to defend themselves and to attack their enemies. This strange feature of Persian law caused much trouble for God's people. For example, Darius had appointed Daniel as a top governor. This made many Persian officials jealous, so they persuaded Darius to decree that for thirty days no one must pray to any god—only to Darius. All offenders were to be thrown to the lions. Darius agreed. When he learned that Daniel had prayed to God, he tried to rescue him, but was also reminded that no law of the Medes and Persians could be annulled (Daniel 6:14–15).

READ ESTHER 8–10.

BASIC SURVEY

JOB

AUTHOR: Not stated.

DATE: Unclear, but many believe Job is one of the oldest stories in the Bible, perhaps from approximately 1700 BC.

IN TEN WORDS OR LESS

God allows human suffering for His own purposes.

DETAILS, PLEASE

Job is a wealthy farmer from Uz. He's "perfect and upright" (1:1 KJV). Satan receives God's permission to attack Job's possessions—and causes the loss of thousands of sheep, camels, oxen, donkeys. . .and worst of all, Job's ten children. Job keeps his faith. Satan then receives God's permission to attack Job's health—but in spite of terrible suffering, Job refuses to "curse God, and die" as his wife suggests (2:9 KJV). Job's suffering is worsened by four "friends" who accuse him of causing his own trouble. In the end, God speaks, implying that Job should simply trust His way. By story's end, God has restored Job's health and possessions and given him ten more children.

QUOTABLE

> "I came naked from my mother's womb, and I will be naked when I leave. The LORD gave me what I had, and the LORD has taken it away. Praise the name of the LORD!" (1:21 NLT).

> Man that is born of a woman is of few days and full of trouble (14:1 KJV).

UNIQUE AND UNUSUAL

The book of Job pictures Satan coming into God's presence (1:6). It also gives a clear Old Testament hint of Jesus' work, when Job says, "I know that my Redeemer lives, and He shall stand at last on the earth" (19:25 NKJV).

SO WHAT?

Trouble isn't necessarily a sign of sin in a person's life. It may be something God allows to draw us closer to Him.

READ JOB 1–2.

● One-Month Course: your next reading is on page 99.   →

● Three-Month Course: your next reading is on page 94.   →

● Six-Month Course: your next reading is on page 94.   →

HEART OF THE BOOK

JOB'S SUFFERING

About 1700 BC, a man named Job lived in the land of Uz, southeast of Canaan. Job was not only an extremely wealthy man, but was very righteous and constantly communed with God. As a result, God put a hedge of protection around Job and everything that he owned.

One day the devil challenged God, "Stretch out Your hand and touch all that he has, and he will surely curse You to Your face!" (Job 1:11 NKJV). So God allowed Satan to take away all of Job's possessions, even to kill his sons and daughters, but still Job worshipped God, even though he was convinced that God Himself had sent this disaster (Job 1:13–21).

Then Satan received permission to strike Job with disgusting, painful boils from head to toe, but still Job refused to curse God. Job suffered for *months* before his

Despite all of Job's suffering, he refused to curse God. His wife, who didn't understand his righteousness, is shown here in *Job Mocked by His Wife* by Georges de La Tour (1593–1652).

friends arrived (Job 7:3–5). Day after day, he thought intensely about his suffering. But it made no sense, for Job had been taught to believe that God always rewards righteousness and judges sin, yet he could think of nothing he had done that warranted such punishment.

However, God blessed Job afterward (see Job 42:10–17). James tells us, "As an example of patience in the face of suffering, take the prophets who spoke in the name of the Lord. As you know, we count as blessed those who have persevered. You have heard of Job's perseverance and have seen what the Lord finally brought about. The Lord is full of compassion and mercy" (James 5:10–11 NIV).

READ JOB 3–4.

● Three-Month Course: your next reading is on page 99.   →

● Six-Month Course: your next reading is on page 95.   →

CLOSER LOOK

JOB'S FRIENDS ACCUSE HIM

When Job's friends heard about his troubles, they came to comfort him. And at first they did. They saw how great his grief was, so they sat with him for seven days saying nothing (Job 2:11–13). At first they encouraged him that because he *was* righteous, all he needed to do was persevere, and God would again bless him (Job 4:3–7; 8:6, 21). But after months of intense suffering, Job was no longer convinced that God was obligated to bless him, even if he remained faithful (Job 6:11).

Eventually, however, a friend named Zophar became convinced that since no man was completely righteous, Job *must* actually be guilty of secret sins—in fact, God wasn't even judging him as much as he deserved (Job

Job Speaks with His Friends, by Gustave Doré (1832–1883), depicts the friends who came to comfort Job but who ultimately accused him of sinning against God.

11:6). Zophar urged Job to repent. From then on, Job continued to protest his innocence, and his three friends ganged up on him and all began insisting that he must be guilty. They argued from every possible angle that God always judges wickedness—and even though they couldn't think of any sin Job had committed, they were convinced that he *must* have sinned. Why? Because he was suffering.

Finally, a frustrated Eliphaz let loose a vehement tirade, accusing Job of a whole litany of sins—perhaps hoping that if he hurled enough accusations his way, something would stick (Job 22:5–11). Job told them, "Miserable comforters are you all!" (Job 16:2 NKJV). He added, "If only you could be silent! That's the wisest thing you could do" (Job 13:5 NLT).

READ JOB 11 AND 15.

● Six-Month Course: your next reading is on page 96.   →

CLOSER LOOK

THE REASON FOR JOB'S SUFFERING

Job's friends continually argued that Job must have sinned for God to bring trouble into his life, but Job knew that he hadn't sinned so seriously that it merited such suffering. Disobedience *is* a reason for suffering, but it's not the only one. Sometimes the righteous suffer through no fault of their own. Why would God allow this? Often it's because He's working out a plan.

Job recognized that God was the One allowing all his troubles, and stated, "When He has tested me, I shall come forth as gold" (Job 23:10 NKJV). God knows that, painful as our experiences can be, good can come from them. He told the Jews: "I have refined you, but not as silver is refined. Rather, I have refined you in the furnace of suffering" (Isaiah 48:10 NLT). When we pass through the furnace of suffering, it has the potential of purifying us. It can also bring out virtues such as patience and endurance (Romans 5:3).

At the end of the book of Job, God Himself spoke, vindicating Job before his friends and also addressing the overarching issue of human suffering. God didn't explain Job's suffering, but asked a series of questions that showed His vast knowledge—implying that Job should simply trust God's way. And Job did, telling God, "I know that you can do all things" (Job 42:2 NIV).

Yes, people do sin and God does judge sin, but when all was said and done, the entire point of the book of Job was to show that this scenario doesn't always apply.

READ JOB 38 AND 42.

● Six-Month Course: your next reading is on page 99.

SATAN NEEDS PERMISSION

The unsaved are outside of God's protection, and the devil works freely in their lives (Ephesians 2:2–3). And although Satan also causes trouble for the saved, he must get permission from God first. When Satan told God that if Job were put to the test, he would curse God, the Lord said, "Behold, all that he has is in your power, only do not put forth your hand on him" (Job 1:12 NASB). So Satan then caused calamity in Job's life. Satan is "the accuser of our brethren" (Revelation 12:10 NKJV). He accuses

Since Job believed in God, Satan had to seek God's permission before testing him. William Blake (1757–1827) depicted Satan and Job in his painting *Satan Smiting Job with Sore Boils.*

God's people of breaking His laws and then demands the right to punish them. This will only cease when Satan is cast down to the earth at the beginning of the Tribulation period.

READ GENESIS 3 AND REVELATION 12.

JOB'S DISEASE

Job was covered with "painful boils from the sole of his foot to the crown of his head" (Job 2:7–8 NKJV) and constantly scraped the pus-filled scabs with a piece of broken pottery. They were so painful that he couldn't sit on the ground, but sat in a soft heap of ashes. His disease is thought to have been a disgusting form of leprosy, possibly combined with elephantiasis. Small wonder that his friends didn't even *recognize* him when they first saw him! Job said, "My body is clothed with worms and scabs, my skin is broken and festering" (Job 7:5 NIV). Apparently flies laid their eggs in his open sores and maggots hatched in them and covered his body at times. (See also Job 30:30.) Yet God completely healed him!

READ JOB 7 AND MARK 1:21–44.

ELIHU WAS RIGHT

Elihu was the youngest of Job's friends, so he respectfully waited while the older men spoke. But when he saw that they accused Job without any proof, and that Job was more intent on proclaiming his own righteousness than in giving God praise, he finally spoke (Job 32:1–6). Elihu disagreed with Job's statement, "I am innocent, and there is no iniquity in me. Yet He finds occasions against me" (Job 33:9–10 NKJV). In saying this, Job had succumbed

to the sin of self-righteousness. Elihu then justified God's wisdom and actions, and proclaimed that He never did wickedness and never oppressed the righteous (Job 34:12; 37:23). In the end, although God rebuked Job (Job 38:1–3; 42:1–6) *and* his three older friends (Job 42:7–9), the Lord never rebuked Elihu, because what he'd said was right.

God did not rebuke Elihu because the words he spoke to Job were true. He is shown here speaking with Job in *The Wrath of Elihu* by William Blake (1757–1827).

READ JOB 32 AND 34–35.

BEHEMOTH AND LEVIATHAN

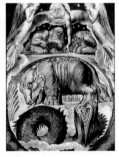

As proof of His great power and wisdom, God pointed out two of the greatest living creatures that He had created—behemoth and leviathan. Many people believe that behemoth refers to an elephant or a hippopotamus, and that leviathan was an oversized Nile crocodile. But other Christians point out that behemoth "moves his tail like a cedar" (Job 40:17 NKJV). Rather than a mere hippo, God seems to be describing something like an Apatosaurus. This giant

God used the behemoth and the leviathan—two unknown creatures—as examples of His power and wisdom in His creation. William Blake (1757–1827) painted his own idea of what these creatures might look like in *Behemoth and Leviathan*.

dinosaur truly *was* the most impressive beast God created and "ranks first among the works of God" (Job 40:19 NIV). Also, leviathan sounds far more like a gigantic water-dwelling Plesiosaurus—or some as-yet-undiscovered, fire-breathing swamp dragon. Many Christians believe that a few dinosaurs survived the Flood and lived into early patriarchal times.

READ JOB 40–41.

BASIC SURVEY

PSALMS

AUTHOR: Various, with nearly half attributed to King David. Other names noted include Solomon, Moses, Asaph, Ethan, and the sons of Korah. Many psalms don't mention an author.

DATE: Approximately 1400s BC (Moses' time) through the 450s BC (when the Jews were under Persian rule).

IN TEN WORDS OR LESS

Ancient Jewish songbook showcases prayers, praise—and complaints—to God.

DETAILS, PLEASE

Over several centuries, God led various individuals to compose emotionally charged poems—of which 150 were later compiled into the book we know as the Psalms. Many of the psalms are described as "of David," meaning they could be by, for, or about Israel's great king. Highlights of the book include the "shepherd psalm" (23), which describes God as protector and provider; David's cry for forgiveness after his sin with Bathsheba (51); psalms of praise (100 is a powerful example); and the celebration of scripture found in Psalm 119, with almost all of the 176 verses making some reference to God's laws, statutes, commandments, precepts, word, etc. Some psalms, called "imprecatory," call for God's judgment on enemies (see Psalms 69 and 109, for example). Many psalms express agony of spirit on the writer's part—but nearly every psalm returns to the theme of praise to God. That's the way the book ends: "Let every thing that hath breath praise the LORD. Praise ye the LORD" (150:6 KJV).

QUOTABLE

> O LORD, our Lord, how excellent is Your name in all the earth (8:1 NKJV).

> The LORD is my shepherd; I shall not want (23:1 KJV).

> Create in me a clean heart, O God; and renew a right spirit within me (51:10 KJV).

> I have hidden your word in my heart that I might not sin against you (119:11 NIV).

> I look up to the mountains—does my help come from there? My help comes from the LORD, who made heaven and earth! (121:1–2 NLT).

> Behold, how good and how pleasant it is for brethren to dwell together in unity! (133:1 KJV).

UNIQUE AND UNUSUAL

The book of Psalms is the Bible's longest, both in terms of chapters (150) and total word count. It contains the longest chapter in the Bible (Psalm 119, with 176 verses) and the shortest (Psalm 117, with 2 verses). Psalm 117 is also the midpoint of the Protestant Bible, with 594 chapters before it and 594 after.

SO WHAT?

The psalms run the gamut of human emotion—which is why so many people turn to them in times of both joy and sadness.

READ PSALMS 1 AND 69.

- One-Month Course: your next reading is on page 106.   →
- Three-Month Course: your next reading is on page 101.   →
- Six-Month Course: your next reading is on page 101.   →

HEART OF THE BOOK

DAVID THE SWEET PSALMIST

David was an anointed musician who wrote many songs called psalms, which are a mixture of honest complaints, wholehearted cries for help, declarations of trust, and beautiful praises to God. Many people read the psalms when troubled or fearful and find great comfort. In addition, many portions of joyful psalms have been set to music once again and used to worship God.

Because David was also a prophet (Acts 2:30), some psalms were prophetic declarations about the coming Messiah. Psalms 16 and 22 are the most outstanding examples. David himself recognized this anointing, and wrote, "David the son of Jesse declares, the man who was raised on high declares,

King David wrote many of the psalms. He is pictured here in *David Playing the Harp* by Jan de Bray (1627–1697).

the anointed of the God of Jacob, and the sweet psalmist of Israel, 'The Spirit of the LORD spoke by me, and His word was on my tongue'" (2 Samuel 23:1–2 NASB).

Some psalms were also written by Levites called the "sons of Korah" (see Psalms 42–49). These Kohathites were inspired musicians and singers whom David appointed to worship the Lord after the ark of the covenant was brought to Jerusalem (1 Chronicles 6:31–43). They apparently wrote while David himself was alive and writing.

Other psalms were written by unknown musicians who had been carried away captive to Babylon in 586 BC (see Psalm 137). Still others were written by poor, faithful Levites during the days of the Persian Empire (see Psalm 119). All these other psalmists were inspired by David's example—and most of all, inspired by God.

READ PSALMS 95–96.

● Three-Month Course: your next reading is on page 106. →

● Six-Month Course: your next reading is on page 102. →

CLOSER LOOK

SHEPHERDS AND SHEEP

David was a shepherd before he became a king. Jesus described Himself as a shepherd who would lay down His life to save His sheep.

David's family owned sheep, and as the youngest son, David was obligated to spend his days shepherding the flock. But God then highly exalted him by choosing him as the next king of Israel (1 Samuel 16:11–13). "He chose David also his servant, and took him from the sheepfolds: from following the ewes great with young he brought him to feed Jacob his people, and Israel his inheritance" (Psalm 78:70–71 KJV).

After he was anointed king, "the Spirit of the LORD came upon David from that day forward" (1 Samuel 16:13 KJV). He had already been musically inclined, like so many shepherds, but now the songs he wrote were inspired by God. Though he was king, David remained a shepherd at heart, and when God wanted to touch him deeply with a strong message, He had Nathan tell him a story about a small ewe lamb (2 Samuel 12:1–9).

From David's rich experience as a shepherd comes some of the most profound and moving imagery in the Psalms. Psalm 23, called "the Shepherd Psalm," begins with the words, "The LORD is my shepherd, I lack nothing. He makes me lie down in green pastures, he leads me beside quiet waters" (Psalm 23:1–2 NIV).

Jesus, the "son of David," declared that He Himself was the Good Shepherd who guarded His sheep and would lay down His life to defend them (John 10:1–18). He told a tender story about a shepherd who went to great lengths to rescue a lost lamb (Luke 15:3–7).

READ PSALMS 23 AND 41.

● Six-Month Course: your next reading is on page 103.   →

Lost Books and Missing Epistles

The title above Psalm 90 reads, "A Prayer of Moses the man of God." This is the only psalm written by Moses in the book of Psalms. But the amazing thing is that it wasn't included in the books of the Law written by Moses, but was floating on its own for hundreds of years until the Levites who compiled the book of Psalms included it. Otherwise, it probably would have been lost.

The Book of Jasher is an example of an entire book that never made it into the Bible. Small portions of it are quoted in Joshua 10:12–13 and in 2 Samuel 1:17–27, but that's all we have. It was apparently a book of poetry extolling Israel's battles. So why didn't it survive? Why wasn't it included? Apparently, God knew it wasn't necessary, so He only had scribes preserve the portions that we needed.

Think about this: after writing twenty-one chapters of his Gospel, the apostle John added that he could have gone on virtually *forever* had it been God's will: "And there are also many

There are several books quoted in the Bible that are not included in the biblical canon.

other things that Jesus did, which if they were written one by one, I suppose that even the world itself could not contain the books that would be written" (John 21:25 NKJV).

This also explains why Paul's epistle to the Laodiceans (Colossians 4:16) wasn't preserved in the New Testament. However, if we want to, we'll have eternity to read all these missing books in heaven.

READ PSALM 90 AND 2 SAMUEL 1:17–27.

 Six-Month Course: your next reading is on page 106. →

PROPHECIES OF CRUCIFIXION

Some one thousand years before Jesus' death, Psalm 22 gave a detailed description of crucifixion, a form of execution that wasn't practiced in Israel then. The following quotes are from Psalm 22:14–18 (NIV). "They pierce my hands and my feet" (v. 16). This is precisely what the Romans did. "All my bones are out of joint" (v. 14). As victims hung on the cross, their arms were dislocated from their sockets. "All my bones are on display" (v. 17). Christ's muscles were so cut open from whipping that His underlying bones were visible. "My mouth is dried up" (v. 15). Crucified people experienced dehydration (see John 19:28). "They divide my clothes among them and cast lots for my garment" (v. 18). This is precisely what the Romans did (see John 19:23–24).

Although written about 1,000 years before the crucifixion, Psalm 22 describes Jesus' death. The crucifixion is depicted in *Christ on the Cross between Two Thieves* by Peter Paul Rubens (1577–1640).

READ PSALM 22 AND MARK 15:1–39.

THE PROTECTION PSALM

Psalm 91 is called "the Protection Psalm," and during times of war or danger, many people claim its promises of protection for themselves or their loved ones. It states: "You shall not be afraid of the terror by night, nor of the arrow that flies by day, nor of the pestilence that walks in darkness, nor of the destruction that lays waste at noonday" (Psalm 91:5–6 NKJV). It further promises that although people may be dying all around you, God will spare you. But there is a condition to these promises: you must habitually "dwell" with God and must continuously "abide" with the Almighty (Psalm 91:1 NKJV). It doesn't work to be God's fair-weather friend and only cry out to Him when you desperately need Him.

READ PSALMS 91 AND 140–141.

HIDDEN TREASURE

LOVE FOR GOD'S WORD

Psalm 119 is the longest chapter in the Bible and is a complex poem proclaiming the psalmist's love for God's Word. There is one section for each letter of the Hebrew alphabet, and the verses of each stanza all begin with the same Hebrew letter. This psalm was probably written by a devout Levite after the Jews had returned from Babylon but were oppressed by their enemies. Nehemiah

describes such circumstances: "The survivors. . .are there in great distress and reproach" (Nehemiah 1:3 NKJV). This psalm contains many beautiful promises and declarations, such as: "Your word I have treasured in my heart, that I may not sin against You" (Psalm 119:11 NASB). Also: "Open my eyes, that I may behold wonderful things from Your law" (Psalm 119:18 NASB).

Psalm 119 is the longest chapter in the Bible and focuses on a love for God's Word.

READ PSALM 119:1–56.

HIDDEN TREASURE

SONGS OF ASCENT

Psalms 120–134 are mostly very short psalms, and each one bears the title "A song of ascents." Jerusalem was on a higher elevation than the surrounding land, and the Bible often speaks of "going up to Jerusalem" (Matthew 20:18 NIV). These psalms were probably sung by Jewish pilgrims as they drew near to Jerusalem to attend the three great annual feasts (Exodus 23:14–17). As they began the ascent to the city, the crowds rejoiced and sang these songs together. "You shall have a song. . .when a holy festival is kept" (Isaiah 30:29 NKJV). Jesus and His family would have sung these psalms as they approached Jerusalem for the annual Feast of the Passover (Luke 2:41), and He and His disciples would've sung them as well.

READ PSALMS 120–134.

BASIC SURVEY

PROVERBS

AUTHOR: Solomon, primarily (1:1), with sections attributed to "the wise" (22:17), Agur (30:1), and King Lemuel (31:1). Little is known of the latter two.

DATE: Solomon reigned approximately 970–930 BC. The scribes of King Hezekiah, who lived about two hundred years later, "copied out" the latter chapters of the book we have today (25:1).

IN TEN WORDS OR LESS

Pithy, memorable sayings encourage people to pursue wisdom.

DETAILS, PLEASE

Proverbs is simply a collection of practical tips for living. Mainly from the pen of King Solomon, the wisest human being ever (God said, in 1 Kings 3:12 NKJV, "I have given you a wise and understanding heart"), the Proverbs speak to issues like work, money, sex, temptation, drinking, laziness, discipline, and child rearing. Underlying each proverb is the truth that "the fear of the LORD is the beginning of knowledge" (1:7 KJV).

QUOTABLE

> Trust in the LORD with all your heart and do not lean on your own understanding (3:5 NASB).

> Go to the ant, thou sluggard; consider her ways, and be wise (6:6 KJV).

> Whoever spares the rod hates their children, but the one who loves their children is careful to discipline them (13:24 NIV).

UNIQUE AND UNUSUAL

The final chapter of Proverbs includes a long poem in praise of wives, rather unusual for that time and culture.

SO WHAT?

Wisdom, as Proverbs 4:7 (KJV) indicates, "is the principal thing. . .with all thy getting get understanding." If you need help with that, just ask God (James 1:5).

READ PROVERBS 4 AND 15.

● One-Month Course: your next reading is on page 111.   →

● Three-Month Course: your next reading is on page 107.   →

● Six-Month Course: your next reading is on page 107.   →

HEART OF THE BOOK

SEEKING WISDOM AND UNDERSTANDING

When God asked Solomon what he desired more than anything else, Solomon asked for wisdom—so God granted his request and made him the wisest man who had ever lived. This wisdom is evident in the book of Proverbs (1 Kings 3:5–12; 4:29–34).

We, too, do well to recognize the importance of wisdom in our daily lives. Solomon repeatedly advises, "Get wisdom! Get understanding!" (Proverbs 4:5 NKJV). He emphasizes this point, saying, "Wisdom is the principal thing; therefore get wisdom. And in all your getting, get understanding" (Proverbs 4:7 NKJV). When we get wisdom, we do ourselves a great favor. "He who gets wisdom loves his own soul; he who keeps understanding will find good" (Proverbs 19:8 NKJV).

Solomon demonstrated great wisdom and understanding. He is depicted here in *The Wisdom of Solomon* by James Tissot (1836–1902).

How do we get wisdom? By listening closely to wise men and women, and learning from them. Also, one of the best things we can do to gain wisdom and understanding is to meditate daily on God's Word. "If you receive my words, and treasure my commands within you. . . . Yes, if you cry out for discernment, and lift up your voice for understanding. . .then you will understand the fear of the LORD, and find the knowledge of God. For the LORD gives wisdom" (Proverbs 2:1, 3, 5–6 NKJV). As the psalmist says, "I have more understanding than all my teachers, for Your testimonies are my meditation" (Psalm 119:99 NKJV).

In Proverbs chapters 1, 3, and 8, Wisdom is personified as a beautiful woman whom men are advised to desire more than any other treasure on earth.

READ PROVERBS 1 AND 3.

● Three-Month Course: your next reading is on page 111.   →

● Six-Month Course: your next reading is on page 108.   →

CLOSER LOOK

THE FEAR OF THE LORD

Wisdom is more than just amassing facts and figures. That's mere head knowledge. It's also more than discovering clever ways to apply knowledge to life situations. In its most basic form, true wisdom is grasping this one simple fact—that the Lord created the entire universe and is not only all-knowing but all-powerful. When we can say like Job, "I know that You can do everything" (Job 42:2 NKJV), we'll not only worship God, but fear (deeply respect and revere) Him.

This is why Solomon wrote, "The fear of the LORD is the beginning of knowledge" (Proverbs 1:7 NKJV). He also stated, "The fear of the LORD is the beginning of wisdom" (Proverbs 9:10 NKJV). God Almighty is the ultimate source of all wisdom and knowledge. If we trust in our own intelligence, we may *think* that we're wise—and others may consider us wise—but we won't be. "When pride comes, then comes shame; but with the humble is wisdom" (Proverbs 11:2 NKJV).

Some Christians point out, however, that the Bible says that "God is love" and that "there is no fear in love. . . . The one who fears is not made perfect

We must revere, worship, and respect God in order to be wise.

in love" (1 John 4:8, 18 NIV). So they wonder why the Bible tells us to "fear" God. But this verse tells us that we are not to fear *people* because "the fear of man brings a snare" (Proverbs 29:25 NKJV). On the other hand, "the fear of the LORD is clean" (Psalm 19:9 NKJV). There's nothing negative about worshipping and fearing God.

READ PROVERBS 8–9.

● Six-Month Course: your next reading is on page 111.　　　→

HARD WORK VERSUS LAZINESS

Solomon emphasized the importance and value of hard work.

Solomon gave frank advice on the merits of hard work. He wrote, "Lazy people are soon poor; hard workers get rich," and "Lazy people irritate their employers" (Proverbs 10:4, 26 NLT). He also wouldn't have had much sympathy for people lying around all day doing nothing, hoping to set themselves for life by buying the winning lottery ticket: "Lazy people want much but get little, but those who work hard will prosper" (Proverbs 13:4 NLT). Solomon urged people to learn from the hardworking ants: "Take a lesson from the ants, you lazybones. Learn from their ways and become wise!" (Proverbs 6:6 NLT). The apostle Paul agreed, saying, "The one who is unwilling to work shall not eat" (2 Thessalonians 3:10 NIV).

READ PROVERBS 6 AND 10.

AVOIDING FOOLISHNESS

Solomon constantly warned against engaging in foolish behavior. He particularly warned against having the mind-set of a fool. What is a fool? A fool is typically a proud, stubborn, loudmouthed person who thinks he's right and won't listen to reason. Solomon wrote, "The way of a fool is right in his own eyes" (Proverbs 12:15 NKJV), and "The lazy man [*and* the fool] is wiser in his own eyes than seven men who can answer sensibly" (Proverbs 26:16 NKJV). You simply can't talk sense to a foolish person, so the Bible advises: "Do not speak in the hearing of a fool, for he will despise the wisdom of your words" (Proverbs 23:9 NKJV). Unfortunately, a truly foolish person can usually only learn from life's hard lessons.

READ PROVERBS 10 AND PSALMS 45–47.

SEEKING WISE COUNSEL

One of the wisest things that any of us can do is to have the humility to admit that we don't know everything—and to seek wise advice from mature brothers and sisters in the Lord. The Bible calls this "seeking counsel," and Solomon wrote, "Without counsel, plans go awry, but in the multitude of counselors they are established" (Proverbs 15:22 NKJV). He also stated, "Where there is no counsel, the people fall; but in the multitude of counselors there is safety" (Proverbs 11:14 NKJV). Those who wish to succeed in life—and in business ventures—are wise to remember that "plans are established by counsel; by wise counsel wage war" (Proverbs 20:18 NKJV). In fact, Solomon candidly stated, "He who heeds counsel is wise" (Proverbs 12:15 NKJV).

READ PROVERBS 12 AND 20.

WISE SPEECH

You can generally tell whether someone is wise or foolish by the way they speak, and what they say. Solomon said, "The mouth of fools poureth out foolishness" (Proverbs 15:2 KJV). Fools make little effort to control their tongues. Their pride compels them to boast and make rash accusations, and their anger causes them to speak hurtful words. A wise man, however, chooses his words carefully. "A soft answer turneth away wrath: but grievous words stir up anger" (Proverbs 15:1 KJV). In the New Testament, Paul advises us to "speak the truth in love" (Ephesians 4:15 NLT). We also must know when to be silent. James says, "If you claim to be religious but don't control your tongue, you are fooling yourself, and your religion is worthless" (James 1:26 NLT).

The Bible instructs us to choose our words carefully and to control our tongues.

READ PROVERBS 21–22.

BASIC SURVEY

ECCLESIASTES

AUTHOR: Not stated, but probably Solomon. The author is identified as the "son of David" (1:1 KJV) and "king over Israel in Jerusalem" (1:12 NIV), and says he had "more wisdom than all they that have been before me" (1:16 KJV).

DATE: 900s BC.

IN TEN WORDS OR LESS

Apart from God, life is empty and unsatisfying.

DETAILS, PLEASE

A king pursues the things of this world, only to find them unfulfilling. Learning, pleasure, work, laughter—"all is vanity" (1:2 KJV). The king also laments the inequities of life: people live, work hard, and die, only to leave their belongings to someone else; the wicked prosper over the righteous; the poor are oppressed. Nevertheless, the king realizes "the conclusion of the whole matter: Fear God, and keep his commandments: for this is the whole duty of man" (12:13 KJV).

QUOTABLE

> To every thing there is a season, and a time to every purpose under the heaven (3:1 KJV).

> Remember now your Creator in the days of your youth (12:1 NKJV).

UNIQUE AND UNUSUAL

The book's generally negative tone makes some readers wonder if Solomon wrote it late in life, after his hundreds of wives led him to stray from God.

SO WHAT?

Life doesn't always make sense. . .but there's still a God who understands.

READ ECCLESIASTES 4 AND 12.

● One-Month Course: your next reading is on page 114.   →

● Three-Month Course: your next reading is on page 114.   →

● Six-Month Course: your next reading is on page 112.   →

CLOSER LOOK

FUTILITY OF LIFE WITHOUT GOD

Ecclesiastes is often considered the most depressing book in the Bible. In it, King Solomon declares the utter futility and uselessness of every human activity. He says, "I have seen all the works that are done under the sun; and,

behold, all is vanity and vexation of spirit" (Ecclesiastes 1:14 KJV). The NIV states, "I have seen all the things that are done under the sun; all of them are meaningless, a chasing after the wind."

Solomon lamented, "As I looked at everything I had worked so hard to accomplish, it was all so meaningless" (Ecclesiastes 2:11 NLT). Solomon was the richest, wisest man on earth, yet he concluded that life was pointless and not worth living. Many Christians

This stained glass—displayed in a cathedral in Bayeux, Calvados, France—depicts Solomon, the author of Ecclesiastes.

wonder what such a glum book is doing in the Bible. But it must be remembered that Solomon went through a period when he backslid from the Lord (1 Kings 11:1–9), when he became like any other worldly man living a futile life. Without God, life has no purpose.

Ecclesiastes isn't alone in declaring the futility of life without God. David said, "Surely every man is vanity," and "The thoughts of man. . .are vanity" (Psalm 39:11; 94:11 KJV). David also declared that when people abandoned God, "their days did he consume in vanity, and their years in trouble" (Psalm 78:33 KJV).

However, Solomon ends this dismal book on a powerful, upbeat note, saying, "The conclusion, when all has been heard, is: fear God and keep His commandments, because this applies to every person" (Ecclesiastes 12:13 NASB).

READ ECCLESIASTES 1–2.

● Six-Month Course: your next reading is on page 114. →

A SEASON FOR EVERYTHING

We must turn to God to determine whether it is the right time or season for us to act.

Solomon wisely observed, "To everything there is a season, a time for every purpose under heaven: a time to be born, and a time to die; a time to plant, and a time to pluck what is planted. . .a time to weep, and a time to laugh; a time to mourn, and a time to dance. . .a time to gain, and a time to lose; a time to keep, and a time to throw away. . .a time to keep silence, and a time to speak" (Ecclesiastes 3:1-2, 4, 6–7 NKJV). But the question is: how do we know when it's the right time to do one of these two very different actions? Solomon answered this, saying, "A wise man's heart discerns both time and judgment" (Ecclesiastes 8:5 NKJV).

READ ECCLESIASTES 3 AND 8.

LIFE AFTER DEATH

In the book of Ecclesiastes, Solomon seems to argue against the immortality of the soul. He states, "For the living know they will die; but the dead do not know anything, nor have they any longer a reward" (Ecclesiastes 9:5 NASB). He emphasizes this by saying, "Whatever your hand finds to do, do it with all your might, for in the realm of the dead. . .there is neither working nor planning nor knowledge nor wisdom" (Ecclesiastes 9:10 NIV). However, in the same book, Solomon asks, "Who knows if the human spirit rises upward and if the spirit of the animal goes down into the earth?" (Ecclesiastes 3:21 NIV). Certainly death terminates this physical life. For our bodies, it *is* the end. But our spirit lives on.

READ ECCLESIASTES 9–10.

BASIC SURVEY

SONG OF SOLOMON

AUTHOR: Solomon (1:1), though some wonder if the song "of Solomon" is like the psalms "of David"—which could mean they're *by, for,* or *about* him.

DATE: Solomon ruled around 970 to 930 BC.

IN TEN WORDS OR LESS

Married love is a beautiful thing worth celebrating.

DETAILS, PLEASE

A dark-skinned beauty is marrying the king, and both are thrilled. "Behold, thou art fair, my love; behold, thou art fair; thou hast doves' eyes," he tells her (1:15 KJV). "Behold, thou art fair, my beloved, yea, pleasant: also our bed is green," she responds (1:16 KJV). Through eight chapters and 117 verses, the two lovers admire each other's physical beauty, expressing their love and devotion.

QUOTABLE

> "Let him kiss me with the kisses of his mouth—for your love is better than wine" (1:2 NKJV).

> "He brought me to the banqueting house, and his banner over me was love" (2:4 KJV).

> "Many waters cannot quench love, neither can the floods drown it" (8:7 KJV).

UNIQUE AND UNUSUAL

Like the book of Esther, Song of Solomon never mentions the name "God."

SO WHAT?

God made marriage for the husband and wife's enjoyment—and that marital love can be a picture of God's joy in His people.

READ SONG OF SOLOMON 1–2.

● One-Month Course: your next reading is on page 117. →

● Three-Month Course: your next reading is on page 117. →

● Six-Month Course: your next reading is on page 115. →

Love Poetry and God's Bride

Some scholars say that the Song of Solomon resembles ancient Egyptian and Babylonian love poetry—and that it's simply a sensuous love song celebrating love between a man and a woman. Actually, however, the closest literary comparison is found in the proverbs of Solomon, where people are admonished to enjoy amorous bliss within an exclusive marriage relationship (see Proverbs 5:15–20; 6:24–29; 7:6–23).

The Song of Solomon was painted by Gustave Moreau (1826–1898).

God surely intended a spiritual meaning as well. He talked about Israel as His bride, saying, "I remember the devotion of your youth, how as a bride you loved me and followed me through the wilderness" (Jeremiah 2:2 NIV). He also stated, "For as a young man marries a virgin, so shall your sons marry you; and as the bridegroom rejoices over the bride, so shall your God rejoice over you" (Isaiah 62:5 NKJV). (See also Hosea 2:16, 19.)

Christians also see this love song as a celebration of the love between Christ and His bride, the Church. Paul wrote, "'For this reason a man shall leave his father and mother and be joined to his wife, and the two shall become one flesh.' This is a great mystery, but I speak concerning Christ and the church" (Ephesians 5:31–32 NKJV). We have been betrothed to Christ, and one day in heaven the marriage will take place (2 Corinthians 11:2; Revelation 19:7).

Of course, we shouldn't overlook that this book is also intended to be a celebration of pure marital love between a husband and wife.

READ SONG OF SOLOMON 3–4.

● Six-Month Course: your next reading is on page 117.   →

IDENTITY OF SOLOMON'S BELOVED

Solomon wrote of his most cherished bride, "I liken you, my darling, to a mare among Pharaoh's chariot horses" (Song of Solomon 1:9 NIV). This may indicate that this dark-skinned beauty (v. 6) was Solomon's Egyptian wife. "Solomon made a treaty with Pharaoh king of Egypt, and married Pharaoh's daughter" (1 Kings 3:1 NKJV). He gave the Egyptian princess preferential treatment and built her a palace of her own (1 Kings 7:8; 2 Chronicles 8:11). Other Bible scholars think that her title, "Shulamite" (Song of Solomon 6:13), may mean "Shunammite," a native of Shunem in Israel, renowned for its beautiful women (1 Kings 1:3–4). On the other hand, "Shulamite" is likely a pet name meaning "Solomon's girl." Whatever her identity, this beautiful lady captured the heart of Israel's king.

READ SONG OF SOLOMON 5–6.

PARADISE GARDENS IN ISRAEL

The author of Song of Solomon used beautiful imagery—such as pomegranates that were found in Israel's gardens—to describe his love.

Israel has the perfect climate for many kinds of fruits, nuts, and spices, and in Solomon's day people cultivated gardens, orchards, and vineyards. The Hebrew word *pardes* means "paradise," and in the Song of Solomon 4:13 (NIV) Solomon speaks of "an orchard [*pardes*] of pomegranates with choice fruits." Elsewhere he wrote, "I made gardens and parks [*pardes*] and planted all kinds of fruit trees in them" (Ecclesiastes 2:5 NIV). Solomon describes "henna blossoms from the vineyards of En Gedi" (Song of Solomon 1:14 NIV), fig trees and vines (Song of Solomon 2:13), and "an orchard of pomegranates with choice fruits, henna with nard plants, nard and saffron, calamus and cinnamon, with all the trees of frankincense, myrrh and aloes, along with all the finest spices" (Song of Solomon 4:13–14 NASB). (See also Song of Solomon 6:2, 11; 7:12–13.)

READ SONG OF SOLOMON 7–8.

BASIC SURVEY

ISAIAH

AUTHOR: Isaiah, the son of Amoz (1:1).

DATE: Around 740 to 680 BC, starting "in the year that king Uzziah died" (6:1 KJV).

IN TEN WORDS OR LESS

A coming Messiah will save people from their sins.

DETAILS, PLEASE

Like most prophets, Isaiah announced the bad news of punishment for sin. But he also described a coming Messiah who would be "wounded for our transgressions. . .bruised for our iniquities. . .and with his stripes we are healed" (53:5 KJV). Called to the ministry through a stunning vision of God in heaven (chapter 6), Isaiah wrote a book that some call "the fifth Gospel" for its predictions of the birth, life, and death of Jesus Christ some seven hundred years later. These prophecies of redemption balance the depressing promises of God's discipline against Judah and Jerusalem, which were overrun by Babylonian armies about a century later. Isaiah's prophecy ends with a long section (chapters 40–66) describing God's restoration of Israel, His promised salvation, and His eternal kingdom.

QUOTABLE

> "Holy, holy, holy, is the LORD of hosts; the whole earth is full of His glory" (6:3 NKJV).

> Behold, a virgin shall conceive, and bear a son, and shall call his name Immanuel (7:14 KJV).

> For unto us a child is born, unto us a son is given: and the government shall be upon his shoulder: and his name shall be called Wonderful, Counsellor, The mighty God, The everlasting Father, The Prince of Peace (9:6 KJV).

> We all, like sheep, have gone astray, each of us has turned to our own way; and the LORD has laid on him the iniquity of us all (53:6 NIV).

UNIQUE AND UNUSUAL

Isaiah had two children with strange, prophetic names. Shear-jashub (7:3) means "a remnant shall return," and Maher-shalal-hash-baz (8:3) means "haste to the spoil." Shear-jashub's name carried God's promise that exiled Jews would one day return home. Maher-shalal-hash-baz's name assured the king of Judah that his country's enemies would be attacked by Assyrian armies.

SO WHAT?

Early in His ministry, Jesus said He fulfilled the prophecies of Isaiah: "The Spirit of the Lord GOD is upon Me, because the LORD has anointed Me to preach good tidings to the poor; He has sent Me to heal the brokenhearted, to proclaim liberty to the captives, and the opening of the prison to those who are bound; to proclaim the acceptable year of the LORD" (61:1–2 NKJV). It's amazing how much God cares about us!

READ ISAIAH 1–2.

● One-Month Course: your next reading is on page 124.   →

● Three-Month Course: your next reading is on page 119.   →

● Six-Month Course: your next reading is on page 119.   →

HEART OF THE BOOK

ISAIAH—THE ROYAL PROPHET

Isaiah saw visions of God "during the years when Uzziah, Jotham, Ahaz, and Hezekiah were kings of Judah" (Isaiah 1:1 NLT). This was from approximately 740 to 680 BC. At the beginning of this time, the powerful northern kingdom of Aram was the greatest threat to Israel and Judah. But during Ahaz's reign, in 732 BC, the Assyrians conquered Aram. From then on, Assyria was the main enemy of God's people.

Isaiah is called "the royal prophet" because, according to rabbinic tradition, his father, Amoz, was the brother of Amaziah, king of Judah. This is not known for certain, however. Isaiah's unnamed wife is called "the prophetess" (Isaiah 8:3 KJV), indicating that she may have had a prophetic anointing as well. They had two sons, both named after major historical events.

More than any other prophet, Isaiah spoke about the coming Messiah, and his many prophecies were fulfilled in the birth, life, and death of Jesus Christ. He also wrote detailed descriptions of the coming kingdom of heaven (Isaiah 2:1–5; 65:17–25). In addition, he mentioned the destruction of the wicked in hell (Isaiah 66:24), and Jesus quoted him in Mark 9:47–48.

Scholars believe that Isaiah wrote his book between 701 and 681 BC. Many people argue that Isaiah didn't compose the entire book, but only wrote chapters 1–39, and that a later writer penned chapters 40–66.

Isaiah was a prophet who spoke about the coming of Jesus.

But the unique expression "the Holy One of Israel," used almost exclusively in Isaiah, appears throughout the entire book, arguing strongly for its unity.

READ ISAIAH 3 AND 8.

● Three-Month Course: your next reading is on page 124.   →

● Six-Month Course: your next reading is on page 120.   →

Prophecies of the Messiah

Isaiah's prophecy describes the suffering that Christ would endure on the cross, which is shown in the painting *The Raising of the Cross* by Peter Paul Rubens (1577–1640).

Isaiah 53 is an astonishingly accurate prophecy about the coming Messiah. Isaiah wrote it about 680 BC, some 710 years before Jesus' trial, crucifixion, and burial, yet it was fulfilled in minute detail in His life. The early Christians declared clearly that this was about Jesus (Acts 8:32–35; 1 Peter 2:21–25).

It begins in Isaiah 52:13–15, particularly in verse 14 (NIV), which says that "his appearance was so disfigured. . .and his form marred beyond human likeness." Before His crucifixion, Jesus was beaten and His body mutilated by Roman whips.

The prophecy states, "He was led as a lamb to the slaughter, and as a sheep before its shearers is silent, so He opened not His mouth" (Isaiah 53:7 NKJV). When Jesus was accused of many crimes before Pilate, he remained silent, to the governor's astonishment (Matthew 27:13–14). "He was taken from prison and from judgment" (Isaiah 53:8 NKJV). Jesus didn't receive a fair trial (Matthew 27:24; John 19:12–16).

Isaiah continued, "And they made His grave with the wicked—but with the rich at His death" (Isaiah 53:9 NKJV). Jesus died between two criminals; then a rich disciple, Joseph of Arimathea, received permission to bury Him in his own new tomb (Matthew 27:38, 57–60).

Why did Jesus suffer so? The prophecy explains: "He was wounded for our transgressions, He was bruised for our iniquities. . .we have turned, every one, to his own way; and the LORD has laid on Him the iniquity of us all. . . . He bore the sin of many" (Isaiah 53:5–6, 12 NKJV).

READ ISAIAH 52:13–53:12 AND ACTS 8:26–40.

● Six-Month Course: your next reading is on page 121.   →

GOD'S COMING KINGDOM

Genesis 2–3 described a paradise lost, and Isaiah wrote that paradise will be restored on earth: "The wolf also shall dwell with the lamb, the leopard shall lie down with the young goat, the calf and the young lion and the fatling together; and a little child shall lead them. . . . They shall not hurt nor destroy in all My holy mountain" (Isaiah 11:6, 9 NKJV).

The departed of all ages will resurrect from the dead (Isaiah 26:19), and death will also be no more: "He will swallow up death forever. The Sovereign LORD will wipe away the tears from all faces" (Isaiah 25:8 NIV).

After the Messiah defeats all their enemies and there is no more war, blacksmiths will busily transform swords into plowshares. People will be occupied with peaceful farming. The Messiah will "settle disputes for many peoples. They will beat their swords into plowshares and their spears into pruning hooks. Nation will not take up sword against nation, nor will they train for war anymore" (Isaiah 2:4 NIV).

God declared: "Behold, I create new heavens and a new earth; and the former things will not be remembered or come to mind. But be glad and rejoice forever in what I create; for behold, I create Jerusalem for rejoicing and her people for gladness. I will also rejoice in Jerusalem and be glad in My people; and there will no longer be heard in her the voice of weeping and the sound of crying" (Isaiah 65:17–19 NASB). (See also Isaiah 11:1–10.)

Isaiah described God's coming kingdom as a place where wolves and lambs could dwell together.

READ ISAIAH 61 AND 65.

 Six-Month Course: your next reading is on page 124.   →

A Ready, Willing Spirit

Isaiah wrote, "I heard the voice of the Lord, saying: 'Whom shall I send, and who will go for Us?' Then I said, 'Here am I! Send me'" (Isaiah 6:8 NKJV). So God made him a prophet and a messenger. One thing God loves greatly is a willing spirit, especially when it comes to speaking His word to others. Isaiah also prophesied, "How lovely on the mountains are the feet of him who brings good news. . .who announces salvation" (Isaiah 52:7 NASB). This is why Paul says that a vital part of every Christian's spiritual armor is to have our "feet fitted with the readiness that comes from the gospel of peace" (Ephesians 6:15 NIV). It is our obligation and privilege to preach the Gospel.

READ ISAIAH 5–6.

Satan's Fall from Heaven

Isaiah gave a prophecy against the king of Babylon (Isaiah 14:4), but this also describes the fall of Satan who empowered him: "How you are fallen from heaven, O Lucifer, son of the morning! . . . For you have said in your heart: 'I will ascend into heaven, I will exalt my throne above the stars of God. . . . I will be like the Most High'" (Isaiah 14:12–14 NKJV). The devil's sin was being "puffed up with pride" (1 Timothy 3:6 NKJV). Ezekiel also described his fall: "You were in Eden. . . . You were the anointed cherub. . . . And you sinned; therefore I have cast you as

The fall of Satan is described by Isaiah and Ezekiel. Gustave Doré (1832–1883) depicted Satan in Milton's *Paradise Lost.*

profane from the mountain of God" (Ezekiel 28:13–14, 16 NASB). Satan still has access to heaven to accuse the saints, but this will soon end (Revelation 12:7–10).

READ ISAIAH 14 AND EZEKIEL 28.

GOD'S WONDERFUL THOUGHTS

One of the most profound passages in the Bible is this: "'My thoughts are not your thoughts, neither are your ways my ways,' declares the LORD. 'As the heavens are higher than the earth, so are my ways higher than your ways and my thoughts than your thoughts'" (Isaiah 55:8–9 NIV). God is aware of facts that we can't possibly know. That's why we must look to Him for wisdom. This is also why Solomon said, "Trust in the LORD with all your heart, and lean not on your own understanding" (Proverbs 3:5 NKJV). We can trust Him because He loves us. "I know the thoughts that I think toward you, saith the LORD, thoughts of peace, and not of evil" (Jeremiah 29:11 KJV). (See also Romans 8:28.)

READ ISAIAH 40 AND 55.

PROPHECIES ABOUT CYRUS

The king of the Persians, Cyrus II, founded the vast Persian Empire. Some 140 years previously, Isaiah prophesied about him: "Thus says the LORD to His anointed, to Cyrus, whose right hand I have held—to subdue nations before him. . . . I have even called you by your name" (Isaiah 45:1, 4 NKJV). Also Isaiah prophesied, "He shall build my city, and he shall let go my captives" (Isaiah 45:13 KJV). God also declared, "He. . .shall [say] to Jerusalem, 'You shall be built,' and to the temple, 'Your foundation shall be laid'" (Isaiah 44:28 NKJV). In fulfillment, in 539 BC Cyrus issued a decree allowing the Jews to return home. God accurately declares the future far in advance—then moves mightily to bring about His will.

READ ISAIAH 44:1–45:13.

BASIC SURVEY

JEREMIAH

AUTHOR: Jeremiah (1:1), with the assistance of Baruch, a scribe (36:4).

DATE: Approximately 585 BC.

IN TEN WORDS OR LESS

After years of sinful behavior, Judah will be punished.

DETAILS, PLEASE

Called to the ministry as a youth (1:6), Jeremiah prophesied bad news to Judah: "Lo, I will bring a nation upon you from far, O house of Israel, saith the LORD" (5:15 KJV). Jeremiah was mocked for his prophecies, occasionally beaten, and imprisoned in a muddy well (chapter 38). But his words came true with the Babylonian invasion of chapter 52.

QUOTABLE

> "Look, as the clay is in the potter's hand, so are you in My hand, O house of Israel!" (18:6 NKJV).

UNIQUE AND UNUSUAL

The book of Jeremiah that we read is an expanded, second version of a destroyed first draft. King Jehoiakim, angry with Jeremiah for his dire prophecies, cut the scroll with a penknife "and cast it into the fire" (36:23 KJV). At God's command, Jeremiah produced a second scroll with additional material (36:32).

SO WHAT?

Through Jeremiah, God gave Judah some forty years to repent. God is "patient toward you, not wishing for any to perish but for all to come to repentance" (2 Peter 3:9 NASB).

READ JEREMIAH 1–2.

● One-Month Course: your next reading is on page 130.   →

● Three-Month Course: your next reading is on page 130.   →

● Six-Month Course: your next reading is on page 125.   →

JEREMIAH—THE PROPHET OF DOOM

Jeremiah was only a youth when God called him to be a prophet to the people of Judah. When Jeremiah protested that he was too young, the Lord told him, "Do not say, 'I am too young.' You must go to everyone I send you to and say whatever I command you" (Jeremiah 1:7 NIV).

At that time, the Assyrian Empire had just fallen. Good King Josiah ruled (Jeremiah 1:1–2) and was on an ambitious program of destroying

The prophet Jeremiah warned the people of Judah about Jerusalem's destruction.

idol worship throughout Judah and Israel. Unfortunately, however, the Israelites were deeply entrenched in Baal worship, and only halfheartedly went along with Josiah's sweeping reforms.

Jeremiah then began to prophesy that doom was coming. Around 605 BC, he went to the temple and warned that it would be destroyed and Jerusalem would be abandoned. The priests and prophets shouted, "You must die!" (Jeremiah 26:8 NIV). Fortunately, some nobles stood up for him, and his life was spared. But down through the years Jeremiah was repeatedly reproached, locked up in stocks, and threatened.

In the end, King Zedekiah rebelled, so the Babylonians besieged Jerusalem. Then Pharaoh led an army out of Egypt, and the Babylonians broke off their siege. But Jeremiah warned Zedekiah that God was still determined to judge them for their sins (Jeremiah 37:9–10). Sure enough, the Babylonians returned. Jeremiah was arrested, flogged, then imprisoned in a dungeon cell where he remained for many days. He survived the famine and the fall of Jerusalem, and was released and allowed to live in Judah.

READ JEREMIAH 4–5.

● Six-Month Course: your next reading is on page 126. →

CLOSER LOOK

Babylon Creates an Empire

For two hundred years the Assyrians had ruled Babylon. Then around 630 BC, Nabopolassar, king of Babylon, revolted. He began to build an empire and by 610 BC had advanced north and conquered Nineveh itself. In 609 BC, Pharaoh Neco led an Egyptian army to help the Assyrians fight the Babylonians. But the Babylonian army, under Prince Nebuchadnezzar, defeated them.

To the south in Judah, the Egyptians set up Jehoiakim as a puppet king. Then in 606 BC, Pharaoh Neco again attacked the Babylonians. At the Battle

Nebuchadnezzar took the people of Judah into captivity, which is portrayed in this lithograph titled *The Captivity of Judah.*

of Carchemish in 605 BC, his army was badly mauled (Jeremiah 46:2). That same year, Nabopolassar died and Nebuchadnezzar became king of Babylon. Following this battle, Pharaoh Neco lost control of all Syria, Phoenicia, and Judah (2 Kings 24:7). When Nebuchadnezzar conquered Judah in 605 BC, he took several members of the royal house and noble families back to Babylon—among them Daniel and his friends (Daniel 1:1–2).

King Jehoiakim later rebelled against the Babylonians, so Nebuchadnezzar took him to Babylon. His son Jehoiachin then reigned. But only three months later, in 597 BC, Jehoiachin was also taken to Babylon. Several Jews went with him—among them Ezekiel. Zedekiah then became king, but after nine years he, too, rebelled, so Nebuchadnezzar sent an army to besiege Jerusalem. They conquered the city in 586 BC and burned the temple, the palace, and all the houses of Jerusalem. They broke down the city's walls and took most of the survivors as prisoners to Babylon.

READ 2 KINGS 24 AND JEREMIAH 52.

● Six-Month Course: your next reading is on page 127.   →

CLOSER LOOK

THE NEW COVENANT

Jean-Baptiste Jouvenet (1644–1717) painted *The Last Supper*. During Jesus' last supper with His disciples, He established God's new covenant with His people.

Jeremiah prophesied six hundred years before Jesus' day, "'Behold, days are coming,' declares the LORD, 'when I will make a new covenant with the house of Israel. . . . I will put My law within them and on their heart I will write it; and I will be their God, and they shall be My people. . . . For I will forgive their iniquity, and their sin I will remember no more'" (Jeremiah 31:31, 33–34 NASB).

After the last Passover meal, Jesus broke the bread and gave it to His disciples, saying, "Take, eat; this is My body." Then He passed the cup, saying, "Drink from it, all of you. For this is My blood of the new covenant, which is shed for many for the remission of sins" (Matthew 26:26–28 NKJV). The following day, Jesus' body was broken with scourging and crucifixion, and His blood was poured out so that our sins could be forgiven.

God *has* now written his law on our hearts. As Paul tells us, "You are a letter from Christ. . .written not with ink but with the Spirit of the living God, not on tablets of stone but on tablets of human hearts" (2 Corinthians 3:3 NIV). We *are* now His people. He promised, "I will dwell in them and walk among them. I will be their God, and they shall be My people" (2 Corinthians 6:16 NKJV). And He *has* completely forgiven our sins. "In Him [Jesus] we have redemption through His blood, the forgiveness of sins" (Ephesians 1:7 NKJV).

READ JEREMIAH 31 AND HEBREWS 8.

● Six-Month Course: your next reading is on page 130.   →

HIDDEN TREASURE

BURNING JEREMIAH'S SCROLL

One day, God told Jeremiah to record all the prophecies he'd received, so Jeremiah dictated them to the scribe Baruch, who wrote them in a scroll. Jeremiah then sent Baruch to the temple to read his warnings. Jehudi and other noblemen heard Baruch, took the scroll to Jehoiakim's palace, and began reading it to him. It was wintertime, so the king had a fire burning, and every time Jehudi read three or four columns, Jehoiakim cut that section off and tossed it in the fire. He did this until the entire scroll was burned. If Jehoiakim had repented at the warnings, God would've had mercy. But because he rejected God's word, his judgment was certain. Jeremiah then gave Baruch another scroll and had him write the words again.

READ JEREMIAH 36.

HIDDEN TREASURE

CAST INTO DEEP MUD

As the Babylonian siege of Jerusalem continued and famine racked the city, Jeremiah prophesied: "Whoever stays in this city will die by the sword, famine or plague, but whoever goes over to the Babylonians will live" (Jeremiah 38:2 NIV). Finally, the enraged Jewish officials insisted that Jeremiah be put to death, so King Zedekiah handed him over. They dropped him into a large cistern (reservoir). All the water was gone and there was only deep mud there, so Jeremiah sank in it and couldn't get free. This looked like the end. But an Ethiopian named Ebed-melech heard what they'd done, went to the king, and got permission to rescue Jeremiah. With the help of several men, Ebed-melech lowered a rope then pulled him up.

READ JEREMIAH 37–38.

JEREMIAH IS VINDICATED

Finally the besieging army broke through the walls. Zedekiah fled the city, but the Babylonians pursued, scattered his army, killed his sons, blinded him, and took him to Babylon. The conquerors also took many other Jews with him. Jeremiah was still in prison, so the Babylonians released him. They knew that Jeremiah had warned the Jews to surrender to them, so they let him live wherever he wished to. It was harvesttime, and the land was overflowing with ripe figs, grapes, and dates, so Jeremiah and the survivors had their pick of the best of the land. The Jewish governor, appointed by Babylon, urged everyone to settle down peacefully and serve the Babylonians.

READ JEREMIAH 39–40.

THE BROKEN PROMISE

An Israelite prince named Ishmael had the Jewish governor and his Babylonian guards murdered, but an army officer named Johanan rescued Jeremiah and the other Jews from him. Then Johanan and his officers worried that the Babylonians would retaliate against *them*. So they took the people and headed for Egypt, then stopped and asked Jeremiah if God had a message for them. They vowed, "Whether it is pleasing or displeasing, we will obey the voice of the LORD our God" (Jeremiah 42:6 NKJV). After ten days, God told them to stay in Judah and He would be merciful and bless them. This was *not* the answer Johanan and his fellow officers had wanted or expected, so they broke their promise and continued on to Egypt.

READ JEREMIAH 41–42.

BASIC SURVEY

LAMENTATIONS

AUTHOR: Not stated, but traditionally Jeremiah.

DATE: Probably around 586 BC, shortly after the fall of Jerusalem to the Babylonians.

IN TEN WORDS OR LESS

A despairing poem over the destruction of Jerusalem.

DETAILS, PLEASE

Jeremiah witnesses the punishment he'd long threatened. Judah's "enemies prosper; for the LORD has afflicted her because of the multitude of her transgressions," Jeremiah wrote. "Her children have gone into captivity before the enemy" (1:5 NKJV). The sight brings tears to Jeremiah's eyes ("My eye, my eye overflows with water," 1:16 NKJV). Lamentations ends with the cry: "You have utterly rejected us and are angry with us beyond measure" (5:22 NIV).

QUOTABLE

> Restore us, O LORD, and bring us back to you again! Give us back the joys we once had! (5:21 NLT).

UNIQUE AND UNUSUAL

Though Lamentations doesn't indicate its author, Jeremiah is described in 2 Chronicles 35:25 as a composer of laments.

SO WHAT?

God's punishment seems severe, but as Hebrews 12:11 (NKJV) says, "No chastening seems to be joyful for the present, but painful; nevertheless, afterward it yields the peaceable fruit of righteousness to those who have been trained by it."

READ LAMENTATIONS 1–2.

● One-Month Course: your next reading is on page 133.　　→

● Three-Month Course: your next reading is on page 133.　　→

● Six-Month Course: your next reading is on page 131.　　→

CLOSER LOOK

God Doesn't Willingly Afflict

God had forewarned His people centuries earlier that if they stubbornly disobeyed, He would send dire judgments upon them (Deuteronomy 28:15–68). The people hadn't repented, "the wrath of the Lord arose against his people" (2 Chronicles 36:16 KJV), and judgment had come in full force. Their city was burned, and their people had starved for months in a siege, only to be finally killed or taken into exile.

It seemed as if God was acting utterly without mercy. Jeremiah complained, "The Lord was like an enemy. He has swallowed up Israel" (Lamentations 2:5 NKJV). The prophet Habakkuk had prayed that God would judge His people, yet when the Babylonians were about to attack, he implored, "O Lord. . .in wrath remember mercy" (Habakkuk 3:2 KJV).

In the midst of this great calamity, Jeremiah declared, "Though He causes grief, yet He will show compassion according to the multitude of His mercies. For He does not afflict willingly, nor grieve the children of men" (Lamentations 3:32–33 NKJV). Referring to this same judgment, he said, "As I live, saith the Lord God, I have no pleasure in the death of the wicked; but that the wicked turn from his way and live" (Ezekiel 33:11 KJV).

This is the heart of God. Even in judgment, God loves for people to repent so He can show mercy (Lamentations 3:40–42). He promises, "With a little wrath I hid My face from you for a moment; but with everlasting kindness I will have mercy on you" (Isaiah 54:8 NKJV).

READ LAMENTATIONS 3 AND PSALM 31.

 Six-Month Course: your next reading is on page 133. →

THE WEEPING PROPHET

Jeremiah loved his people, and though they had mocked him and mistreated him for years, he wept when they were judged. He wrote, "For these things I weep; my eye, my eye overflows with water; because. . .my children are desolate" (Lamentations 1:16 NKJV). Elsewhere he said, "Oh that my head were waters, and mine eyes a fountain of tears, that I might weep day

Jeremiah Lamenting the Destruction of Jerusalem by Rembrandt (1606–1669) shows Jeremiah as he weeps over God's judgment of His people.

and night for the slain of the daughter of my people!" (Jeremiah 9:1 KJV). This is why Jeremiah is called "the weeping prophet." Jesus also lamented, "Jerusalem, Jerusalem, you who kill the prophets and stone those sent to you, how often I have longed to gather your children together, as a hen gathers her chicks under her wings, and you were not willing" (Matthew 23:37 NIV).

READ LAMENTATIONS 4 AND JEREMIAH 9.

FAMINE IN A SIEGE

In Bible times, powerful aggressors frequently invaded other lands. However, most cities—like Jerusalem—were highly fortified and had high, thick walls around them. And they stored up lots of food and had a water supply. Thus Jerusalem withstood a three-year siege by the Babylonians, although toward the end, they had almost completely run out of food. Jeremiah wrote, "All her people groan seeking bread; they have given their precious things for food." He wept for her "little ones who are faint because of hunger" (Lamentations 1:11; 2:19 NASB). People became skin and bones in long sieges, and many died of hunger (Lamentations 4:4–10). Yet God longed for people to obey Him so that He could show mercy to them and provide for them.

READ LAMENTATIONS 5 AND JEREMIAH 14.

BASIC SURVEY

EZEKIEL

AUTHOR: Ezekiel, a priest (1:1–3).

DATE: Approximately 590s–570s BC.

IN TEN WORDS OR LESS

Though Israel is in exile, the nation will be restored.

DETAILS, PLEASE

Ezekiel, an exiled Jew in Babylon, becomes God's spokesman to fellow exiles. He shares unusual (even bizarre) visions with the people, reminding them of the sin that led to their captivity, but also offering hope of national restoration.

QUOTABLE

> "For I have no pleasure in the death of one who dies," says the Lord GOD. "Therefore turn and live!" (18:32 NKJV).

UNIQUE AND UNUSUAL

Ezekiel's vision of a valley of dry bones is one of the Bible's strangest images: "I prophesied as I was commanded: and. . .there was a noise, and behold a shaking, and the bones came together. . .the sinews and the flesh came up upon them, and the skin covered them above. . .and the breath came into them, and they lived, and stood up upon their feet, an exceeding great army" (37:7–8, 10 KJV).

SO WHAT?

Ezekiel strongly teaches personal responsibility: "The soul who sins will die. But if a man is righteous and practices justice. . .he is righteous and will surely live" (18:4–5, 9 NASB).

READ EZEKIEL 18 AND PSALM 102.

● One-Month Course: your next reading is on page 137.   →

● Three-Month Course: your next reading is on page 137.   →

● Six-Month Course: your next reading is on page 134.   →

CLOSER LOOK

EZEKIEL—PROPHET IN BABYLON

Ezekiel was a Levite, one of nearly ten thousand skilled laborers carried captive to Babylon in 597 BC with King Jehoiachin (2 Kings 24:14). He was resettled along the Kebar River in Babylonia, where he and the other captives built houses and lived. Ezekiel was married, but obeyed God's command not to grieve for his wife when she died (Ezekiel 24:15–18).

Ezekiel was commissioned to be a prophet in 592 BC, five years after arriving in Babylon. He was thirty years old (Ezekiel 1:1–3). God told him, "I have made thee a watchman unto the house of Israel: therefore hear the word at my mouth, and give them warning from me"

Ezekiel was living in Babylon when God commissioned him to be a prophet.

(Ezekiel 3:17 KJV). Unfortunately, although the Jews listened, they didn't obey. God told him, "To them you are nothing more than one who sings love songs with a beautiful voice and plays an instrument well, for they hear your words but do not put them into practice" (Ezekiel 33:32 NIV).

God explained, "You dwell in the midst of a rebellious house, which has eyes to see but does not see, and ears to hear but does not hear" (Ezekiel 12:2 NKJV). Since they were shutting out his words, God instructed Ezekiel to do a series of bizarre, silent skits. These mysterious messages grabbed people's attention and forced them to think deeply about what he was trying to convey to them.

Unlike the out-of-order prophecies of Jeremiah, Ezekiel's revelations are all in perfect sequence and meticulously dated, often even to the month and the day.

READ EZEKIEL 2–3.

● Six-Month Course: your next reading is on page 137.　　→

Vision of the Cherubim

Five years after he arrived in Babylonia, Ezekiel was by the Kebar River when the heavens opened and he saw "a whirlwind was coming out of the north, a great cloud with raging fire engulfing itself; and brightness was all around it and radiating out of its midst like the color of amber" (Ezekiel 1:4 NKJV). Ezekiel then saw four heavenly beings called cherubim. Each one had four faces, and "their appearance was like burning coals of fire. . .and out of the fire went lightning" (Ezekiel 1:13 NKJV). Above the four creatures was a throne, and the Lord sat on the throne, gleaming brilliantly like fire with a rainbow around Him. The only other person to see the cherubim was the apostle John, in AD 96.

READ EZEKIEL 1 AND 10.

Digging through the Wall

After Jehoiachin went to Babylon, Zedekiah became king. Then false prophets arose, assuring them that very soon the exiles would return from Babylon. But God warned them through Ezekiel that more disaster was coming. In one pantomime, Ezekiel dug through the clay wall of his house in broad daylight. Then he crawled through the hole with all his belongings, set the pack on his shoulder, and carried it to another place. The Jews asked, "What are you doing?" Ezekiel answered, "I am a sign to you. As I have done, so shall it be done to them; they shall be carried away into captivity" (Ezekiel 12:9, 11 NKJV). Sure enough, Zedekiah later rebelled, Jerusalem was besieged, and the *rest* of the Jews went into exile in Babylon.

READ EZEKIEL 4 AND 12.

THE VALLEY OF DRY BONES

This was one of Ezekiel's weirdest visions, yet it's filled with beautiful meaning. In the spirit God took Ezekiel to a valley full of scattered, dry bones. The bones came together into skeletons and were covered with flesh and skin, then life came into the bodies! Here's what it meant: The

Israelites had been exiled from their land to Babylon. They were saying, "Our bones are dried up and our hope is gone" (Ezekiel 37:11 NIV). This was true. But God showed them that even though it looked like all hope was gone, He still loved them and was going to do a miracle: they would eventually obey Him, and He would bring them back to their own land.

Ezekiel's vision of the dry bones is one of many events depicted in the Knesset Menorah in Jerusalem.

READ EZEKIEL 37 AND JEREMIAH 29.

GOG AND MAGOG

Ezekiel chapters 38–39 describe a great northern power invading Israel "in the latter years" (Ezekiel 38:8 NKJV). God told him, "Set your face against Gog, of the land of Magog, the prince of Rosh, Meshech, and Tubal" (Ezekiel 38:2 NKJV). Now, the Russians descend from an ancient people called the *Rus*, so this may well be what *Rosh* refers to. Many Bible prophecy teachers also think that Meshech means Moscow, so teach that Russia will invade Israel in the end time. However, "the prince of Rosh, Meshech" could also be translated "chief prince of Meshech." While these chapters *may* describe a Russian invasion, it's not absolutely certain. According to Revelation 20:7–8 this refers to a battle at the end of the thousand-year rule of Christ on earth.

READ EZEKIEL 38–39.

BASIC SURVEY

DANIEL

AUTHOR: Likely Daniel, but although chapters 7–12 are written in the first person ("I Daniel," 7:15 KJV), the first six chapters are in the third person ("Then Daniel answered," 2:14 KJV).

DATE: The period of the "Babylonian captivity," approximately 605–539 BC.

IN TEN WORDS OR LESS

Faithful to God in a challenging setting, Daniel is blessed.

DETAILS, PLEASE

As a young man, Daniel is taken from Jerusalem to serve the king of Babylon. Daniel's God-given ability to interpret dreams endears him to King Nebuchadnezzar, whose vision of a huge statue represents existing and future kingdoms. A later king gets Daniel to interpret the "writing on the wall," but loses his kingdom that same night. Later, the Median king, Cyrus, keeps Daniel as an adviser but is tricked into passing a law that sends Daniel into a den of lions. The final six chapters contain Daniel's prophetic visions, including that of "seventy weeks" of the end time.

QUOTABLE

> Our God whom we serve is able to deliver us from the burning fiery furnace, and he will deliver us out of thine hand, O king (3:17 KJV).

> "We do not make requests of you because we are righteous, but because of your great mercy" (9:18 NIV).

UNIQUE AND UNUSUAL

The book was originally written in two languages: Hebrew (the introduction and most of the prophecies, chapter 1 and chapters 8–12) and Aramaic (the stories of chapters 2–7).

SO WHAT?

God will always take care of the people who "dare to stand alone. . .to have a purpose firm" for Him.

READ DANIEL 1–2.

● One-Month Course: your next reading is on page 142.　→

● Three-Month Course: your next reading is on page 138.　→

● Six-Month Course: your next reading is on page 138.　→

HEART OF THE BOOK

THE PROPHET DANIEL

As a young man, Daniel—along with three other youths later called Shadrach, Meshach, and Abednego—was taken from his home in Jerusalem in 605 BC to serve Nebuchadnezzar the king of Babylon. Daniel was from a noble family (Daniel 1:3–4), and he and his friends started off by taking a courageous stand, refusing to eat the nonkosher food allotted to them. But their risk paid off and God blessed them.

Shadrach, Meshach, and Abednego found trouble when they disobeyed an order to bow before a statue of Nebuchadnezzar; as punishment they were thrown into a fiery furnace, where they were protected by a powerful being "like the Son of God" (Daniel 3:25 NKJV).

Daniel was ignored and almost completely forgotten after Nebuchadnezzar's death, and a number of briefly reigning kings followed. Finally, the last Babylonian king, Belshazzar, threw a drinking party using cups stolen from the temple in Jerusalem; he literally saw "the handwriting on the wall" that Daniel, hastily called out of retirement, interpreted as the imminent takeover of Babylon by the Medes.

The Median king, Cyrus, kept Daniel as an adviser and made him one of the three top rulers of the Babylonian territories. The final six chapters of this book contain Daniel's prophetic visions, including that of "seventy weeks"

Belshazzar's Feast by Rembrandt (1606–1669) illustrates the moment when the Babylonian king saw the writing that appeared on the wall.

of the end time. Daniel also studied the scroll of the prophet Jeremiah and realized that the "seventy years" Jeremiah had prophesied about were almost over, and that it was time for his people to be released from captivity.

READ DANIEL 3–4.

● Three-Month Course: your next reading is on page 142.　→

● Six-Month Course: your next reading is on page 139.　→

CLOSER LOOK

VISIONS OF GREAT EMPIRES

One night, King Nebuchadnezzar had a troubling dream of a statue made of different materials. Daniel first told him what he had dreamed and then gave its interpretation. Its head, made of gold, represented the Babylonian Empire (610–539 BC), which was presently in existence.

The rest of the statue symbolized empires yet to rise: its two arms of silver represented the Medo-Persian Empire (539–333 BC); its belly of bronze was the Grecian Empire (323–146 BC); its two legs of iron were the Roman Empire (27 BC–AD 476)—which later split into two empires, east and west. Finally, the feet and toes made of iron mixed with clay symbolized an end-time federation of ten nations—both dictatorships and democracies.

Several years later Daniel himself had a dream of great empires. The first, a winged lion, symbolized the Babylonians; the second, a bear, was the Medo-Persians; the third, a four-headed leopard, was the Greeks; the fourth, a powerful monster, was the Romans. The fourth beast had ten horns on its head, which again symbolized the final ten-nation empire that would rise out of the Roman Empire.

The bear had three ribs in its mouth: these were the three empires that had come before it—Egypt, Assyria, and Babylon. So there have been a total of *seven* great empires so far. This corresponds to the seven-headed beast that the apostle John described many years later: "I saw. . .a scarlet beast which was full of names of blasphemy, having seven heads and ten horns" (Revelation 17:3 NKJV).

READ DANIEL 7–8.

 Six-Month Course: your next reading is on page 140.   →

CLOSER LOOK

GOD AND THE SON OF MAN

After his vision of four beasts, Daniel's vision continued: "I kept looking until thrones were set up, and the Ancient of Days took His seat; His vesture was like white snow and the hair of His head like pure wool. . . . I kept looking in the night visions, and behold, with the clouds of heaven one like a Son of Man was coming, and He came up to the Ancient of Days and was presented before Him. And to Him was given dominion, glory and a kingdom, that all the peoples. . .might serve Him. His dominion is an everlasting dominion" (Daniel 7:9, 13–14 NASB).

During His earthly ministry, Jesus constantly referred to Himself as the "Son of Man," and most people assumed that He was using God's title for the prophet Ezekiel (Ezekiel 2:1, 3, 6, 8; 3:1, 3, etc.)—but Jesus had the prophecy from Daniel in mind. Thus, when the high priest pointedly asked Jesus whether He was the Son of God, Jesus answered, "You have said it yourself; nevertheless I tell you, hereafter you will see the Son of Man sitting at the right hand of Power, and coming on the clouds of heaven" (Matthew 26:64 NASB).

Jesus also prophesied of His second coming: "And they will see the Son of Man coming on the clouds of heaven" (Matthew 24:30 NLT). And the apostle John wrote: "Behold, he cometh with clouds; and every eye shall see him" (Revelation 1:7 KJV). (See also Luke 1:32–33.)

READ DANIEL 9 AND PSALM 2.

● Six-Month Course: your next reading is on page 142.   →

DANIEL IN THE LIONS' DEN

God's protection of Daniel from hungry lions is depicted in the painting *Daniel in the Lions' Den* by Peter Paul Rubens (1577–1640).

Cyrus placed Darius the Mede in charge of the conquered Babylonian territories, and Darius favored Daniel, appointing him as one of the three top rulers of the kingdom. This made many governors and satraps jealous, so they persuaded Darius to enact a law that no one must pray to any god for thirty days—only to Darius. All offenders should be thrown to the lions. Darius foolishly agreed. Daniel, of course, continued praying faithfully to God. When Daniel's enemies told Darius of it, he reluctantly ordered Daniel placed in the lions' den. Early the next morning, after a sleepless night, Darius called to Daniel, asking if he was still alive. Daniel answered that God had sent an angel to shut the lions' mouths. Darius then threw Daniel's accusers to the lions.

READ DANIEL 5–6.

DANIEL PRAYS FOR THREE WEEKS

The prophet Daniel once prayed for twenty-one days, and God sent an angel with the answer. When the angel finally arrived, he told Daniel that his prayers had been heard from the first day he'd prayed, but that a demon prince had fought him to prevent him from getting through (Daniel 10:1–13). Satan still constantly fights God's will. That's often why people have to pray so much and wait so long for answers to prayer. Paul told the Christians of Thessalonica, "We wanted to come to you—even I, Paul, time and again—but Satan hindered us" (1 Thessalonians 2:18 NKJV). Satan tries to stop God's will by creating obstacles. And sometimes, as in Daniel's and Paul's cases, he delays answers to prayer, even if he can't stop them completely.

READ DANIEL 10 AND 12.

BASIC SURVEY

HOSEA

AUTHOR: Probably Hosea himself, though the text is in both first and third person.

DATE: Somewhere between 760 (approximately when Hosea began ministering) and 722 BC (when Assyria overran Israel).

IN TEN WORDS OR LESS

Prophet's marriage to prostitute reflects God's relationship with Israel.

DETAILS, PLEASE

God gives Hosea a strange command: "Go, marry a promiscuous woman" (Hosea 1:2 NIV). The marriage pictures God's relationship to Israel—an honorable, loving husband paired with an unfaithful wife. Hosea marries an adulteress named Gomer and starts a family with her. When Gomer returns to her life of sin, Hosea—again picturing God's faithfulness—buys her back from the slave market. Much of the book contains God's warnings for disobedience but His promises of blessing for repentance.

QUOTABLE

> For they [Israel] have sown the wind, and they shall reap the whirlwind (8:7 KJV).

> "I [God] led Israel along with my ropes of kindness and love" (11:4 NLT).

UNIQUE AND UNUSUAL

Gomer had three children—perhaps Hosea's, but maybe not—each given a prophetic name. Son Jezreel was named for a massacre, daughter Lo-Ruhamah's name meant "not loved," and son Lo-Ammi's name meant "not my people."

SO WHAT?

God is faithful, even when His people aren't—and He's always ready to forgive. "I will heal their backsliding," God said through Hosea. "I will love them freely" (14:4 KJV).

READ HOSEA 2–3.

- One-Month Course: your next reading is on page 145.   →
- Three-Month Course: your next reading is on page 145.   →
- Six-Month Course: your next reading is on page 143.   →

CLOSER LOOK

HOSEA'S UNFAITHFUL WIFE

Hosea, a prophet from Israel, is shown here in this painting by Duccio di Buoninsegna (1255–1319).

Hosea was the only prophet from the northern kingdom (Israel) to write a book in the Bible. He began his ministry about 760 BC, when Jeroboam II was king of Israel (Hosea 1:1). During this time Amos (to the south, in Judah) was also prophesying against Israel (Amos 1:1). At this point, the oppressive kingdom of Aram was weak and Jeroboam had conquered their territory, including Damascus and as far north as Hamath (2 Kings 14:28). Archaeological evidence confirms that the northern kingdom was then richer and more powerful than they'd ever been.

However, this was also a very sinful period in their history. Idol worship was rampant, and God referred to the noblewomen of Samaria (Israel's capital) as lazy, drunken cows who callously oppressed the poor (Amos 4:1; see also 8:4–6).

Even though their sins were grievous and judgment was looming, God still loved His people. God compared His covenant relationship with them to a marriage, saying, "Turn, O backsliding children, saith the LORD; for I am married unto you" (Jeremiah 3:14 KJV). To illustrate how He was still faithful although Israel had strayed, God told Hosea, "Go, marry a promiscuous woman and have children with her, for like an adulterous wife this land is guilty of unfaithfulness to the LORD" (Hosea 1:2 NIV).

God yearned for His people to repent, but warned that if they refused, they'd be carried away captive to Assyria. This happened a few decades later in 722 BC (2 Kings 17:5–6).

READ HOSEA 4–5.

● Six-Month Course: your next reading is on page 145.   →

BECOMING GOD'S PEOPLE

When Hosea's promiscuous wife, Gomer, conceived and bore a son, God said: "Call his name Lo-Ammi [Not-My-People], for you are not My people, and I will not be your God." Then He added, "Yet the number of the children of Israel shall be as the sand of the sea. . . . And it shall come to pass in the place where it was said to them, 'You are not My people,' there it shall be said to them, 'You are sons of the living God'" (Hosea 1:9–10 NKJV). In Romans 9:24–26, 30–31, Paul said that this prophecy has been fulfilled in the Gentiles who came to faith in Jesus, God's Son. They were formerly *not* God's people, but had become His people.

READ HOSEA 1 AND ROMANS 9.

THE SON OF GOD AND EGYPT

For centuries, many prophecies about the coming Messiah lay in plain sight in the pages of scripture, but weren't recognized for what they were. Consider this one from 760 BC: "When Israel was a child, I loved him, and out of Egypt I called my son" (Hosea 11:1 NIV). It seemed odd because it was the Israelites— the descendants of Israel (Jacob)—that God brought out of Egypt. Israel himself had died

Hosea's prophecy was fulfilled when Jesus' family returned to Israel after fleeing to Egypt, an event that is depicted in *Rest on the Flight into Egypt* by Fra Bartolomeo (1472–1517).

nearly four hundred years previously. Yet God referred to Israel as "a child" and His "son" (singular). As Matthew pointed out, this prophecy was fulfilled *precisely* in Jesus' life: when He was only a child, God indeed called Him out of Egypt to the land of Israel (Matthew 2:14–15).

READ HOSEA 11 AND MATTHEW 2:13-23.

BASIC SURVEY

JOEL

AUTHOR: Joel, son of Pethuel (1:1). Little else is known about him.

DATE: Unclear, but possibly just before the Babylonian invasion of Judah in 586 BC.

IN TEN WORDS OR LESS

Locust plague pictures God's judgment on His sinful people.

DETAILS, PLEASE

A devastating locust swarm invades the nation of Judah, but Joel indicates this natural disaster is nothing compared to the coming "great and very terrible" day of the Lord (2:11 KJV). God plans to judge His people for sin, but they still have time to repent. Obedience will bring both physical and spiritual renewal: "I will pour out my spirit upon all flesh" (2:28 KJV), God says. When the Holy Spirit comes on Christian believers at Pentecost (Acts 2), the apostle Peter quotes this passage to explain what has happened.

QUOTABLE

> "Whoever calls on the name of the LORD shall be saved" (2:32 NKJV).

> Multitudes, multitudes in the valley of decision: for the day of the LORD is near in the valley of decision (3:14 KJV).

UNIQUE AND UNUSUAL

Unlike other prophets, who condemned idolatry, injustice, or other specific sins of the Jewish people, Joel simply called for repentance without describing the sin committed.

SO WHAT?

Though God judges sin, He always offers a way out—in our time, through Jesus.

READ PSALM 79 AND PROVERBS 13.

● One-Month Course: your next reading is on page 148.   →

● Three-Month Course: your next reading is on page 148.   →

● Six-Month Course: your next reading is on page 146.   →

CLOSER LOOK

Locust Plagues in Israel

Every March or April, millions of juvenile locusts leave the northern Sahara desert and swarm like immense, dark clouds throughout the Middle East. They are incredibly voracious and often devour everything in sight. In Moses' day, God sent a great swarm that "invaded all Egypt and settled down in every area of the country in great numbers. Never before had there been such a plague of locusts" (Exodus 10:14 NIV).

Locust plagues frequently caused devastation and destruction of crops in Israel as well. God said that He sent them as judgment (Deuteronomy 28:38–42). One such locust plague is described in the book of Joel, which depicts wave after wave of locusts descending upon the land: "What the locust swarm has left the great locusts have eaten; what the great locusts have left the young locusts have eaten; what the young locusts have left other locusts have eaten" (Joel 1:4 NIV).

God promised, however, that if His people repented He would heal their land (2 Chronicles 7:13–14). Locust swarms sometimes wiped out farmers'

Joel described one of the devastating locust plagues that destroyed Israel's crops.

entire crops, leaving them destitute, and if this happened year after year, people nearly starved. So God promised, "Then I will make up to you for the years that the swarming locust has eaten, the creeping locust, the stripping locust and the gnawing locust" (Joel 2:25 NASB). Or as the NKJV says, "I will restore to you the years that the swarming locust has eaten."

Locust swarms are sometimes still a problem in areas of the Middle East today.

READ JOEL 1 AND EXODUS 10:1–20.

● Six-Month Course: your next reading is on page 148.   →

THE DAY OF THE LORD

The ancient Israelites longed for "the day of the Lord" when God would judge the wicked and provide justice and deliverance for the righteous. But the prophets warned that this day would be a cataclysmic event—nothing to look forward to. There would be terrifying signs in the heavens—the sun turned dark and the moon turned into blood (Joel 2:30–31). Besides, the people who *thought* they were righteous might also be judged. Joel warned, "The day of the LORD is great; it is dreadful. Who can endure it?" (Joel 2:11 NIV). And Amos added, "Woe to you who desire the day of the LORD! For what good is the day of the LORD to you?" (Amos 5:18 NKJV; see also Zephaniah 1:14–18).

READ JOEL 2:1–27 AND REVELATION 6:12–17; 16.

GOD POURS OUT HIS SPIRIT

Joel prophesied about God sending His Spirit upon believers, saying, "And it shall come to pass afterward that I will pour out My Spirit on all flesh; your sons and your daughters shall prophesy, your old men shall dream dreams, your young men shall see visions. And also on My menservants and on My

maidservants I will pour out My Spirit in those days" (Joel 2:28–29 NKJV). This was fulfilled on Pentecost in AD 30 when the Holy Spirit was poured out on 120 disciples of Jesus in Jerusalem (Acts 2:14–21). God continued to send the Holy Spirit upon Christians (Acts 8:14–17; 10:44–46; 19:1–6). This also empowered them to boldly preach the Gospel (Acts 1:8; 4:31).

Joel described how God would pour out His Holy Spirit on believers. A dove is often seen as a symbol of God's presence.

READ JOEL 2:28–32; 3:1–21; AND ACTS 2.

BASIC SURVEY

AMOS

AUTHOR: Amos, a shepherd from Tekoa, near Bethlehem (1:1).

DATE: Approximately the 760s BC.

IN TEN WORDS OR LESS

Real religion isn't just ritual, but treating people with justice.

DETAILS, PLEASE

An average guy—a lowly shepherd, actually—takes on the rich and power-ful of Israelite society, condemning their idol worship, persecution of God's prophets, and cheating of the poor. Though God once rescued the people of Israel from slavery in Egypt, He is ready to send them into new bondage due to their sin. Amos sees visions that picture Israel's plight: a plumb line, indicating the people are not measuring up to God's standards; and a basket of ripe fruit, showing the nation is ripe for God's judgment.

QUOTABLE

> Prepare to meet thy God, O Israel (4:12 KJV).

> Seek good, not evil, that you may live (5:14 NIV).

> "Let justice run down like water, and righteousness like a mighty stream" (5:24 NKJV).

UNIQUE AND UNUSUAL

A native of the southern Jewish kingdom of Judah, Amos was directed by God to prophesy in the northern Jewish nation of Israel.

SO WHAT?

How are you treating the people around you? In God's eyes, that's an indica-tor of your true spiritual condition. For a New Testament perspective, see James 2:14–18.

READ AMOS 1–2.

● One-Month Course: your next reading is on page 151. →

● Three-Month Course: your next reading is on page 151. →

● Six-Month Course: your next reading is on page 149. →

CLOSER LOOK

A Working-Class Prophet

Before he died, around 795 BC, Elisha had prophesied that Israel would defeat the Arameans (2 Kings 13:14–19), and around 775 BC, Jonah prophesied that King Jeroboam would restore Israel to its greatest extent

since the days of Solomon. Sure enough, "he restored the border of Israel from the entrance of Hamath as far as the Sea of the Arabah, according to the word of the LORD. . .which He spoke through His servant Jonah" (2 Kings 14:25 NASB).

The problem was that Israel and Judah considered their prosperity as a sign that God approved of their selfish lifestyles and was blessing them. They were "men of corrupt minds. . .

Amos was a shepherd and an orchard worker. He repeatedly warned the people of Israel to be faithful to God.

supposing that gain is godliness" (1 Timothy 6:5 KJV). In actuality they were idolatrous, extravagant, and oppressors of the poor.

Amos was a common laborer—a shepherd and orchard worker—in the village of Tekoa, six miles south of Bethlehem in Judah (Amos 1:1; 7:14–15). God called him to prophesy against both Israel and Judah, so he went boldly to the religious center at Bethel and preached, "Jeroboam will die by the sword, and Israel will surely go into exile" (Amos 7:11 NIV). He was bluntly warned to head back to Judah.

Amos's message was simple: God was about to bring devastating judgment upon His disobedient people. He had sent them repeated warnings with His prophets, but if the people didn't repent, they'd be conquered and carried into exile and cease existing as a nation.

READ AMOS 3 AND 7.

● Six-Month Course: your next reading is on page 151.   →

God's Merciful Judgments

God is merciful and doesn't immediately send complete destruction even when people persist in disobedience. As Amos explained, God often sends limited judgments as warnings. "'I brought hunger to every city. . . . I kept the rain from falling when your crops needed it the most. . . . I struck your farms and vineyards with blight and mildew. Locusts devoured all your fig and olive trees. . . . I sent plagues on you. . . . I destroyed some of

Amos explained that God used judgments such as failing crops to lead the people of Israel to repent.

your cities. . . . But still you would not return to me,' says the LORD" (Amos 4:6–11 NLT). God is "longsuffering toward us, not willing that any should perish but that all should come to repentance" (2 Peter 3:9 NKJV). But eventually, if people stubbornly refuse to repent, He *will* send final judgment.

READ AMOS 4 AND 8.

Going through the Motions

In Matthew 23, Jesus rebuked the religious leaders for their hypocrisy and hollow religiosity. They thought that just going through the motions and performing the proper rituals would please God, but they failed to have love, mercy, and faith (Matthew 23:23). This problem was nothing new. Nearly eight hundred years earlier God declared, "I hate, I despise your religious festivals; your assemblies are a stench to me. Even though you bring me burnt offerings and grain offerings, I will not accept them. . . . Away with the noise of your songs! I will not listen to the music of your harps. But let justice roll on like a river, righteousness like a never-failing stream!" (Amos 5:21–24 NIV). God wants heartfelt worship, love, and justice most of all (see John 4:23).

READ AMOS 5 AND MATTHEW 23.

BASIC SURVEY

OBADIAH

AUTHOR: Obadiah (1:1), perhaps a person by that name, or maybe an unnamed prophet for whom "Obadiah" (meaning "servant of God") is a title.

DATE: Unclear, but probably within thirty years after Babylon's invasion of Judah in 586 BC.

IN TEN WORDS OR LESS

Edom will suffer for participating in Jerusalem's destruction.

DETAILS, PLEASE

Edom was a nation descended from Esau—twin brother of Jacob, the patriarch of Israel. The baby boys had struggled in their mother's womb (Genesis 25:21–26), and their conflict had continued over the centuries. After Edom took part in the Babylonian ransacking of Jerusalem, Obadiah passed down God's judgment: "For violence against your brother Jacob, shame shall cover you, and you shall be cut off forever" (1:10 NKJV).

QUOTABLE

> Upon Mount Zion shall be deliverance (1:17 KJV).

UNIQUE AND UNUSUAL

Obadiah is the Old Testament's shortest book—only one chapter and twenty-one verses.

SO WHAT?

Obadiah shows God's faithfulness to His people. This prophecy is a fulfillment of God's promise from generations earlier that "I will bless those who bless you, and the one who curses you I will curse" (Genesis 12:3 NASB).

READ PSALMS 3–4 AND PROVERBS 11.

● One-Month Course: your next reading is on page 153.

● Three-Month Course: your next reading is on page 153.

● Six-Month Course: your next reading is on page 153.

AN ECHO OF JEREMIAH

Obadiah lived at the same time as the prophet Jeremiah. We know that there were other prophets besides Jeremiah living then, but they're lesser known because they didn't leave any written prophecies (Jeremiah 26:20–23). One of the most striking things about the short book of Obadiah is that 1:1–9 is, in places, an almost word-for-word repeat of Jeremiah 49:7–22. Obadiah spoke out against Edom, who rejoiced when the Babylonians destroyed Israel. Jeremiah wrote his prophecy first, promising that Edom would be judged—but gave no reasons for this judgment. However, Obadiah later witnessed how mercilessly the Edomites treated the Jews during the Babylonian invasion (see 1:10–16) and prophesied that God would judge Edom for those specific things.

READ OBADIAH 1 AND JEREMIAH 49.

FORTRESSES IN THE HIGH ROCKS

These hills were once part of ancient Edom, whose people believed that they would never be conquered.

Israel was a land of low hills and plains, fairly easily invaded and conquered by the Babylonians, but Edom was a land of lofty plateaus, dotted with cities like Sela hidden among impenetrable defiles and canyons. The Edomites gloated when Israel was destroyed, confident that they themselves could never be conquered. (Years later, the fabulous Rock City of Petra would be built in Edom.) Nevertheless, God gave them this message: "The pride of your heart has deceived you, you who live in the clefts of the rocks and make your home on the heights, you who say to yourself, 'Who can bring me down to the ground?'" (Obadiah 1:3 NIV). God would bring them down, though they made their nest among the stars (v. 4).

READ PSALM 60 AND ISAIAH 34.

BASIC SURVEY

JONAH

AUTHOR: Unclear; the story is Jonah's, but written in the third person.

DATE: Approximately 760 BC. Jonah prophesied during the reign of Israel's King Jeroboam II (see 2 Kings 14:23–25), who ruled from about 793 to 753 BC.

IN TEN WORDS OR LESS

Reluctant prophet, running from God, is swallowed by giant fish.

DETAILS, PLEASE

God tells Jonah to preach repentance in Nineveh, capital of the brutal Assyrian Empire. Jonah disobeys, sailing in the opposite direction—toward a rendezvous with literary immortality. A storm rocks the ship, and Jonah spends three days in a giant fish's belly before deciding to obey God after all. When Jonah preaches, Nineveh repents—and God spares the city from the destruction He'd threatened. But the prejudiced Jonah pouts. The story ends with God proclaiming His concern even for vicious pagans.

QUOTABLE

> "I will pay what I have vowed. Salvation is of the LORD" (2:9 NKJV).

> "Should I not have compassion on Nineveh, the great city in which there are more than 120,000 persons who do not know the difference between their right and left hand?" (4:11 NASB).

UNIQUE AND UNUSUAL

Jonah's prophecy wasn't fulfilled—because of Nineveh's repentance.

SO WHAT?

God loves *everyone*—even the enemies of His chosen people. As Romans 5:8 (NLT) says, "But God showed his great love for us by sending Christ to die for us while we were still sinners."

READ JONAH 1 AND PSALM 9.

● One-Month Course: your next reading is on page 157.   →

● Three-Month Course: your next reading is on page 157.   →

● Six-Month Course: your next reading is on page 154.   →

CLOSER LOOK

Jonah—Prophet of Israel

Jonah, son of Amittai, was from the town of Gath Hepher in Israel. This town was in Zebulun, in northern Israel, west of the Sea of Galilee (Joshua 19:10, 13). The prophet Elisha frequently passed near it as he walked the road from Mount Carmel to Shunem (2 Kings 4:8–9, 25). In fact, it is pos-

Jonah refused to obey God's order to go to Nineveh. He appears in the artwork by Michelangelo (1475–1564) in the Sistine Chapel.

sible that Jonah was influenced by the group of prophets that followed Elisha and learned from him (2 Kings 6:1), since Jonah began his ministry around 775 BC, only twenty years after Elisha died in 795 BC.

Jonah is most famous for refusing to go to Nineveh to warn them about God's impending judgment, but he is also known to have made an amazing prophecy that was fulfilled by King Jeroboam II of Israel. "He was the one who restored the boundaries of Israel from Lebo Hamath to the Dead Sea, in accordance with the word of the LORD, the God of Israel, spoken through his servant Jonah son of Amittai, the prophet from Gath Hepher" (2 Kings 14:25 NIV).

In Jonah's day, the Arameans were weak, and Israel had reconquered much territory to the north that had once been part of Solomon's empire. Israel was powerful and prosperous, and was becoming rich through international trade. There was an international sea port in Joppa, where Phoenician ships carried Israelite produce as far west as Tarshish, in southern Spain. When Jonah attempted to flee from the Lord, he boarded one of these great merchant ships and set sail for the western edge of the known world.

READ JONAH 2 AND 2 KINGS 14.

● Six-Month Course: your next reading is on page 155.   →

Jonah and the Great Fish

In Jonah's day, a mighty warring empire to the north was an imminent threat. The Assyrians were the cruelest, most violent empire the world had ever seen, and Jonah knew this. So at first he was delighted when God told him to go to Nineveh and preach, "Forty days from now Nineveh will be destroyed!" (Jonah 3:4 NLT). Then Jonah got the inescapable feeling that the Assyrians would repent if they heard this warning—and then God would have mercy and *not* destroy them (John 4:2). So Jonah took a ship to Tarshish, to make *sure* Nineveh was destroyed.

However, God sent a great storm, and the sailors hurled Jonah overboard to placate God. But "the LORD had prepared a great fish to swallow up Jonah" (Jonah 1:17 KJV). Now, the Hebrew word in Jonah 1:17 and the Greek word in Matthew 12:40 both mean "great aquatic animal"—so this "fish" could have been a sperm whale or a whale shark, which can grow fifty feet long. Both of these have swallowed animals as big as humans. As long as the animal or person inside the whale's stomach is alive, the digestive juices don't start flowing.

Another thing, the expression "three days and three nights" can also refer to one whole day and *parts* of two other days. So Jonah didn't necessarily spend a full seventy-two hours in the sea creature's belly. He could have spent forty hours and had plenty of oxygen to survive until the sea creature vomited him up.

READ JONAH 3–4.

 Six-Month Course: your next reading is on page 157.   →

HIDDEN TREASURE

THE SHIPS OF TARSHISH

About 775 BC Jonah went to the Israelite port of Joppa, where he found a number of international seafaring vessels, and boarded a ship bound for distant Tarshish (Jonah 1:3). Now, Tarshish was Tartessus in southwest Spain, a kingdom rich in metals, on the river Tartessus west of modern Gibraltar. The Phoenicians had a mining colony there named Gadir. When the Bible speaks of "you ships of Tarshish" (Isaiah 23:1, 14 NIV), it refers to Phoenician ships that sailed to the western end of the known world. The Greeks believed that the paradisiacal Garden of the Hesperides (where golden apples giving immortality grew) was in Tartessus. They thought that the sunset in the west resulted from the sun reflecting off the golden apples.

READ PSALMS 10–11 AND ISAIAH 23.

HIDDEN TREASURE

THE CHILDREN OF PAGANS

It's widely believed that God doesn't hold children responsible for sin until they reach "the age of accountability," the age at which they know the difference between good and evil. In Deuteronomy 1:39 (NKJV), God

speaks of "your little ones. . .who today have no knowledge of good and evil" and speaks of a time "before the child shall know to refuse the evil, and choose the good" (Isaiah 7:16 KJV). God asked Jonah, "Should I not pity Nineveh, that great city, in which are more than one hundred and twenty thousand persons who cannot discern between their right hand and their left?" (Jonah 4:11 NKJV). He was talking about the young children. While the scriptures aren't conclusive, it appears that all very young children go to heaven.

Many people believe that young children will go to heaven because they do not yet understand the difference between good and evil.

READ MATTHEW 18:1–35 AND 19:13–30.

BASIC SURVEY

MICAH

AUTHOR: "The word of the LORD that came to Micah the Morasthite" (1:1 KJV). Micah either wrote the prophecies or dictated them to another.

DATE: Approximately 700 BC.

IN TEN WORDS OR LESS

Israel and Judah will suffer for their idolatry and injustice.

DETAILS, PLEASE

Micah chastises both the northern and southern Jewish nations for pursuing false gods and cheating the poor. The two nations will be devastated by invaders (the Assyrians), but God will preserve "the remnant of Israel" (2:12 KJV).

QUOTABLE

> The LORD has told you what is good, and this is what he requires of you: to do what is right, to love mercy, and to walk humbly with your God (6:8 NLT).

UNIQUE AND UNUSUAL

Centuries before Jesus' birth, Micah predicted the town where that would occur: "But you, Bethlehem Ephrathah, though you are little among the thousands of Judah, yet out of you shall come forth to Me the One to be Ruler in Israel" (5:2 NKJV).

SO WHAT?

Micah shows how God's judgment is tempered by mercy. "Who is a God like you, who pardons sin and forgives the transgression of the remnant of his inheritance? You do not stay angry forever but delight to show mercy" (7:18 NIV).

READ MICAH 1–2.

● One-Month Course: your next reading is on page 159.   →

● Three-Month Course: your next reading is on page 159.   →

● Six-Month Course: your next reading is on page 159.   →

THE MILLENNIUM

Micah prophesied about a peaceful period that will follow a time of great end-time trouble. "Now it shall come to pass in the latter days that the mountain of the LORD's house. . .shall be exalted above the hills; and peoples shall flow to it. . . . For out of Zion the law shall go forth. . . . They shall beat their swords into plowshares, and. . .nation shall not lift up sword against nation, neither shall they learn war anymore" (Micah 4:1–3 NKJV). Then Christ will rule the world during the Millennium. This word comes from the Greek words *mille* (thousand) and *ennium* (years). God will transform the earth into a paradise, and we will help Jesus govern it. "And they lived and reigned with Christ for a thousand years" (Revelation 20:4 NKJV).

READ MICAH 3–4.

THE MESSIAH FROM BETHLEHEM

About 750 years before Jesus was born, the prophet Micah wrote, "But you, Bethlehem Ephrathah, though you are little among the thousands of Judah, yet out of you shall come forth to Me the One to be Ruler in Israel, whose goings forth are from of old, from everlasting" (Micah 5:2 NKJV). Or as the NASB states, "His goings forth are from long ago, from the days of eternity." Jesus has always existed in eternity, one with God His Father, but He was

The prophet Micah foretold that the Messiah would be born in Bethlehem. *The Adoration of the Shepherds* by Gerard van Honthorst (1592–1656) depicts the birth of Jesus.

born as a small baby in the town of Bethlehem. The Jewish chief priests and scribes knew this prophecy of Micah, so they were aware that this was the place the Messiah would be born (Matthew 2:1–6).

READ MICAH 5–6.

BASIC SURVEY

NAHUM

AUTHOR: "The book of the vision of Nahum the Elkoshite" (1:1 KJV). Nahum either wrote the prophecies or dictated them to another.

DATE: Sometime between 663 and 612 BC.

IN TEN WORDS OR LESS

Powerful, wicked Nineveh will fall before God's judgment.

DETAILS, PLEASE

"Woe to the bloody city!" (3:1 KJV), Nahum cries. Nineveh, capital of the brutal Assyrian Empire, has been targeted for judgment by God Himself, who will "cast abominable filth upon you, make you vile, and make you a spectacle" (3:6 NKJV) for sins of idolatry and cruelty. Nahum's prophecy comes true when the Babylonian Empire overruns Nineveh in 612 BC.

QUOTABLE

> The LORD is slow to anger, and great in power, and will not at all acquit the wicked (1:3 KJV).

> The LORD is good, a refuge in times of trouble. He cares for those who trust in him (1:7 NIV).

UNIQUE AND UNUSUAL

Nahum is a kind of Jonah, Part 2. Though the city had once avoided God's judgment by taking Jonah's preaching to heart and repenting, now, more than a century later, it will experience the full consequence of its sins.

SO WHAT?

Even the most powerful city on earth is no match for God's strength. Neither is the biggest problem in our individual lives.

READ NAHUM 1 AND PSALMS 12–15.

● One-Month Course: your next reading is on page 162.   →

● Three-Month Course: your next reading is on page 162.   →

● Six-Month Course: your next reading is on page 160.   →

THE FALL OF MIGHTY NINEVEH

Many people concede that the Bible contains an accurate record of Israel's history. But they're not ready to admit that the Bible is the very Word of God. Fulfilled prophecy, however, is definitive proof of the Bible's divine inspiration.

About 630 BC, when Nahum described the soon-coming doom of Nineveh, capital of the Assyrian Empire, it didn't seem likely. The Assyrians were an oppressive warrior state, they were unspeakably cruel to the nations they conquered—and they were at the very height of their power. Nineveh it-

self was protected by five walls, with the inner wall one hundred feet high and four chariot-widths thick. And since Nineveh was at the junction of two rivers, it was guarded on several sides by water. "The river was her defense, the waters her wall" (Nahum 3:8 NIV).

Nevertheless, Nahum prophesied that Nineveh would be conquered (Nahum 2:1–4; 3:1–3, 14–15). And he predicted exactly how it would fall: "But with an overflowing flood He will make an utter

Babylon conquered Nineveh, possibly with the assistance of Babylonian archers such as the ones shown in this mosaic.

end of its place. . . . The gates of the rivers are opened" (Nahum 1:8; 2:6 NKJV).

Less than twenty years later, armies of Babylonians and Medes surrounded Nineveh. After two years of siege, the attackers built a dam on the Khoser River (which ran through the city). Then, in 612 BC, they opened the river gates and the resulting flood washed away part of the wall, allowing them to enter. So complete was Nineveh's destruction that when Alexander the Great fought a battle nearby in 331 BC, he saw no evidence that a city had ever been there.

READ NAHUM 2 AND PSALMS 24–25.

● Six-Month Course: your next reading is on page 162.   →

HIDDEN TREASURE

GOD PROTECTS HIS PEOPLE

One of the most comforting promises in the Bible is found in the book of Nahum: "The LORD is good, a refuge in times of trouble. He cares for those who trust in him" (Nahum 1:7 NIV). This not only speaks of supernatural protection in times of war and danger, as does Psalm 91, but is a promise we can look to during *any* troubled times—whether periods of economic chaos, family disagreements, when accused by enemies, or anytime things get out of control and we need divine help. God genuinely loves and cares for us. (See Psalm 55:22.) As Peter stated in the New Testament, "Give all your worries and cares to God, for he cares about you" (1 Peter 5:7 NLT).

READ NAHUM 3 AND PSALMS 26–27.

HIDDEN TREASURE

WHEN GOD GETS ANGRY

Many people are troubled by Old Testament images of God as an angry, vengeful deity. Nahum 1:2 (NIV) says, "The LORD takes vengeance and is filled with wrath. The LORD takes vengeance on his foes and vents his wrath against his enemies." Some people wonder if God evolved from a God of wrath into a God of love. No. He says, "I am the LORD, I change not" (Malachi 3:6 KJV). God has *always* been love (1 John 4:8), but He has also always been just. Nahum goes on to say, "The LORD is slow to anger but. . . will not leave the guilty unpunished" (Nahum 1:3 NIV). The Assyrians were vicious and greedy and the Bible states, "The LORD is good. . .but. . .he will make an end of Nineveh" (vv. 7–8 NIV).

READ ISAIAH 30–31.

BASIC SURVEY

HABAKKUK

AUTHOR: Habakkuk (1:1); nothing is known of his background.

DATE: Approximately 600 BC.

IN TEN WORDS OR LESS

Trust God even when He seems unresponsive or unfair.

DETAILS, PLEASE

In Judah, a prophet complains that God allows violence and injustice among His people. But Habakkuk is shocked to learn the Lord's plan for dealing with the problem: sending the "bitter and hasty" (1:6 KJV) Chaldeans to punish Judah. Habakkuk argues that the Chaldeans are far worse than the disobedient Jews, telling God, "You are of purer eyes than to behold evil" (1:13 NKJV). The Lord, however, says He's only using the Chaldeans for His purposes, and will in time punish them for their own sins. It's not Habakkuk's job to question God's ways: "The LORD is in his holy temple: let all the earth keep silence before him" (2:20 KJV). Habakkuk, like Job, ultimately submits to God's authority.

QUOTABLE

> The just shall live by his faith (2:4 KJV).

> I will joy in the God of my salvation (3:18 KJV).

UNIQUE AND UNUSUAL

The apostle Paul quotes Habakkuk 2:4 in his powerful Gospel presentation in Romans 1.

SO WHAT?

Our world is much like Habakkuk's—full of violence and injustice—but God is still in control. Whether we sense it or not, He's working out His own purposes.

READ HABAKKUK 1 AND PSALM 29.

● One-Month Course: your next reading is on page 165.   →

● Three-Month Course: your next reading is on page 165.   →

● Six-Month Course: your next reading is on page 163.   →

CLOSER LOOK

HABAKKUK ASKS GOD QUESTIONS

There's sometimes so much pain around us that we wonder, "If God is love (1 John 4:8), why does He cause all this suffering? And if He doesn't cause it, why does He *allow* it? Since He's all-powerful, He could just stop it, couldn't

He?" Some people are afraid to question God. They think that means that they don't trust Him. So they simply say, "God is good all the time!" and never ask questions. Now, God *is* good, but that didn't stop the prophet Habakkuk from wondering why bad things happened.

First, Habakkuk was dismayed by his people in Judah doing evil and seemingly getting away with it; he wondered why God didn't punish

Habakkuk asked God several difficult questions, but he also accepted that he would not always understand God's ways.

them. Then when God told him that He was going to send the Babylonians to judge them, Habakkuk questioned how God could use such violent, godless pagans to chastise His people.

Habakkuk wasn't afraid to ask God some very tough questions, such as, "How long, LORD, must I call for help, but you do not listen? Or cry out to you, 'Violence!' but you do not save? Why do you make me look at injustice? Why do you tolerate wrongdoing?" (Habakkuk 1:1–3 NIV).

In the end, Habakkuk realized that he couldn't fully understand God's ways, but he still needed to trust God. In the New Testament, Peter declared, "After you have suffered for a little while, the God of all grace, who called you to His eternal glory in Christ, will Himself perfect, confirm, strengthen and establish you" (1 Peter 5:10 NASB).

READ HABAKKUK 2 AND PSALMS 32–33.

 Six-Month Course: your next reading is on page 165.   →

God's Promises Are Sure

God encouraged Habakkuk that His word would be fulfilled in due time, saying, "For the vision is yet for the appointed time; it hastens toward the goal and it will not fail. Though it tarries, wait for it; for it will certainly come, it will not delay" (Habakkuk 2:3 NASB). In Isaiah, God described how the rain watered the earth then stated, "It is the same with my word. I send it out, and it always produces fruit. It will accomplish all I want it to, and it will prosper everywhere I send it" (Isaiah 55:11 NLT). This is why we are told in Hebrews 10:36 (NKJV), "For you have need of endurance, so that after you have done the will of God, you may receive the promise."

READ PSALMS 34 AND 36.

When Everything Goes Wrong

Habakkuk trusted God so much that he said, "Even though the fig trees have no blossoms, and there are no grapes on the vines; even though the olive crop fails, and the fields lie empty and barren; even though the flocks die in the fields, and the cattle barns are empty, yet I will rejoice in the LORD!" (Habakkuk 3:17–18 NLT). He was basically saying, "I don't care if absolutely *everything* goes wrong! Even if I have no food, I'm still going to be happy and love God!" Paul said something similar: "Everywhere and in all things I have learned both to be full and to be hungry, both to abound and to suffer need" (Philippians 4:12 NKJV). Though suffering, they were still thankful.

READ HABAKKUK 3 AND PSALM 38.

BASIC SURVEY

ZEPHANIAH

AUTHOR: Zephaniah (1:1).

DATE: Approximately 640–620 BC, during the reign of King Josiah (1:1).

IN TEN WORDS OR LESS

A coming "day of the Lord" promises heavy judgment.

DETAILS, PLEASE

Zephaniah begins with a jarring prophecy: "I will utterly consume all things from off the land," God declares in the book's second verse (KJV). People, animals, birds, and fish will all perish, victims of God's wrath over Judah's idolatry. Other nearby nations will be punished as well in "the fire of my jealousy" (3:8 KJV), but there is hope: in His mercy, God will someday restore a remnant of Israel that "shall not do iniquity, nor speak lies" (3:13 KJV).

QUOTABLE

> The great day of the LORD is near; it is near and hastens quickly (1:14 NKJV).

> The LORD thy God in the midst of thee is mighty; he will save, he will rejoice over thee with joy (3:17 KJV).

UNIQUE AND UNUSUAL

Zephaniah gives more detail about himself than most of the minor prophets, identifying himself as a great-great-grandson of Hezekiah (1:1), probably the popular, godly king of Judah (2 Chronicles 29).

SO WHAT?

God gave the people of Judah fair warning of His judgment, just as He has done with us. For Christians, the coming "day of the Lord" carries no fear.

READ ZEPHANIAH 1 AND PSALMS 39–40.

● One-Month Course: your next reading is on page 167.   →

● Three-Month Course: your next reading is on page 167.   →

● Six-Month Course: your next reading is on page 167.   →

GOD SHAKES THE COMPLACENT

"I will search Jerusalem with lamps, and punish the men who are settled in complacency, who say in their heart, 'The LORD will not do good, nor

will He do evil'" (Zephaniah 1:12 NKJV). Many people in Zephaniah's day were complacent and self-satisfied. They didn't deny that God existed, but secretly figured that He was either distant or uninvolved in their activities and had left them to their own devices. They didn't believe He would bless them for doing good, nor punish them for doing evil. He was, in a

Zephaniah spoke to those who did not believe that God would punish them for being too complacent.

word, irrelevant. But God is not mocked, and not powerless. He promised to shake up the lives of the self-sufficient and complacent.

READ ZEPHANIAH 2 AND PSALMS 6–7.

GOD PROMISES RELIEF

Zephaniah is a short book with great news: "The LORD your God is with you, the Mighty Warrior who saves. He will take great delight in you; in his love he will no longer rebuke you, but will rejoice over you with singing" (Zephaniah 3:17 NIV). Many people have seen a great deal of trouble in their lives and are used to seeing God's love expressed *this* way: "As many as I love, I rebuke and chasten: be zealous therefore, and repent" (Revelation 3:19 KJV). It's comforting to know that "He will not always chide" (Psalm 103:9 KJV). God promises relief: "For I will not contend forever. . .for the spirit would fail before Me, and the souls which I have made" (Isaiah 57:16 NKJV).

READ ZEPHANIAH 3 AND PSALMS 43–44.

BASIC SURVEY

HAGGAI

AUTHOR: Haggai (1:1).

DATE: 520 BC—a precise date because Haggai mentions "the second year of Darius the king" (1:1 KJV), which can be verified against Persian records.

IN TEN WORDS OR LESS

Jews returning from exile need to rebuild God's temple.

DETAILS, PLEASE

One of three "postexilic" prophets, Haggai encourages former Babylonian captives to restore the demolished temple in Jerusalem. The new world power, Persia, has allowed the people to return to Jerusalem, but they've become distracted with building their own comfortable homes. Through Haggai, God tells the people to rebuild the temple first, to break a drought that's affecting the countryside.

QUOTABLE

> "Be strong, all you people of the land," says the LORD, "and work; for I am with you," says the LORD of hosts (2:4 NKJV).

UNIQUE AND UNUSUAL

Haggai seems to hint at the end-time Tribulation and second coming of Christ when he quotes God as saying, "I will shake the heavens, and the earth, and the sea, and the dry land; and I will shake all nations, and the desire of all nations shall come" (2:6–7 KJV).

SO WHAT?

Priorities are important. When we put God first, He is more inclined to bless us.

READ HAGGAI 1 AND PROVERBS 23.

● One-Month Course: your next reading is on page 170.   →

● Three-Month Course: your next reading is on page 170.   →

● Six-Month Course: your next reading is on page 168.   →

CLOSER LOOK

ENCOURAGING GOD'S WORKERS

When people stopped building the temple, God sent a severe drought. Haggai ordered them to begin working and finish the temple.

The first Persian king, Cyrus, had written an edict telling the Jews to rebuild their temple, so they had a right to build. But after Cyrus died, his edict was forgotten and misplaced. Thus, when the new king, Artaxerxes, was told that the Jews were rebelling by rebuilding their city and temple, he commanded them to stop. So the Jews decided to postpone things for a more favorable season. They reasoned, "The time has not yet come to rebuild the LORD's house" (Haggai 1:2 NIV).

God then began to withhold His blessings and sent a drought to get their attention: As the prophet Haggai told them, "You have planted much but harvest little. . . . Your wages disappear as though you were putting them in pockets filled with holes!" (Haggai 1:6 NLT). Haggai explained that God was withholding His blessings because His people were afraid to stand up for what was right. Worse yet, while they judged it an inopportune time to build the temple, they were building fine dwellings for themselves. They were putting themselves first. God demanded, "Why are you living in luxurious houses while my house lies in ruins?" (Haggai 1:4 NLT).

Haggai ordered them to boldly start building once again. The prophet Zechariah echoed this message. Then Zerubbabel (the Jewish ruler) and Jeshua (the high priest) took courage and started to rebuild, "and the prophets of God were with them, helping them" (Ezra 5:2 NKJV). Soon the people joined them, and the temple was finished.

READ HAGGAI 2 AND PSALM 49.

● Six-Month Course: your next reading is on page 170.   →

HIDDEN TREASURE

THE GLORIOUS TEMPLE

As long as the temple was only a foundation, it wasn't apparent what it would become. But after the Jews began building the walls, it became evident that it simply couldn't compare to the temple Solomon had built. Haggai asked, "Who is left among you who saw this temple in its former glory? And how do you see it now? In comparison with it, is this not in your eyes as nothing?" (Haggai 2:3 NKJV). While admitting that the new temple couldn't compare, Haggai prophesied, "The glory of this latter temple shall be greater than the former" (Haggai 2:9 NKJV). In fact, beginning about 20 BC, King Herod rebuilt this second temple, and eventually it became grander and more glorious than even Solomon's temple (see Luke 21:5).

READ PSALMS 52–54 AND PROVERBS 24.

HIDDEN TREASURE

GOD'S SIGNET RING

God told the prophet Haggai, "Speak to Zerubbabel governor of Judah, saying. . .'I will make you like a signet ring, for I have chosen you,' declares the LORD of hosts" (Haggai 2:21, 23 NASB). A signet ring was an extremely precious ring, expressing the bearer's authority. With this ring a king or wealthy official signed and authorized official documents by pressing its insignia into moist clay or hot wax. God had made Zerubbabel just such an authority and executor of His will. But there was a warning to such men: maintaining such an exalted position was contingent upon their continuing obedience—if they disobeyed God, He would remove their authority and anointing (see Jeremiah 22:24).

READ PSALMS 57–58 AND PROVERBS 25.

BASIC SURVEY

ZECHARIAH

AUTHOR: Zechariah, son of Berechiah (1:1); some believe a second, unnamed writer contributed chapters 9–14.

DATE: Approximately 520–475 BC.

IN TEN WORDS OR LESS

Jewish exiles should rebuild their temple—and anticipate their Messiah.

DETAILS, PLEASE

Like Haggai, another postexilic prophet, Zechariah urges Jewish people to rebuild the Jerusalem temple. He also gives several prophecies of the coming Messiah, including an end-times vision of a final battle over Jerusalem: Then "shall the LORD go forth, and fight against those nations. . . . And his feet shall stand in that day upon the mount of Olives. . . . And the LORD shall be king over all the earth" (14:3–4, 9 KJV).

QUOTABLE

> "'Return to me,' declares the LORD Almighty, "and I will return to you'" (1:3 NIV).

UNIQUE AND UNUSUAL

Zechariah's prophecy of the Messiah riding a donkey into Jerusalem (9:9) was fulfilled to the letter in Jesus' "triumphal entry" (Matthew 21:1–11). The prophecy "They shall look upon me whom they have pierced" (12:10 KJV) refers to the Roman soldiers' spearing of Christ after the Crucifixion (John 19:34).

SO WHAT?

Knowing that many of Zechariah's specific prophecies were fulfilled in Jesus, we can trust that his other predictions—of the end time—will come true, too.

READ ZECHARIAH 1 AND 8.

- One-Month Course: your next reading is on page 173.   →
- Three-Month Course: your next reading is on page 173.   →
- Six-Month Course: your next reading is on page 171.   →

ZECHARIAH'S MESSIANIC PROPHECIES

The book of Zechariah makes some astonishing prophecies about Jesus. First, it says, "Rejoice greatly, Daughter Zion! Shout, Daughter Jerusalem! See, your king comes to you, righteous and victorious, lowly and riding on a donkey, on a colt, the foal of a donkey" (Zechariah 9:9 NIV). As Matthew 21:1–5 states, these things were fulfilled to the letter in Jesus' triumphal entry into Jerusalem.

Another prophecy says, "So they counted out for my wages thirty pieces of silver. And the LORD said to me, 'Throw it to the potter'—this magnificent

The book of Zechariah features prophecies about Jesus, including the betrayal of Judas. This painting by Rembrandt (1606–1669) is titled *Judas Returning the Thirty Silver Pieces.*

sum at which they valued me! So I took the thirty coins and threw them to the potter in the Temple of the LORD" (Zechariah 11:12–13 NLT). This was fulfilled when Judas betrayed Jesus in Matthew 26:14–16; 27:3–10.

In Mark 14:27 (NKJV) Jesus predicted that all His disciples would abandon Him, saying, "All of you will be made to stumble because of Me this night, for it is written: 'I will strike the Shepherd, and the sheep will be scattered.'" He was quoting Zechariah 13:7. And it was fulfilled. When the mob came and arrested Jesus, "all the disciples forsook Him and fled" (Matthew 26:56 NKJV).

Finally, a fourth prophecy states, "Then they will look on Me whom they pierced. Yes, they will mourn for Him as one mourns for his only son, and grieve for Him as one grieves for a firstborn" (Zechariah 12:10 NKJV). The Gospel of John explains how this prophecy was fulfilled after Jesus had died on the cross (see John 19:31–37).

READ ZECHARIAH 9 AND 11.

● Six-Month Course: your next reading is on page 173. →

JOSHUA THE HIGH PRIEST

God had highly exalted Zerubbabel, the Jewish governor. God now exalted Joshua the high priest and described his great value. The Lord planned on mightily using Joshua, yet Zechariah saw Satan standing at his right hand, accusing him of sin and of being unworthy. But the Angel of the Lord rebuked Satan and called Joshua "a burning stick that has been snatched from the fire" (Zechariah 3:2 NLT). God then forgave Joshua's sins and had him clothed in clean garments. He instructed Zechariah, "Take the silver and gold, make an elaborate crown, and set it on the head of Joshua. . .the high priest. . . . He shall bear the glory, and shall sit and rule on His throne" (Zechariah 6:11, 13 NKJV).

READ ZECHARIAH 3 AND 6.

WHERE SPIRITS COME FROM

Some people imagine that human spirits preexist with God before coming to earth and are sent from heaven into a human body sometime before birth. However, if all spirits originate in heaven, this would mean that all human spirits are saved. All come from heaven and are therefore automatically destined to return there. Many people would gladly agree with this thought, but this isn't the picture scripture gives. Where then do human spirits come from? The prophet Zechariah said that the Lord "stretches out the heavens, lays the foundation of the earth, and forms the spirit of man within him" (Zechariah 12:1 NKJV). God literally forms a new eternal human spirit within the fertilized egg at the moment of conception.

READ ZECHARIAH 10 AND 12.

BASIC SURVEY

MALACHI

AUTHOR: Malachi (1:1), meaning "my messenger." No other details are given.

DATE: Approximately 433 BC, likely after Nehemiah returned to Persia (Nehemiah 13:6).

IN TEN WORDS OR LESS

The Jews have become careless in their attitude toward God.

DETAILS, PLEASE

Prophesying a century after the return from exile, Malachi chastises the Jews for offering "lame and sick" sacrifices (1:8 KJV); for divorcing their wives to marry pagan women; and for failing to pay tithes for the temple. The Lord was angry with the attitude, "It is vain to serve God" (3:14 KJV), but promised to bless the obedient: "To you who fear My name the Sun of Righteousness shall arise with healing in His wings" (4:2 NKJV).

QUOTABLE

> "'Return to me, and I will return to you,' says the LORD Almighty'" (3:7 NIV).

UNIQUE AND UNUSUAL

Malachi, the last book of the Old Testament, contains the final word from God for some four hundred years, until the appearance of John the Baptist and Jesus, the Messiah, as prophesied in Malachi 3:1 (KJV): "I will send my messenger, and he shall prepare the way before me, and the LORD, whom ye seek, shall suddenly come to his temple."

SO WHAT?

God doesn't want empty religious rituals—He wants people to worship Him in spirit and in truth. (See John 4:24.)

READ MALACHI 1 AND PSALMS 61–63.

● One-Month Course: your next reading is on page 176.   →

● Three-Month Course: your next reading is on page 176.   →

● Six-Month Course: your next reading is on page 174.   →

What Are We Doing Wrong?

Malachi was the last prophet before John the Baptist. After Malachi, God simply stopped speaking to His people for 430 years. When you read the following verses, you'll understand why.

"'I have loved you,' says the LORD. Yet you say, 'In what way have You loved us?'" (Malachi 1:2 NKJV). "Where is My reverence? says the LORD of hosts to you priests who despise My name. Yet you say, 'In what way have we despised Your name?'" (Malachi 1:6 NKJV). "You offer defiled food on My altar, but say, 'In what way have we defiled You?'" (Malachi 1:7 NKJV). "You have wearied the LORD with your words; yet you say, 'In what way have we wearied Him?'" (Malachi 2:17 NKJV).

"'You have gone away from My ordinances and have not kept them. Return to Me, and I will return to you,' says the LORD of hosts. But you said, 'In what way shall we return?'" (Malachi 3:7 NKJV). "Will a man rob God? Yet you have robbed Me! But you say, 'In what way have we robbed You?'" (Malachi 3:8 NKJV). "'Your words have been harsh against Me,' says the LORD, yet you say, 'What have we spoken against You?'" (Malachi 3:13 NKJV).

After Malachi, God did not speak to His people through prophets until the arrival of John the Baptist. God was waiting for His people to return to Him. The act of returning to God is pictured in *The Return of the Prodigal Son* by Pompeo Batoni (1708–1787).

In answer to their last impudent question, the Lord reminded them that they'd been saying, "It is vain to serve God" (Malachi 3:14 KJV). They had become discouraged with serving God, so although they were still going through the motions, their hearts were no longer in it.

READ MALACHI 2 AND PROVERBS 26.

● Six-Month Course: your next reading is on page 176. →

GIVING GOD THE LEFTOVERS

The Jews in Malachi's day were cheating God at every turn. God had said that His people were to give Him a tenth of all their increase and profit. This went to support the Levites (Deuteronomy 14:22–29). Yet they were negligent in their tithing (Malachi 3:8–11). The Law also stated that if an animal "has any defect, such as lameness or blindness, or any serious defect, you shall not sacrifice it to the LORD your God" (Deuteronomy 15:21 NASB). Yet the Jews gave God their rejects. Through Malachi, the Lord demanded, "When you offer blind animals for sacrifice, is that not wrong? When you sacrifice lame or diseased animals, is that not wrong? Try offering them to your governor! Would he be pleased with you?" (Malachi 1:8 NIV).

READ MALACHI 3 AND DEUTERONOMY 14.

THE COMING OF ELIJAH

This stained glass is a picture of Elijah. Christ himself and the people of His day noted similarities between Elijah and John the Baptist.

In the last prophecy in the Old Testament, God promised, "Behold, I am going to send you Elijah the prophet before the coming of the great and terrible day of the LORD" (Malachi 4:5 NASB). The angel Gabriel declared that this would be fulfilled in John the Baptist, saying, "He will also go before Him [the Messiah] in the spirit and power of Elijah. . .to make ready a people prepared for the LORD" (Luke 1:17 NKJV). And Jesus twice stated that John was Elijah who had been prophesied to come (Matthew 11:13–14; 17:10–13). Yet John himself denied that he was Elijah (John 1:19–21). He didn't merely doubt what God had said about *him*; he eventually doubted what God had said about Jesus (John 1:29–34; Matthew 11:2–3).

READ MALACHI 4 AND MATTHEW 11.

BASIC SURVEY

MATTHEW

AUTHOR: Not stated, but traditionally Matthew, a tax collector (9:9). Matthew is also known as "Levi" (Mark 2:14 KJV).

DATE: Approximately AD 55, before all the apostles left Jerusalem to evangelize the world.

IN TEN WORDS OR LESS

Jesus fulfills the Old Testament prophecies of a coming Messiah.

DETAILS, PLEASE

The first of the four *Gospels* (meaning "good news"), Matthew is written primarily to a Jewish audience, so it quotes numerous Old Testament references to prove that Jesus is the promised Messiah. Beginning with a genealogy that shows Jesus' ancestry, Matthew then details the angelic announcement of His conception. He introduces John the Baptist and describes the calling of key disciples Peter, Andrew, James, and John. Jesus' teachings are emphasized, with long passages covering His "Sermon on the Mount" (chapters 5–7), including the Beatitudes and the Lord's Prayer. Matthew also details the death, burial, and resurrection of Jesus.

QUOTABLE

> "And she will bring forth a Son, and you shall call His name JESUS, for He will save His people from their sins" (1:21 NKJV).

> "Therefore go and make disciples of all nations, baptizing them in the name of the Father and of the Son and of the Holy Spirit" (28:19 NIV).

UNIQUE AND UNUSUAL

Matthew is the only biographer of Jesus to mention unusual miracles—the tearing of the temple curtain, the breaking open of tombs, and the raising to life of dead saints—that occurred during that time (27:50–54).

SO WHAT?

As Messiah, Jesus is also king—and worthy of our worship.

READ MATTHEW 3–4.

● One-Month Course: your next reading is on page 183. →

● Three-Month Course: your next reading is on page 177. →

● Six-Month Course: your next reading is on page 177. →

HEART OF THE BOOK

FULFILLING MESSIANIC EXPECTATIONS

Matthew repeatedly quotes Old Testament scriptures to prove that Jesus was the long-awaited Messiah—and Jesus fulfilled *many* prophecies. However, He also surprised the Jews by fulfilling promises that they hadn't realized were about the Messiah. They hadn't expected, for example, that He would be a healer and a teacher (Acts 10:38; Luke 4:18–19), and they certainly weren't expecting that He'd be rejected by the religious leaders, be crucified, die, then resurrect from the dead.

The Jews envisioned a charismatic king like David who would rally Israel, vanquish the foreign oppressors, and reestablish the greatness and glory of the kingdom of Israel. That's why the disciples repeatedly asked Jesus, "Lord, are you at this time going to restore the kingdom to Israel?" (Acts 1:6 NIV). God had promised David: "I will raise up your offspring to succeed you, one of your own sons. . . . I will set him over my house and my kingdom forever; his throne will be established forever" (1 Chronicles 17:11, 14 NIV). That's why, when Jesus spoke of His death, the Jews said, "We have heard from the law that the Christ remains forever" (John 12:34 NKJV).

Jesus wasn't quite doing what people expected the Messiah would do. Nevertheless, the common people reasoned, "When the Messiah comes, will he perform more signs than this man?" (John 7:31 NIV). They hoped that this gentle carpenter would eventually rise to the occasion and fulfill *all* their Messianic expectations. So the crowds shouted, "Son of David!" when He rode into Jerusalem (Matthew 21:9 NIV). The expression "Son of David" literally meant "Messiah."

READ MATTHEW 16 AND 21.

● Three-Month Course: your next reading is on page 180.   →

● Six-Month Course: your next reading is on page 178.   →

CLOSER LOOK

THE SERMON ON THE MOUNT

Sermon on the Mount by Carl Heinrich Bloch (1834–1890) portrays Jesus delivering His most famous teaching.

Jesus' most famous teaching is commonly called the Sermon on the Mount and is found in Matthew 5–7. This sermon contains the heart of Christ's teaching—on love, forgiveness, prayer, and obedience. Although all these varied teachings are presented *here*, we can be sure that He repeated these thoughts on many occasions in numerous towns, villages, and open-air settings. For example, the shorter version in Luke 6:20–49 was clearly given in another setting at another time. Jesus repeated these basic teachings because it was vital that *everyone* hear them.

The following are just a few examples of what Jesus taught: "Love your enemies, bless them that curse you, do good to them that hate you, and pray for them which despitefully use you, and persecute you" (Matthew 5:44 KJV). "Judge not, that you be not judged" (Matthew 7:1 NKJV). "Ask, and it shall be given you; seek, and ye shall find; knock, and it shall be opened unto you" (Matthew 7:7 KJV).

Jesus often taught the opposite of what people expected to hear. They were used to hearing "an eye for an eye," but Jesus told them not to retaliate, but that if someone struck them on one cheek, to let them slap the other as well. Instead of hating enemies, He commanded us to love them. Instead of covetously and stingily saving, He commanded us to be generous and freely give to those who asked of us (Matthew 5:38–42). These counterintuitive teachings nevertheless make great sense in God's larger scheme of things.

READ MATTHEW 6–7.

● Six-Month Course: your next reading is on page 179.   →

CLOSER LOOK

Jesus' Healing Miracles

Matthew's Gospel describes Jesus performing miracle after miracle, healing people's physical infirmities and sicknesses, and for three and a half years, sick people crowded around Him.

Jesus was an outstanding healer and had power and authority over the devil. "God anointed Jesus of Nazareth with the Holy Spirit and with power. Then Jesus went around doing good and healing all who were oppressed by the devil" (Acts 10:38 NLT). He said, "The Spirit of the LORD is upon Me, because He anointed Me to. . .proclaim release to the captives, and recovery of sight to the blind, to set free those who are oppressed" (Luke 4:18 NASB).

The Jews hadn't visualized their Messiah coming as a healer, but there were certainly prophecies that He would do exactly that. Matthew tells us that Jesus "healed all the sick. This was to fulfill what was spoken through the prophet Isaiah: 'He took up our infirmities and bore our diseases'" (Matthew 8:16–17 NIV).

Besides demonstrating God's love and concern for His people, Jesus' miracles—healing people, giving sight to the blind, and raising the dead— were powerful proof that Jesus was who He claimed to be. And people who were honest recognized this. Nicodemus admitted, "Rabbi, we know that you are a teacher who has

Gebhard Fugel (1863–1939) painted *Miracles of Jesus,* which illustrates Jesus healing the sick.

come from God. For no one could perform the signs you are doing if God were not with him" (John 3:2 NIV). After Jesus raised Lazarus from the dead, "many of the Jews who had. . .seen the things Jesus did, believed in Him" (John 11:45 NKJV).

READ MATTHEW 8–9.

● Six-Month Course: your next reading is on page 180. →

HEART OF THE BOOK

JESUS' DEATH AND RESURRECTION

God sent His Son to earth to become a man, to experience all the pain and sorrow that humans experience, and to be our Savior. But to the utter surprise of many Jews, to save us He had to die on the cross for our sins. And to be crucified, He had to be rejected by His own people. Now, the "common people heard him gladly" (Mark 12:37 KJV), but the corrupt religious leaders, motivated by jealousy, plotted against Him, had Him arrested, and after conducting a fake trial, handed Him over to the Romans to be crucified. Jesus first suffered severe pain and blood loss from a flogging, then endured excruciating pain on the cross. As a result, after only six hours, He died.

Two wealthy disciples buried Jesus in a tomb in a garden near the place of execution, and that seemed to be the end of any hope that Jesus would deliver His people. But on the third day, early in the morning, the Spirit of God raised His corpse to life and Jesus Christ "was declared the Son of God with power by the resurrection from the dead" (Romans 1:4 NASB). Small wonder that Thomas bowed down before Him and declared, "My Lord and my God!" (John 20:28 NIV).

Jesus' resurrection gives hope of eternal life to all humankind: "God. . .has given us new birth into a living hope through the resurrection of Jesus Christ from the dead" (1 Peter 1:3 NIV).

READ MATTHEW 27:11–28:20.

● Three-Month Course: your next reading is on page 183.   →

● Six-Month Course: your next reading is on page 183.   →

HIDDEN TREASURE

THE VIRGIN BIRTH

Over seven hundred years before Jesus' birth, Isaiah prophesied, "Behold, the virgin shall conceive and bear a Son" (Isaiah 7:14 NKJV). Now, after Joseph became engaged to a young woman named Mary, the angel Gabriel told Mary, "You will conceive and give birth to a son, and you are to call him Jesus. He will be. . .the Son of the Most High" (Luke 1:31–32 NIV). Mary was a virgin, but the Spirit of God miraculously caused her to conceive. Joseph was troubled by Mary's pregnancy, but the angel told him, "That which is conceived in her is of the Holy Spirit. And she will bring forth a Son, and. . .He will save His people from their sins" (Matthew 1:20–21 NKJV). This is exactly what happened.

READ MATTHEW 1 AND ISAIAH 7.

HIDDEN TREASURE

THE WISE MEN

Balaam prophesied, "A star will rise from Jacob; a scepter will emerge from Israel" (Numbers 24:17 NLT). Some fourteen hundred years later, wise men known as Magi saw a bright star in the skies over Israel. They knew that a great king had been born in Israel. When the Magi arrived in Jerusalem, they asked King Herod, "Where is the newborn king of the Jews? We saw his star as it rose" (Matthew 2:2 NLT). Herod summoned the priests and scribes and asked, "Where is the Messiah supposed to be born?" They answered, "In Bethlehem in Judea" (Matthew 2:4–5 NLT). The Magi then went to Bethlehem, found Jesus, worshipped Him, and gave Him gifts of gold, frankincense, and myrrh, fulfilling Isaiah 60:6.

The Magi went to worship the King whose birth had been prophesied. This painting titled *Adoration of Magi* was created by Giacomo Cavedoni (1577–1660).

READ MATTHEW 2:1–12 AND ISAIAH 60.

THE PARABLE OF THE SOWER

Jesus frequently taught the crowds using parables. This is His most famous parable: "A sower went out to sow his seed. And as he sowed, some fell
by the wayside; and it was trampled down, and the birds of the air devoured
it. Some fell on rock; and as soon as it sprang up, it withered away because
it lacked moisture. And some fell among thorns, and the thorns sprang up
with it and choked it. But others fell on good ground, sprang up, and yielded
a crop a hundredfold" (Luke 8:5–8 NKJV). Jesus explained this parable to His
disciples, but not to the crowds. He wanted them to think and pray about
it until they finally understood it. Being practical farmers, many of them
eventually got it (See Matthew 11:25 NLT.)

READ MATTHEW 12–13.

THE END TIME

Jesus' disciples asked, "What sign will signal your return and the end of the
world?" (Matthew 24:3 NLT). Jesus answered that there would be many false
Messiahs, wars, famines, and earthquakes, but the end would not be yet.
He warned, "You will be hated all over the world." After Christians preach
the Gospel in all nations, "then the end will come" (Matthew 24:9, 14 NLT).
When the Abomination of Desolation is set up in God's temple, believers
must flee, for then the Great Tribulation begins (Matthew 24:15–21). Then
immediately after those days "they will see the Son of Man coming on the
clouds of the sky with power and great glory" (Matthew 24:30 NASB) and
Jesus will gather all believers to Himself.

READ MATTHEW 24 AND LUKE 21.

BASIC SURVEY

MARK

AUTHOR: Not stated, but traditionally John Mark, companion of Paul and Barnabas (Acts 12:25) and associate of Peter (1 Peter 5:13).

DATE: Probably AD 50s or 60s, before the destruction of Jerusalem.

IN TEN WORDS OR LESS

Jesus is God's Son, a suffering servant of all people.

DETAILS, PLEASE

This second Gospel is believed by many to be the first one written. The book of Mark is the briefest and most active of the four biographies of Jesus. Mark addresses a Gentile audience, portraying Jesus as a man of action, divinely capable of healing the sick, controlling nature, and battling the powers of Satan. Mark's theme of the suffering servant comes through in Jesus' interaction with hostile doubters—the Jewish leaders, who want to kill Him (9:31); His neighbors, who take offense at Him (6:3); and even His own family members, who think He's crazy (3:21).

QUOTABLE

> "Follow Me, and I will make you become fishers of men" (1:17 NKJV).

> "It is easier for a camel to go through the eye of a needle, than for a rich man to enter into the kingdom of God" (10:25 KJV).

UNIQUE AND UNUSUAL

Many believe the unnamed spectator at Jesus' arrest was Mark himself: "And there followed him a certain young man, having a linen cloth cast about his naked body; and the young men laid hold on him: and he left the linen cloth, and fled from them naked" (14:51–52 KJV).

SO WHAT?

Suffering and loss aren't necessarily bad things—in fact, for Christians, they're the pathway to real life (8:35).

READ MARK 1:1–20 AND 4.

- One-Month Course: your next reading is on page 189. →
- Three-Month Course: your next reading is on page 189. →
- Six-Month Course: your next reading is on page 184. →

CLOSER LOOK

POWER OVER THE DEVIL

At the very beginning of His ministry, "the Spirit. . .compelled Jesus to go into the wilderness, where he was tempted by Satan for forty days" (Mark 1:12–13

NLT). The devil tried to tempt Jesus to use His power for His own benefit, but Jesus resisted all his deceitful tricks (Matthew 4:1–11). Having passed these tests, Jesus then launched His ministry. As John declared: "The Son of God appeared for this purpose, to destroy the works of the devil" (1 John 3:8 NASB).

This fresco of Jesus resisting the devil is located in Antwerp, Belgium.

Repeatedly, "people brought to Jesus all the sick and demon-possessed. . .and Jesus healed many who had various diseases. He also drove out many demons" (Mark 1:32, 34 NIV). "Whenever the unclean spirits saw Him, they would fall down before Him and shout, 'You are the Son of God!'" (Mark 3:11 NASB). One day in a synagogue, a demon-possessed man tried to defy Jesus, "but Jesus rebuked him, saying, 'Be quiet, and come out of him!' And when the unclean spirit had convulsed him and cried out with a loud voice, he came out of him" (Mark 1:25–26 NKJV).

One of the most dramatic confrontations happened on the east bank of the Sea of Galilee. Jesus met the man possessed by a huge multitude of demons, and the man fell down before Jesus and begged Him not to torment him. Jesus cast the demons out, and they entered a herd of two thousand swine that immediately rushed down a steep bank and drowned in the sea (Mark 5:1–20).

READ MARK 5:1–20 AND 9:1–29.

● Six-Month Course: your next reading is on page 185.   →

CLOSER LOOK

LEGALISM AND THE SABBATH

Repeatedly in the Gospels we see Jesus running afoul of the religious authorities because He wasn't super-scrupulous about keeping the Sabbath. (See examples in Mark 2:23–27; 3:1–6; Luke 13:10–17; 14:1–6; John 9:1–16).

Now, Moses' Law commanded, "Remember the Sabbath day, to keep it holy. Six days you shall labor and do all your work, but the seventh day is the Sabbath of the LORD your God. In it you shall do no work" (Exodus 20:8–10 NKJV). And there was a serious penalty: "Observe the Sabbath, because it is holy to you. Anyone who desecrates it is to be put to death; those who do any work on that day must be cut off from their people" (Exodus 31:14 NIV).

Now, for the *most* part, Jesus and His disciples did faithfully and gladly rest on the Sabbath, along with the rest of the Jewish nation. For example, He only healed multitudes of people *after* the Sabbath ended at sundown (Mark 1:21, 32–34). But the Pharisees had added thousands of tiny rules to Moses' Law, redefining perfectly harmless, good activities as "work." Then, because Jesus didn't follow their legalistic interpretations, they argued, "This man is not from God, because He does not keep the Sabbath" (John 9:16 NASB).

Because Jesus sometimes healed the sick on the Sabbath, His critics confidently stated, "We know this man is a sinner" (John 9:24 NIV). And because the Law advocated the death penalty for those who "profaned" the Sabbath, they felt justified in hating and persecuting Him—and eventually killing Him.

READ MARK 2:23–3:6 AND JOHN 9.

● Six-Month Course: your next reading is on page 186.

CLOSER LOOK

GREATNESS IN SERVING

One time, after Jesus and His disciples entered Capernaum, He asked, "What were you discussing on the way?" But they were too embarrassed to answer, because they'd been arguing about which of them was the greatest. Jesus turned the concept of ruling and reigning on its head when He told the Twelve, "If anyone wants to be first, he shall be last of all and servant of all" (Mark 9:33, 35 NASB).

Later on, two ambitious disciples, James and John, forgot Jesus' admonition and boldly requested to sit on His right and left hand in His kingdom—thoroughly upsetting the other ten apostles—and Jesus once again taught, "Whosoever will be great among you, shall be your minister: and whosoever of you will be the chiefest, shall be servant of all. For even the Son of man came not to be ministered unto, but to minister, and to give his life a ransom for many" (Mark 10:43–45 KJV).

Paolo Veronese (1528–1588) painted *Christ Washing the Feet of the Disciples*, which illustrates Jesus' humility and willingness to serve others.

Unbelievably, they still didn't get the point. At the Last Supper, while Jesus was focused on His coming suffering and death, the Twelve were once again arguing which of them was the greatest. Once again Jesus pointed them to His own example, saying, "I am among you as the One who serves" (Luke 22:27 NKJV). And despite the fact that He was their Lord and Master, He washed their feet like a common servant (John 13:1–16). He made it clear by His own example the kind of humility that His disciples should pursue.

READ MARK 9:30–50 AND 10:1–45.

● Six-Month Course: your next reading is on page 189.   →

HIDDEN TREASURE

JESUS FORGIVES SIN

Once when the people heard that Jesus was in a house, such large crowds gathered that no one could enter by the door. Four men brought a paralyzed friend, but when they couldn't get in, they broke through the ceiling and lowered him by ropes on his mat. Jesus looked upon the paralyzed man and declared, "Son, your sins are forgiven" (Mark 2:5 NIV). Some scribes were scandalized, thinking, "Why does this Man speak blasphemies like this? Who can forgive sins but God alone?" (Mark 2:7 NKJV). However, to prove that He had authority to forgive sins, Jesus immediately commanded the man's healing—and he *was* healed! Jesus, like God, can forgive sins because He is the Son of God, *one* with His Father (John 10:30).

READ MARK 2:1–22 AND 6.

HIDDEN TREASURE

RAISING THE DEAD

When Jesus was asked if He was the Messiah, His proof was that "the dead are raised" (Luke 7:22 NKJV). Jesus had just finished raising a dead man in the village of Nain. Just as He had arrived there, a funeral procession came out, carrying a man to his tomb. Jesus commanded, "Young man, I say to you, get up!" (Luke 7:14 NIV). He immediately returned to life. Later, in Capernaum, Jairus begged Jesus to come heal his dying daughter, but by the time Jesus arrived she had already died. Jesus took her by the hand and said, "Little girl, I say to you, get up!" (Mark 5:41 NIV). Immediately her life returned, and she arose.

READ MARK 5:21–43 AND LUKE 7:1–23.

BLIND BARTIMAEUS IS HEALED

Jesus and His disciples were leaving Jericho followed by a large crowd when a blind man named Bartimaeus heard the excited people and asked what was happening. When the crowd told him who was passing, Bartimaeus cried out to Jesus to have mercy on him. Jesus couldn't hear him, so Bartimaeus kept shouting. Many in the crowd sternly warned him to be quiet, but Bartimaeus shouted even *louder*, "Son of David, have mercy on me!" (Mark 10:48 NKJV). At that, Jesus heard him, so He stopped, called him up, and healed him. Matthew says there were *two* blind men (Matthew 20:30), but Mark only mentions Bartimaeus since he was apparently the most insistent and the loudest of the two.

READ MARK 10:46–52 AND PSALMS 148–150.

ALL THINGS ARE POSSIBLE

Jesus commanded a fig tree to never bear fruit again, and it immediately withered. He then told His astonished disciples, "Whoever says to this mountain, 'Be removed and be cast into the sea,' and does not doubt in

his heart, but believes that those things he says will be done, he will have whatever he says. Therefore I say to you, whatever things you ask when you pray, believe that you receive them, and you will have them" (Mark 11:23–24 NKJV). Jesus' statement is so powerful that it's worth rereading and studying carefully. He was saying that faith in God is mighty. Without

Jesus demonstrated the importance of having faith in God's power by commanding a fig tree to wither.

it, however, people miss out on answers to prayer. In fact, James 1:6–7 tells us that doubt literally sabotages faith.

READ MARK 11 AND PSALMS 64–65.

BASIC SURVEY

LUKE

AUTHOR: Not stated, but traditionally Luke, a Gentile physician (Colossians 4:14), and missionary companion of the apostle Paul (2 Timothy 4:11).

DATE: Probably by AD 60, while Paul was under house arrest in Rome.

IN TEN WORDS OR LESS

Jesus is Savior of all people, whether Jew or Gentile.

DETAILS, PLEASE

Luke's Gospel is addressed to Theophilus (1:3), who may have been a Roman official. Luke's book is the most universal of the four Gospels, and shows Jesus' compassion for all people: Roman soldiers (7:1–10), widows (7:11–17), the "sinful" (7:36–50), the chronically ill (8:43–48), lepers (17:11–19), and others. Luke also describes Jesus' resurrection, adding detailed accounts of His appearances to two believers on the Emmaus road and the remaining eleven disciples.

QUOTABLE

> Whosoever shall seek to save his life shall lose it; and whosoever shall lose his life shall preserve it (17:33 KJV).

> For the Son of man is come to seek and to save that which was lost (19:10 KJV).

UNIQUE AND UNUSUAL

Luke is the only Gospel to share Jesus' stories ("parables") of the good Samaritan (10:25–37), the prodigal son (15:11–32), and the rich man and Lazarus (16:19–31). Luke is also the only Gospel to detail Jesus' actual birth and the words He spoke in childhood (both in chapter 2).

SO WHAT?

It doesn't matter who you are, where you come from, or what you've done— Jesus came to seek and to save you.

READ LUKE 1–2.

● One-Month Course: your next reading is on page 195.   →

● Three-Month Course: your next reading is on page 195.   →

● Six-Month Course: your next reading is on page 190.   →

CLOSER LOOK

A GOSPEL FOR THE GREEKS

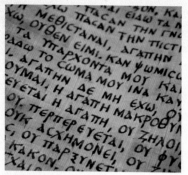

Luke, a Greek physician, addressed his written account to a man named Theophilus. This parchment of 1 Corinthians 13 is written in Greek.

Luke was a Greek, the only non-Jewish Gospel writer, and a physician (Colossians 4:14). He was a traveling companion and personal aide of the apostle Paul for many years and apparently worked in the church in Philippi when not journeying with Paul. (Compare Acts 16:10–12; 17:1; 20:1–6, and notice the difference in "we/us" and "they.")

Luke's Gospel is addressed to a man named Theophilus. In his introduction, he states, "I. . .decided to write an orderly account for you, most excellent Theophilus, so that you may know the certainty of the things you have been taught" (Luke 1:3–4 NIV). We don't know who Theophilus was, though some believe he was a wealthy Greek or a Roman official in Philippi who had sponsored Luke's trip to Judea to research his Gospel. Hence the Gospel was dedicated to him.

The Gospel of Matthew was too distinctly Jewish for many Gentiles—and it was the larger Gentile audience that Luke was writing for. They not only spoke and read Greek, but understood the world from a Greek worldview. Among other things, they had a concept of an "ideal man," so Luke stressed Jesus' love, compassion, and humanity. Luke traced Jesus' genealogy beyond Abraham, the patriarch of the Jews, all the way back to Adam, "the son of God" (Luke 3:38 NIV), the common ancestor of everyone.

Luke's Gospel, not surprisingly, uses Greek medical terms to describe the diseases that Jesus healed and avoids saying that the woman with the bleeding problem "suffered many things of many physicians" (Mark 5:26 KJV; see also Luke 8:43).

READ LUKE 12 AND 16.

● Six-Month Course: your next reading is on page 191.   →

CLOSER LOOK

Jesus' Love and Compassion

The Pharisees believed in God and knew that they must serve Him. But they weren't motivated by love, rather by fear and religious duty. They were convinced that they were saved by their own righteousness—by scrupulously observing the Law of Moses and the many traditions and regulations that they had added to God's Law.

Jesus pointed out that the greatest commandment was to love God with all their hearts and love their fellow man as themselves (Mark 12:28–31), but many Jews were focused on rigidly keeping the Law. This led them to judge and condemn the common poor who so often fell short. On the other hand, Jesus emphasized the centrality of love and taught the importance of mercy and forgiveness. This led to His reaching out to "sinners" whom the Pharisees pulled their robes away from in disgust (Matthew 9:9–13).

Jesus publicly showed great compassion and mercy toward a prostitute (Luke 7:36–50), and this scandalized righteous Jews. Later, Jesus had mercy on an adulterous woman, again upsetting the religious leaders because He refused to condemn her (John 8:2–11). They labeled Jesus "a friend of tax collectors and sinners" (Matthew 11:19 NIV).

The Samaritans were a mixed race of Jews and Gentiles, and believed only in the first five books of Moses, so that Jews despised them and had nothing to do with them. But Jesus associated with an adulterous Samaritan woman (John 4:1–42) and taught that Samaritans motivated by love were truly obeying God's commands (Luke 10:25–37).

READ LUKE 7:29–50 AND 10:1–37.

 Six-Month Course: your next reading is on page 192.   →

THE COST OF DISCIPLESHIP

Jesus told those who desired to follow His teachings, "If you want to be my disciple, you must hate everyone else by comparison—your father and mother, wife and children, brothers and sisters—yes, even your own life.

Otherwise, you cannot be my disciple" (Luke 14:26 NLT). He added, "You cannot become my disciple without giving up everything you own" (Luke 14:33 NLT). A disciple, Jesus stipulated, must "seek. . .first the kingdom of God" in all things (Matthew 6:33 KJV) and give God's desires priority.

Jesus elaborated on this, saying, "If anyone desires to come after Me, let him deny himself, and take up his cross daily, and follow Me. For whoever

In this painting, Jesus and His disciples are walking through a meadow. Jesus explained that to follow Him, a disciple must be willing to give up many comforts.

desires to save his life will lose it, but whoever loses his life for My sake will save it" (Luke 9:23–24 NKJV). People often felt a desire to follow Jesus, but He warned that to be a Christian meant death to self on a daily basis. Seeking to preserve one's life and live for the good things and the pleasures of this world short-circuit discipleship.

Jesus gave practical examples of what discipleship entailed. "As they were going along the road, someone said to Him, 'I will follow You wherever You go.' And Jesus said to him, 'The foxes have holes and the birds of the air have nests, but the Son of Man has nowhere to lay His head'" (Luke 9:57–58 NASB). Being a disciple often means doing without the comforts and conveniences that most people take for granted.

READ LUKE 9 AND 14.

● Six-Month Course: your next reading is on page 195.   →

SPIRITUAL FRUIT

Jesus gave a simple explanation of who is righteous and who is not. He said, "A good tree does not bear bad fruit, nor does a bad tree bear good fruit. For every tree is known by its own fruit" (Luke 6:43–44 NKJV). He then explained that whatever you have stored in your heart in "abundance" will eventually come out of your mouth. If you have evil thoughts and evil "treasure" stored up in your mind, it will manifest in your life. By the same token, if good thoughts and good "treasure" fill your heart, they, too, soon become evident. (See also Matthew 7:15–23.) Solomon warned, "Guard your heart above all else, for it determines the course of your life" (Proverbs 4:23 NLT).

READ LUKE 6 AND PROVERBS 27.

FEMALE DISCIPLES

Jesus had many female followers. When He toured Galilee, "he took his twelve disciples with him, along with some women who had been cured of evil spirits and diseases. Among them were Mary Magdalene. . .Joanna, the wife of Chuza, Herod's business manager; Susanna; and many others who were contributing from their own resources to support Jesus and his disciples" (Luke 8:1–3 NLT). Mark also names Salome and Mary the mother of Joses (Mark 15:40). Salome was believed to be the mother of James and John (Matthew 20:20–21; 27:56). These six women "and *many* others" traveled with Jesus, and their financial support kept everyone going.

READ LUKE 8:1–3; 10:38–41; AND PROVERBS 31.

HIDDEN TREASURE

THE PRODIGAL SON

Jesus told a parable about a wealthy man with two sons. The youngest son begged his father to give him his share of the estate early, so the father did. Not long after, the youngest son left for a far country where he wasted his money on parties and prostitutes. After he had squandered everything, there was a famine, so half starving, he set out for his father's estate, intent on working as his hired servant. But his father kissed him and welcomed him

This stained glass depicts the return of the prodigal son, a parable Jesus told to help His followers better understand that God will always welcome back those who have strayed from Him.

back as his son. The older brother was indignant, but the father insisted, "We had to celebrate and be glad, because this brother of yours was dead and is alive again; he was lost and is found" (Luke 15:32 NIV).

READ LUKE 15 AND PROVERBS 7.

HIDDEN TREASURE

PERSISTENT PRAYER

Jesus urged His disciples to pray persistently. First, He told them to imagine themselves like a man who banged on the door of his friend's house at midnight, demanding bread. He concluded, "Because of your shameless audacity he will surely get up and give you as much as you need. So I say to you: Ask and it will be given to you" (Luke 11:8–9 NIV). Jesus told another parable "to show them that they should always pray and not give up" (Luke 18:1 NIV). He described a widow who kept going to a judge, demanding that he give her justice. Even though he refused to listen at first, he eventually realized she wasn't going to give him any peace—so he answered her request.

READ LUKE 11 AND 18.

BASIC SURVEY

JOHN

AUTHOR: Not stated, but traditionally John, the "disciple whom Jesus loved" (21:7 KJV), brother of James and son of Zebedee (Matthew 4:21).

DATE: Around AD 85, as the last Gospel written.

IN TEN WORDS OR LESS

Jesus is God Himself, the only Savior of the world.

DETAILS, PLEASE

While the books of Matthew, Mark, and Luke have many similarities (they're called the "synoptic Gospels," meaning they take a common view), the book of John stands alone. The fourth Gospel downplays Jesus' parables (none are recorded) and miracles (only seven are featured). Instead, John provides more extensive treatments of Jesus' reasons for coming to earth ("I am come that they might have life, and that they might have it more abundantly," 10:10 KJV), His intimate relationship with God the Father ("I and my Father are one," 10:30 KJV), and His own feelings toward the job He had come to do ("Father, the hour has come. Glorify your Son, that your Son may glorify you. For you granted him authority over all people that he might give eternal life to all those you have given him," 17:1–2 NIV). John also gives special emphasis to Jesus' patient treatment of the disciples Thomas, who doubted the resurrection (20:24–29), and Peter, who had denied the Lord (21:15–23).

QUOTABLE

> In the beginning was the Word, and the Word was with God, and the Word was God (1:1 KJV).

> "For God so loved the world that He gave His only begotten Son, that whoever believes in Him should not perish but have everlasting life" (3:16 NKJV).

> I am the bread of life (6:35 KJV).

> "I am the good shepherd. The good shepherd lays down his life for the sheep" (10:11 NIV).

> "I am the way, the truth, and the life: no man cometh unto the Father, but by me" (14:6 KJV).

UNIQUE AND UNUSUAL

Jesus' very first miracle, changing water into wine at a wedding in Cana, is recorded only in John's Gospel (2:1–12). So is His raising of Lazarus from the dead (11:1–44), His healing of a man born blind (9:1–38), and His long-distance healing of a nobleman's son (4:46–54). John is also the only Gospel to mention Nicodemus, who heard Jesus' teaching that "you must be born again" (3:7 NKJV).

SO WHAT?

"These have been written so that you may believe that Jesus is the Christ, the Son of God; and that believing you may have life in His name" (20:31 NASB).

READ JOHN 10 AND 17.

● One-Month Course: your next reading is on page 202.   →

● Three-Month Course: your next reading is on page 197.   →

● Six-Month Course: your next reading is on page 197.   →

HEART OF THE BOOK

THE WORD OF GOD

John's Gospel begins with this declaration: "In the beginning was the Word, and the Word was with God, and the Word was God. He was in the beginning with God. All things were made through Him, and without Him nothing was made that was made. . . . And the Word became flesh and dwelt among us" (John 1:1–3, 14 NKJV). This is clearly talking about Jesus.

"Word" comes from the Greek word *Logos*. In addition to meaning "word," it also means "the reason, the divine principle behind everything." Philo (30 BC–AD 50), a Jewish philosopher, wrote that "the Logos of the living God is the bond of everything, holding all things together and binding all the parts." He added that the Logos was "the firstborn of God." Paul declared that Jesus "is the image of the invisible God, the firstborn of all creation. For by Him all things were created. . . . He is before all things, and in Him all things hold together" (Colossians 1:15–17 NASB).

Jesus, the Word, is the image of the invisible God. He is the express image of the Father and the brightness of His glory. Just as our words express *our* character, the Word of God expresses God's character. "The Son radiates God's own glory and expresses the very character of God" (Hebrews 1:3 NLT). John also states, "No one has ever seen God, but the one and only Son, who is himself God and is in closest relationship with the Father, has made him known" (John 1:18 NIV).

READ JOHN 1 AND 5.

● Three-Month Course: your next reading is on page 202.   →

● Six-Month Course: your next reading is on page 198.   →

CLOSER LOOK

BEING BORN AGAIN

Nicodemus and Jesus on a Rooftop by Henry Ossawa Tanner (1859–1937) shows Jesus teaching the religious leader about how we must be "born of the Spirit" (John 3:8).

One night a wealthy Jewish religious leader named Nicodemus came to Jesus secretly. During the course of their conversation, Jesus told him, "Very truly I tell you, no one can see the kingdom of God unless they are born again" (John 3:3 NIV). At first Nicodemus thought that Jesus was referring to a second *physical* birth, but Jesus meant that although we've all been born physically, we *also* need to be born spiritually. We must be "born of the Spirit" (John 3:8 NIV). This is what is meant by being born *again*.

How is someone "born of the Spirit"? Paul tells us that when you open your heart to Jesus, "Christ [will] dwell in your hearts through faith" (Ephesians 3:17 NKJV). Paul further explained that "he who is joined to the Lord is one spirit with Him" (1 Corinthians 6:17 NKJV). God sends the Spirit of His Son into our hearts (Galatians 4:6), and because Jesus is the source of eternal life, when His Spirit enters our hearts and is joined to our spirits, He gives *our* spirits everlasting life.

We receive eternal life when we have faith in Jesus. The following verses express this so simply: "For God so loved the world that He gave His only begotten Son, that whoever believes in Him should not perish but have everlasting life" (John 3:16 NKJV). "He who believes in the Son has everlasting life; and he who does not believe the Son shall not see life" (John 3:36 NKJV).

READ JOHN 2–3.

● Six-Month Course: your next reading is on page 199.   →

CLOSER LOOK

ABIDING IN JESUS

Jesus told His disciples, "Abide in Me, and I in you. As the branch cannot bear fruit of itself, unless it abides in the vine, neither can you, unless you abide in Me" (John 15:4 NKJV). *Abide* is not a commonly used word today, so the NIV translates it, "Remain in me, as I also remain in you."

Now, John 15:6 (NIV) states, "If you do not remain in me, you are like a branch that is thrown away and withers; such branches are picked up, thrown into the fire and burned." Because of this verse, many people reason that remaining in Jesus is something that we must do to remain saved. To cease remaining in Jesus is to "fall away" or be "cut off" from Christ (see Matthew 10:22; Romans 11:21–22; Hebrews 6:4–8).

However, many other Christians believe that our standing and salvation in Christ are eternally secure, and that "abiding" in Him refers to spending time in His presence and being filled with His Spirit and His peace—and that this determines their closeness to Him and the degree of blessing that they experience. This seems to be borne out by Jesus' words: "If you abide in Me, and My words abide in you, ask whatever you wish, and it will be done for you" (John 15:7 NASB). And as John 15:4 states, if we abide in Him we will "bear fruit."

Whatever the exact meaning of "abiding," it's clear that all Christians are to abide (remain) in Christ—and that there are tremendous benefits for doing so.

READ JOHN 14–15.

● Six-Month Course: your next reading is on page 202.

HIDDEN TREASURE

THE LIGHT OF THE WORLD

In the middle of a Jewish feast, Jesus cried out, "I am the Light of the world; he who follows Me will not walk in the darkness, but will have the Light of life" (John 8:12 NASB). (See also John 1:4–9; 9:5; 12:46.) The apostle John wrote, "God is Light, and in Him there is no darkness at all" (1 John 1:5 NASB). The Psalms say of the Lord: "You are radiant with light," and "The LORD wraps himself in light as with a garment" (Psalm 76:4; 104:2 NIV). When Ezekiel saw God, he remarked that "brilliant light surrounded him" (Ezekiel 1:27 NIV). Jesus is the Son of God and is therefore "the brightness of His glory" (Hebrews 1:3 NKJV).

READ JOHN 8 AND 12:20-50.

HIDDEN TREASURE

RAISING LAZARUS FROM THE DEAD

When their brother Lazarus was deathly sick, Mary and Martha sent a messenger to Jesus telling Him. But Jesus waited two more days before going there. When He arrived, Lazarus had already been buried for four days. Martha and Mary went out to meet Jesus. When Jesus arrived at the tomb, He told them to move the stone, but Martha replied, "Lord, by this time

Many witnesses believed in Jesus when they saw Him raise Lazarus from the dead, a miracle depicted in *The Resurrection of Lazarus* by Léon Bonnat (1833–1922).

there will be a stench, for he has been dead four days" (John 11:39 NASB). Jesus reminded her to believe. Then He shouted, "Lazarus, come out!" (John 11:43 NIV). And Lazarus, bound with grave wrappings, walked out. Many Jews had come to comfort the sisters, and they all witnessed this, so many of them believed in Him.

READ JOHN 11:1-12:19.

VICTORY IN JESUS

Jesus told His disciples, "Here on earth you will have many trials and sorrows. But take heart, because I have overcome the world" (John 16:33 NLT). He told them this so that they would have peace in Him, and this peace comes from knowing that because Christ was in them, they had access to His overcoming power. They, too, could overcome the world. As John wrote, "You are of God, little children, and have overcome them, because He who is in you is greater than he who is in the world" (1 John 4:4 NKJV). "For whatever is born of God overcomes the world; and this is the victory that has overcome the world—our faith" (1 John 5:4 NASB).

READ JOHN 16–17.

THE RESURRECTION APPEARANCES

After being crucified and buried, Jesus rose from the dead and shocked His disciples by appearing bodily to them. He first appeared to Mary Magdalene, then to other women. Then He visited Peter, then walked and talked with two disciples on the road to Emmaus. That same evening, He suddenly appeared in the midst of the apostles as they sat inside a house. He let them touch Him, and even ate food. One week later in Galilee, He showed up again, and this time Thomas was there. Later Jesus met nine disciples beside the Sea of Galilee. After that, He appeared to five hundred disciples at one time. Finally, He showed Himself to His disciples near Jerusalem and ascended from the Mount of Olives up to heaven.

READ JOHN 20–21.

BASIC SURVEY

ACTS

AUTHOR: Not stated, but since it's *also* addressed to Theophilus, it's traditionally attributed to Luke, the author of the Gospel of Luke.

DATE: Covering events of the AD 30s to 60s, Acts was probably written before AD 62.

IN TEN WORDS OR LESS

The Holy Spirit's arrival heralds beginning of Christian Church.

DETAILS, PLEASE

The book of Acts is a bridge between the story of Jesus in the Gospels and the life of the Church in the letters that follow. Luke begins with Jesus' ascension into heaven. Ten days later, God sends the Holy Spirit on the day of Pentecost—and the Church is born. The disciples are empowered to preach boldly about Jesus. Jewish leaders, fearing the new movement called "the Way" (9:2 NLT), begin persecuting believers, who scatter and spread the Gospel. The greatest persecutor, Saul, becomes a Christian himself and ultimately joins Peter and other Christians in preaching, working miracles, and strengthening the Church.

QUOTABLE

> "Repent and be baptized, every one of you, in the name of Jesus Christ for the forgiveness of your sins. And you will receive the gift of the Holy Spirit" (2:38 NIV).

UNIQUE AND UNUSUAL

Acts tells of the Gospel's transition from a purely Jewish message to one for all people (9:15; 10:45), and the beginning of the Christian missionary movement (chapter 13).

SO WHAT?

Christians today can have the same anointing that Acts describes: "You shall receive power when the Holy Spirit has come upon you" (1:8 NKJV).

READ ACTS 1 AND 20.

● One-Month Course: your next reading is on page 209.   →

● Three-Month Course: your next reading is on page 203.   →

● Six-Month Course: your next reading is on page 203.   →

HEART OF THE BOOK

THE APOSTLE PAUL

The apostle Paul was born in the city of Tarsus in the Roman province of Cilicia (in southern Turkey) and was named Saul. His father had Roman citizenship, so although he was a Jew, Saul was born a Roman citizen. His Latin name was Paul. Saul was raised a Pharisee and as a young man went to Jerusalem to study under Gamaliel, a leading rabbi. He excelled in these studies and was extremely zealous for the Law of Moses (Acts 22:3, 27–28; Galatians 1:14).

Paul persecuted Christians before he became an apostle. This painting titled *Saint Paul Writing His Epistles* is by Valentin de Boulogne (1591–1632).

Saul agreed to the stoning of Stephen, the first martyr, and went on to lead an intense persecution against Christians throughout Israel. As he was traveling to Damascus to persecute Christians, a bright light shone around him and Jesus appeared and spoke with him. Saul immediately believed and became a disciple (Acts 8–9).

After spending a few years in Arabia and Tarsus, Saul was invited to Antioch to teach and preach. From there, he and Barnabas were sent out as missionaries to both Jews and Gentiles living in the Roman provinces. At this point Saul began using his Roman name, Paul. Paul not only was an effective speaker, but did many mighty miracles. He later traveled with Timothy and Silas and evangelized Greece and Turkey (Acts 11:25–27; 13:1–3).

Paul was eventually arrested and stood trial in Rome before Nero. He was released and apparently traveled west to Spain. Upon returning to the eastern Mediterranean, however, he was rearrested, once again taken to Rome, and this time executed.

READ ACTS 9 AND 26.

● Three-Month Course: your next reading is on page 209.   →

● Six-Month Course: your next reading is on page 204.   →

CLOSER LOOK

PREACHING THE GOSPEL

The first disciples personally witnessed Jesus' miracles and saw Him alive again after His crucifixion and resurrection. That's why they repeatedly declared, "We are His witnesses to these things" (Acts 5:32 NKJV). (See also Acts 2:32; 3:15; 10:39.) In the same way, all believers are to be a witness of the change that Jesus has brought to their lives, to "tell what great things God has done for [them]" (Luke 8:39 NKJV).

We should preach the Gospel not only with words, but by our loving attitude and lifestyle. If we're focused on the wonderful things Jesus has done for us, we'll naturally talk about them, "for out of the abundance of the heart the mouth speaks" (Matthew 12:34 NKJV). As Peter said, "We cannot stop speaking about what we have seen and heard" (Acts 4:20 NASB).

Paul said, "I am not ashamed of the gospel, because it is the power of God that brings salvation to everyone who believes" (Romans 1:16 NIV). But at times we *do* worry about what others will think of us. Also, we often may not know what to say or how to say it. That's why God desires to empower us for this task with His Holy Spirit. As Jesus said, "You will receive power when the Holy Spirit comes upon you. And you will be my witnesses, telling people about me everywhere" (Acts 1:8 NLT). The Holy Spirit gave the first Christians great power and enabled them to be effective witnesses, and He will do the same for us today.

READ ACTS 3 AND 19.

● Six-Month Course: your next reading is on page 205.   →

CLOSER LOOK

SALVATION ONLY IN JESUS

The apostle Peter, who is portrayed in this painting titled *Peter the Apostle* by Giuseppe Nogari (1699–1766), openly stated that Jesus is the only way to salvation.

When Peter and John were brought before the religious council, Peter boldly declared Jesus as the Messiah and Savior, saying, "There is salvation in no one else; for there is no other name under heaven that has been given among men by which we must be saved" (Acts 4:12 NASB). Jesus is not simply one of *many* ways to heaven. As He Himself said, "I am the way, the truth, and the life. No one can come to the Father except through me" (John 14:6 NLT). And this is the message Jesus' disciples preached.

Paul explained, "For there is one God and one mediator between God and mankind, the man Christ Jesus" (1 Timothy 2:5 NIV). A mediator is someone who deals with a problem or issue that separates two people—or two groups of people. The problem between us and God is our sin, and Jesus was the only mediator who could resolve this. Only Jesus can rescue us from death and give us eternal life. The apostle John declared, "God hath given to us eternal life, and this life is in his Son" (1 John 5:11 KJV).

Why is Jesus so special? Why can only *He* save us? The reason is simple: other so-called saviors and gurus may have some good moral teachings, but only Jesus can forgive our sin. As John the Baptist said, "Behold! The Lamb of God who takes away the sin of the world!" (John 1:29 NKJV). Jesus is *the* Lamb of God—the only acceptable sacrifice for our sins. We can only find forgiveness in Jesus.

READ ACTS 4–5.

● Six-Month Course: your next reading is on page 209.   →

THE HOLY SPIRIT

God consists of three persons—God the Father, God the Son (Jesus Christ), and God the Holy Spirit. The Holy Spirit is also called the Spirit of God *and* the Spirit of Christ (Romans 8:9). Some people think the Holy Spirit is just some kind of power or force, but the Bible makes it clear that the Spirit is a person and is equal in power and wisdom and holiness to God. The Spirit knows everything that God knows (1 Corinthians 2:10–11). That's why He is also called "the Spirit of truth" (John 16:13 NIV). The moment we accept Jesus as Lord, God sends the Spirit to live in our hearts (Galatians 4:6). All believers must have the Spirit living in them to be saved (Romans 8:9), but many Christians believe that being "baptized with the Holy Spirit" is a separate event. In the Bible people sometimes received the Holy Spirit after they became Christians (Acts 8:14–17; 19:1–6).

READ ACTS 8 AND 19.

MIRACLES OF HEALING

When Jesus commissioned His twelve apostles to be witnesses and to preach, He also gave them the power to do healing miracles. Jesus later gave this power to seventy other disciples (Matthew 10:1; Luke 10:1, 9). In the book of Acts, the Twelve did many mighty miracles. "Many wonders and signs were done through the apostles" (Acts 2:43 NKJV; see also Acts 5:12).

Jesus had said, "And these signs will follow those who believe. . .they will lay hands on the sick, and they will recover" (Mark 16:17–18 NKJV). And James gave instructions for elders to heal (James 5:14–15). But apparently not *all* Christians had healing powers. For example, when Tabitha became sick and died, none of the Christians of Joppa were able to heal her—but Peter came and raised her from dead (Acts 9:36–41).

The apostles were given the power to heal others. This painting by Karel Dujardin (1626–1678) is titled *Saint Paul Healing the Cripple at Lystra.*

READ ACTS 14 AND 17.

PREACHING TO THE GENTILES

Peter was staying in Joppa when three Romans, sent by the Roman centurion Cornelius, arrived at the door. God told Peter to go with them, even though Jews were forbidden to keep company with Gentiles, or non-Jews (Acts 10:28). So Peter and several other Jews entered his house. Cornelius had invited all of his relatives and close friends, and explained that an angel had appeared to him, telling him to listen to what Peter had to say. When Peter said that "everyone who believes in him [Jesus] will have their sins forgiven" (Acts 10:43 NLT), the Holy Spirit entered the listeners' hearts. The Jewish Christians were amazed and said, "We can see that God has also given the Gentiles the privilege of. . .receiving eternal life" (Acts 11:18 NLT).

READ ACTS 11 AND PSALM 102.

TROUBLE FOR BELIEVERS

Is it actually God's plan for His people to suffer trouble, stress, and persecution? Yes. Paul warned, "We must go through many hardships to enter the kingdom of God" (Acts 14:22 NIV). God often uses troubles, pressures, setbacks, and even persecution to test our faith and refine us. Christians are literally destined for trouble. Paul wrote to Christians to keep them from being shaken by the troubles they were going through, saying, "But you know that we are destined for such troubles" (1 Thessalonians 3:3 NLT). We're not even supposed to think it odd. "Beloved, think it not strange concerning the fiery trial which is to try you, as though some strange thing happened unto you" (1 Peter 4:12 KJV).

READ ACTS 12 AND 16.

JEWS OF THE DIASPORA

There were over five million Jews living scattered throughout the Roman Empire. They were called the Diaspora, or the "dispersed among the Gentiles" (John 7:35 KJV). They met weekly in synagogues, and as James said, "The law of Moses has been preached in every city from the earliest times" (Acts 15:21 NIV). Many Greeks called *proselytes* converted to the Jewish faith, and those who didn't go through with circumcision, but who nevertheless believed in God, were referred to as "God-fearers." When Saul persecuted the Jewish Christians in Judea, many of them fled to Phoenicia, Cyprus, and Antioch and preached to these Jews and God-fearers. Every time they entered a new city, Paul and his companions preached the Gospel to them first as well.

READ ACTS 13 AND 18.

THE STORM AND SHIPWRECK

Paul was being taken to Rome as a prisoner, and they were sailing south of Crete when a powerful wind drove them out to sea. "The terrible storm raged for many days, blotting out the sun and the stars, until at last all hope was gone" (Acts 27:20 NLT). After two weeks, the sailors realized that they were approaching land. So they hoisted the foresail, hoping to be driven up onto the beach. But they got stuck on a sandbar

Paul survived a severe storm and shipwreck while he was being transported as a prisoner to Rome. *Saint Paul Shipwrecked on Malta* is by Laurent de la Hyre (1606–1656).

some ways out and the stern began breaking to pieces in the heavy surf. The centurion ordered everyone who could swim to make it to the beach. Those who couldn't swim hung onto planks and were washed ashore. Miraculously, everyone made it to land safely.

READ ACTS 27–28.

BASIC SURVEY

ROMANS

AUTHOR: The apostle Paul (1:1), with the secretarial assistance of Tertius (16:22).

DATE: Approximately AD 57, near the conclusion of Paul's third missionary journey.

IN TEN WORDS OR LESS

Sinners are saved only by faith in Jesus Christ.

DETAILS, PLEASE

Some call Romans a "theology textbook" for its thorough explanation of the Christian life. Paul describes God's righteous anger against human sin (chapters 1–2), noting everyone falls short of God's standard (3:23). But God Himself provides a way to overcome that sin: "the righteousness of God which is by faith of Jesus Christ unto all that believe" (3:22 KJV). Being justified (made right) through faith in Jesus, we can consider ourselves "to be dead indeed unto sin, but alive unto God through Jesus Christ our Lord" (6:11 KJV). God's Spirit will give life to all who believe in Jesus, allowing us to "present [our] bodies a living sacrifice, holy, acceptable unto God" (12:1 KJV).

QUOTABLE

> And we know that in all things God works for the good of those who love him, who have been called according to his purpose (8:28 NIV).

> Love does no wrong to a neighbor; therefore love is the fulfillment of the law (13:10 NASB).

UNIQUE AND UNUSUAL

Unlike Paul's other letters, Romans was addressed to a congregation he'd never met. He was hoping to see the Roman Christians personally while traveling west to Spain (15:23–24).

SO WHAT?

In Paul's own words, "Therefore being justified by faith, we have peace with God through our Lord Jesus Christ" (5:1 KJV).

READ ROMANS 1–2.

● One-Month Course: your next reading is on page 215.   →

● Three-Month Course: your next reading is on page 210.   →

● Six-Month Course: your next reading is on page 210.   →

HEART OF THE BOOK

SALVATION BY GRACE

The Bible tells us that we're "saved by grace," but what does that mean? Well, grace means several things in the New Testament. When we say that someone is "gracious" or "full of grace," we mean that they're good, kind, and merciful. This is what John meant when he said that Jesus was "full of grace and truth" (John 1:14 KJV).

In New Testament times, "grace" also meant the kindness and mercy of a master toward a servant. The Bible says, "By grace you have been saved through faith, and that not of yourselves; it is the gift of God" (Ephesians 2:8 NKJV). Paul emphasizes this teaching in the book of Romans. First he writes, "All have sinned, and come short of the glory of God" (Romans 3:23 KJV). Then he tells us, "For the wages of sin is death; but the gift of God is eternal life through Jesus Christ our Lord" (Romans 6:23 KJV).

We've been saved from spiritual death by God's grace—His kindness and mercy. He doesn't expect us to work for eternal life or to do enough good deeds to earn it as a reward. We couldn't earn it no matter how hard we worked, so God graciously gave us salvation free, as a gift. All we need to do is open our hearts and receive it.

God offered this gift of grace before we were even seeking Him: "But God demonstrates His own love toward us, in that while we were still sinners, Christ died for us" (Romans 5:8 NKJV).

READ ROMANS 3 AND 6.

● Three-Month Course: your next reading is on page 215.   →

● Six-Month Course: your next reading is on page 211.   →

CLOSER LOOK

Abraham—the Father of Faith

Abraham had great faith in God and is considered the father of both Jews and Gentiles. He is depicted in this painting by Rembrandt (1606–1669) titled *The Sacrifice of Abraham.*

Paul discusses Abraham in Romans 4 and declares when and why God found him righteous. Surprisingly, although Abraham was the forefather of the Jews and was the first Hebrew to be circumcised (Genesis 17:9–26), it was *not* obeying the command to become circumcised that made him righteous in God's eyes. Rather, he was declared righteous because of his faith in the promises of God. "Abraham believed God, and it was credited to him as righteousness" (Romans 4:3 NASB).

The first promise that God made to Abraham was that his descendants would be as numerous as the stars—even though he didn't have any children yet (Genesis 15:4–6). And Abraham believed this. The second promise that God made to Abraham was that his barren wife, Sarah, would bear a son, and that nations would come from that son (Genesis 17:15–22). Again Abraham believed God. Both these promises were given *before* Abraham was circumcised.

This took great faith. Abraham, "contrary to hope, in hope believed, so that he became the father of many nations, according to what was spoken, 'So shall your descendants be.' . . . He did not waver at the promise of God through unbelief, but was strengthened in faith, giving glory to God" (Romans 4:18, 20 NKJV). Then Paul brings out his final point: since Abraham was considered righteous while he was still uncircumcised, he is the father of both the circumcised Jews and the uncircumcised Gentiles. All men are made righteous by putting their faith in Jesus Christ, the Son of God.

READ ROMANS 4–5.

● Six-Month Course: your next reading is on page 212.   →

CLOSER LOOK

OVERCOMING EVIL WITH GOOD

In Romans 12:21 (KJV) Paul writes, "Be not overcome of evil, but overcome evil with good." What exactly does he mean? Paul goes into detail in the verses leading up to this. First he states, "Bless those who persecute you; bless and do not curse" (Romans 12:14 NIV). This is an excellent way of overcoming evil with good. In writing this, of course, Paul is quoting Jesus who said, "Love your enemies, do good to those who hate you, bless those who curse you, pray for those who mistreat you" (Luke 6:27–28 NIV).

Paul then gives another example of how to overcome evil with good, saying, "Dear friends, never take revenge. Leave that to the righteous anger of God. For the Scriptures say, 'I will take revenge; I will pay them back,' says the LORD. Instead, 'If your enemies are hungry, feed them. If they are thirsty, give them something to drink'" (Romans 12:19–20 NLT). To treat your enemies so kindly, you have to be following Jesus' command to love them.

Many people feel that this is simply too idealistic. They think that only Jesus and holy saints can actually love their enemies, but that surely God doesn't expect ordinary people to do that. But even in the Old Testament, God commanded *everyone*, "You shall not take vengeance, nor bear any grudge against the children of your people, but you shall love your neighbor as yourself" (Leviticus 19:18 NKJV). And Jesus explained that your "neighbor" was anyone you came across (Luke 10:25–37).

READ ROMANS 12 AND PSALM 67.

● Six-Month Course: your next reading is on page 215.

GOD WORKS FOR OUR GOOD

Many Christians are comforted by the following promise: "And we know that all things work together for good to those who love God, to those who are the called according to His purpose" (Romans 8:28 NKJV). A good example of this was when Joseph's brothers maliciously sold him into slavery in Egypt, but then God used Joseph to save many nations from famine. Joseph told his brothers, "You meant evil against me, but God meant it for good in order to bring about this present result, to preserve many people alive" (Genesis 50:20 NASB). Of course, not everything believers experience is good in *itself*, but God is able to redeem any situation and use even suffering and hardship to produce beneficial results.

While Joseph suffered greatly at the hands of his brothers, God redeemed him by using him to save nations. Giovanni Andrea de Ferrari (1598–1669) depicted Jacob's grief when he learned of Joseph's fate in the painting *Joseph's Coat Brought to Jacob.*

READ ROMANS 7–8.

CONFESSING CHRIST

Paul writes, "If you openly declare that Jesus is Lord and believe in your heart that God raised him from the dead, you will be saved. For it is by believing in your heart that you are made right with God, and it is by openly declaring your faith that you are saved" (Romans 10:9–10 NLT). We understand that it's vital to believe in Jesus to be saved, but why must we also confess our faith with our mouths? As 2 Corinthians 4:13 (KJV) says, "I believed, and therefore have I spoken." And Jesus explained, "Out of the abundance of the heart the mouth speaks" (Matthew 12:34 NKJV). He also promised that He would personally acknowledge whoever confessed faith in Him (Luke 12:8).

READ ROMANS 10 AND PSALM 119:57–96.

SUBMIT TO THE GOVERNMENT

When Jesus sets up His kingdom, it will be a perfect government. But until that day, nations will be ruled by imperfect rulers. Even the best leaders sometimes make poor decisions. But the Bible tells us, "Everyone must submit to governing authorities. For all authority comes from God, and those in positions of authority have been placed there by God" (Romans 13:1 NLT). Paul goes on to say that there are two reasons to obey the law: to avoid being punished by the authorities and because it's the right way to live. Some of the only times we should *not* obey a government are when it commands us to deny our faith and forbids us to tell others about Jesus (Daniel 3:1–18; 6:1–13; Acts 4:18–20).

READ ROMANS 11 AND 13.

THINKING OF OTHERS

Paul's writings tell us to love, honor, and help one another rather than think only of ourselves.

Paul wrote to the Romans, "Be devoted to one another in love. Honor one another above yourselves" (Romans 12:10 NIV). He expounded on how to do this, saying, "We who are strong ought to bear with the failings of the weak and not to please ourselves. Each of us should please our neighbors for their good, to build them up" (Romans 15:1–2 NIV). How can we honor others above ourselves? By having God's love. "Love is patient and kind. . . . It does not demand its own way" (1 Corinthians 13:4–5 NLT). This goes against the grain of demanding our rights. Most people are so determined to not let others take advantage of them that they won't put up with anything. But God has a different way of operating.

READ ROMANS 14–15.

BASIC SURVEY

1 CORINTHIANS

AUTHOR: The apostle Paul, with the assistance of Sosthenes (1:1).

DATE: Approximately AD 55–57.

IN TEN WORDS OR LESS

An apostle tackles sin problems in the church at Corinth.

DETAILS, PLEASE

Paul had helped found the church in Corinth (Acts 18) but then moved on to other mission fields. In Ephesus, he learns of problems in the Corinthian congregation and writes a letter to address those issues. Paul first deals with sectarianism and then addresses a situation of sexual immorality. He also warns Christians involved in lawsuits against fellow believers and teaches on marriage, Christian liberty, the Lord's Supper, spiritual gifts, and the resurrection of the dead. In the famous thirteenth chapter, Paul describes the "more excellent way" (12:31 KJV): that of charity, or love.

QUOTABLE

> For the preaching of the cross is to them that perish foolishness; but unto us which are saved it is the power of God (1:18 KJV).

> For other foundation can no man lay than that is laid, which is Jesus Christ (3:11 KJV).

UNIQUE AND UNUSUAL

Refuting opponents who questioned Paul's apostleship, he insists that he is as much an apostle as Jesus' original disciples. "Am I am not an apostle?" he asks in 1 Corinthians 9:1 (KJV). "Have I not seen Jesus Christ our Lord?"

SO WHAT?

Church problems are nothing new—neither is the way to correct them. Personal purity, self-discipline, and love for others are vital to a congregation's success.

READ 1 CORINTHIANS 1–2.

- One-Month Course: your next reading is on page 220.   →
- Three-Month Course: your next reading is on page 216.   →
- Six-Month Course: your next reading is on page 216.   →

HEART OF THE BOOK

LOVE—THE GREATEST VIRTUE

The kind of love Paul describes in 1 Corinthians 13 (the "Love Chapter") is so great that many people think they'll never be able to overcome all their anger, jealousy, and prejudices and have that kind of love. Well, they might not have it at the beginning, but as they continue to yield their hearts to God on a daily basis, they will. The Bible says, "God's love has been poured out into our hearts through the Holy Spirit, who has been given to us" (Romans 5:5 NIV). So Christians need to pray for God to give them more of His Spirit and His love.

Remember, Paul didn't come up with these thoughts on his own. He taught them because they're the most basic of all Christian teachings. Jesus declared that the greatest commandments were to love God with all our

Love is at the heart of all of Jesus' teachings. We set ourselves apart from the world as Christians by loving others as God loves us.

hearts and to love our neighbor as much as we love ourselves (Matthew 22:35–40). Jesus also taught that love should be the distinguishing virtue of all Christians: "Your love for one another will prove to the world that you are my disciples" (John 13:35 NLT). This is because, as the Bible tells us, God Himself is love (1 John 4:8 KJV).

The presence of genuine love is one of the proofs that someone has God in his or her life: "The fruit of the Spirit is love" (Galatians 5:22 KJV). And John tells us that the surest evidence that a person loves God is if they love others (1 John 3:10–23; 4:7–19).

READ 1 CORINTHIANS 9 AND 13.

● Three-Month Course: your next reading is on page 220.   →

● Six-Month Course: your next reading is on page 217.   →

CLOSER LOOK

Our Resurrection Bodies

Hendrick ter Brugghen (1588–1629) depicted Thomas seeking proof of Christ's resurrection in the painting *The Incredulity of Saint Thomas*. We, too, will have resurrected bodies when Jesus returns.

Some people think that Jesus saves just their spirit, so when their body dies, they leave it behind forever and only their spirit lives eternally in heaven. They guess that it sort of floats around on clouds forever, because it is just a spirit, after all. Christians' spirits *do* go to heaven at first, but God has a long-term plan: He wants to save their physical bodies, too, and reunite them with their spirits. To do this He will resurrect their bodies. To "resurrect" means to bring back to life.

For their bodies to live forever, God must *change* them to make them powerful and indestructible and eternal—just like Jesus' resurrection body. "If the Spirit of Him who raised Jesus from the dead dwells in you, He who raised Christ from the dead will also give life to your mortal bodies" (Romans 8:11 NKJV). "The Lord Jesus Christ. . . will transform our lowly bodies so that they will be like his glorious body" (Philippians 3:20–21 NIV).

Although they're natural physical bodies now, perishable and weak, they will become glorious, powerful, eternal bodies. "So will it be with the resurrection of the dead. The body that is sown is perishable, it is raised imperishable; it is sown in dishonor, it is raised in glory; it is sown in weakness, it is raised in power; it is sown a natural body, it is raised a spiritual body" (1 Corinthians 15:42–44 NIV).

The resurrection will happen at the very end of time when Jesus returns (1 Thessalonians 4:14–17).

READ 1 CORINTHIANS 14–15.

● Six-Month Course: your next reading is on page 220.   →

AVOIDING SECTARIANISM

Paul warned the Christians of Corinth against divisions. Some of them were insisting, "I follow Paul." Others were arguing, "I follow Peter," and others were boasting, "I follow Apollos." Paul asked, "Was Paul crucified for you?" (1 Corinthians 1:12–13 NIV). Of course not. Jesus was, so we should all follow Jesus. We should respect every person who truly follows Him, no matter which pastor they prefer to listen to or which church they attend. We might think that our pastor is better, but it's wrong to think that only the people in our church are true Christians. We should accept other Christians who have different opinions (Romans 14:1–6). If we agree on the important things about Jesus, we can be in unity and love one another (Ephesians 4:3–6).

READ 1 CORINTHIANS 3–4.

JOINED TO THE LORD

Many Christians think that the description of Jesus "living in their heart" is simply a poetic phrase and that it can't mean that literally. After all, as far as they understand, God is up in a distant heaven and they are down here on earth. But the Bible says, "He who is joined to the Lord is one spirit with Him" (1 Corinthians 6:17 NKJV). The Spirit of Christ truly *does* live in our hearts (Galatians 4:6). In fact, He is inseparably united with our spirit. This is

Jesus described Himself as the true vine, and we are His branches because we draw life from Him.

precisely what gives us eternal life. Jesus taught this same concept in John 15 when He described Himself as the true vine and described individual believers as branches *joined* to Him and receiving His life.

READ 1 CORINTHIANS 6 AND 8.

OLD TESTAMENT EXAMPLES

Some Christians wonder whether the Old Testament is still relevant now that Jesus has come and fulfilled the requirements of the Law and the prophecies of the prophets. After all, the Bible says, "He cancels the first covenant in order to put the second into effect" (Hebrews 10:9 NLT). But Paul explains that the entire Old Testament was written for our benefit and that there is much that we can learn from it. After discussing the example of the children of Israel, Paul stated, "Now these things happened to them as an example, and they were written for *our* instruction" (1 Corinthians 10:11 NASB, emphasis added). We can even draw new lessons from old commandments in the scriptures (see 1 Corinthians 9:6–11).

READ 1 CORINTHIANS 10–11.

WE ARE ONE BODY

One of the results of being joined to Christ is that the same Spirit who's in us is *also* in other sincere believers. So in a very real sense, the Spirit unites us with *them* as well. Paul described this, saying, "For as the body is one and has many members, but all the members of that one body, being many, are one body, so also is Christ. . . . Now you are the body of Christ and members individually" (1 Corinthians 12:12, 27 NKJV). He then drew the logical conclusion: just as an entire body looks out for one member that is in pain, so the body of Christ should care for each individual member (vv. 25–26). Jesus is the head (Ephesians 4:15–16), and we are the body, His to command.

READ 1 CORINTHIANS 12 AND 16.

BASIC SURVEY

2 CORINTHIANS

AUTHOR: The apostle Paul, with Timothy's assistance (1:1).

DATE: Approximately AD 55–57, shortly after the writing of 1 Corinthians.

IN TEN WORDS OR LESS

Paul defends his ministry to the troubled Corinthian church.

DETAILS, PLEASE

Corinthian believers had apparently addressed some of the problems Paul's first letter mentioned—though there were still troublemakers who questioned his authority. He was forced to "speak foolishly" (11:21 KJV), boasting of hardships he'd faced serving Jesus: "I have worked harder, been put in prison more often, been whipped times without number, and faced death again and again" (11:23 NLT). Paul even suffered a "thorn in the flesh" (12:7 KJV), which God refused to take away, telling him instead, "My grace is sufficient for thee: for my strength is made perfect in weakness" (12:9 KJV). His parting warning: "Examine yourselves as to whether you are in the faith. Test yourselves" (13:5 NKJV).

QUOTABLE

> God made him who had no sin to be sin for us, so that in him we might become the righteousness of God (5:21 NIV).

UNIQUE AND UNUSUAL

Paul never identifies his "thorn in the flesh," though some speculate it may have been bad eyesight, temptations, even physical unattractiveness.

SO WHAT?

Christians should respect authority—whether in the church, the home, or society at large.

READ 2 CORINTHIANS 2–3.

- One-Month Course: your next reading is on page 224. →
- Three-Month Course: your next reading is on page 224. →
- Six-Month Course: your next reading is on page 221. →

CLOSER LOOK

THE JUDGMENT SEAT OF CHRIST

Believers must one day give an account of their lives—both their words and their deeds. Paul wrote, "For we must all appear before the judgment seat of Christ, so that each of us may receive what is due us for the things done while in the body, whether good or bad" (2 Corinthians 5:10 NIV). Paul adds: "We will all stand before the judgment seat of God. . . . Yes, each of us will give a personal account to God" (Romans 14:10, 12 NLT).

We will not only be required to give an account of how we lived our lives, but we will then be rewarded in proportion to the good we have done, or suffer loss for the wrong we have done, or the good we failed to do. This judgment is not to determine whether we go to heaven or to hell. Believers' names are already written in the Lamb's Book of Life.

This judgment will determine *how much* we're rewarded. It will be a very loving and fair judgment—but it will be thorough. As Paul wrote: "If anyone's work which he has built. . .endures, he will receive a reward. If anyone's work is burned, he will suffer loss; but he himself will be saved, yet so as through fire" (1 Corinthians 3:14–15 NKJV).

Even if we lived futile lives, doing little for Christ, our salvation remains secure. But what a terrible, needless loss to see the selfish ambition and self-seeking works of years burned away. Nevertheless, we are forgiven and will remain in Christ's love.

READ 2 CORINTHIANS 5–6.

● Six-Month Course: your next reading is on page 222.

CLOSER LOOK

CHRISTIANS GIVING GENEROUSLY

In the Old Testament, God promised, "Bring all the tithes into the storehouse so there will be enough food in my Temple. If you do. . .I will open the windows of heaven for you. I will pour out a blessing so great you won't have enough room to take it in!" (Malachi 3:10 NLT). That is a powerful promise, and many Christians have faithfully given a tenth of their earnings and have been blessed mightily in return—not entirely with financial benefits, but often in other ways. They count themselves abundantly blessed already if God keeps accidents, financial disasters, and sickness away.

We should be willing to give generously to others, and we should do so with a cheerful heart.

While Jesus had almost nothing to say about tithing, He constantly spoke about giving generously. For example, He said, "Give, and you will receive. Your gift will return to you in full—pressed down, shaken together to make room for more, running over, and poured into your lap. The amount you give will determine the amount you get back" (Luke 6:38 NLT). Part of this return will be financial since God *has* promised to supply all our physical needs (Philippians 4:13), but remember that we're often simply blessed spiritually because, as Jesus said, "It is more blessed to give than to receive" (Acts 20:35 KJV).

However God blesses us for giving, He *does* bless us. Paul wrote, "Whoever sows sparingly will also reap sparingly, and whoever sows generously will also reap generously. Each of you should give what you have decided in your heart to give, not reluctantly or under compulsion, for God loves a cheerful giver" (2 Corinthians 9:6–7 NIV).

READ 2 CORINTHIANS 8–9.

● Six-Month Course: your next reading is on page 224.   →

HIDDEN TREASURE

CAST DOWN BUT VICTORIOUS

Life for Christians isn't always easy, contrary to what you may have heard. There will be times when God allows very heavy circumstances to press you down. As Paul said, "We were under great pressure, far beyond our ability to endure" (2 Corinthians 1:8 NIV). At times, God allows things in our lives that, if they continued, would be literally unbearable. Most of the time, however, our situation resembles this: "We are hard-pressed on every side, yet not crushed; we are perplexed, but not in despair" (2 Corinthians 4:8 NKJV). Only Christ in us can give us the strength to make it (Philippians 4:19). Therefore "cast all your anxiety on him because he cares for you" (1 Peter 5:7 NIV).

READ 2 CORINTHIANS 1 AND 4.

HIDDEN TREASURE

SPIRITUAL WAR

We should always be prepared to defend God's truth and to fight the temptations of the devil. This painting titled *Saint Michael Vanquishing Satan* is by Raffaello Sanzio (1483–1520).

We are engaged in a war "against the rulers of the darkness of this world, against spiritual wickedness in high places" (Ephesians 6:12 KJV). The apostle Peter warns, "Your enemy the devil prowls around like a roaring lion" (1 Peter 5:8 NIV), so we're commanded, "Resist the devil, and he will flee from you" (James 4:7 KJV). To do this, we must take up spiritual weapons (Ephesians 6:17–18). Paul tells us that "the weapons of our warfare are not of the flesh, but divinely powerful for the destruction of fortresses. We are destroying. . .every lofty thing raised up against the knowledge of God" (2 Corinthians 10:4–5 NASB). While this refers primarily to demolishing arguments against God, it also applies to our spiritual battle against the enemy.

READ 2 CORINTHIANS 10–11.

BASIC SURVEY

GALATIANS

AUTHOR: The apostle Paul (1:1).

DATE: Perhaps around AD 49, as one of Paul's earliest letters.

IN TEN WORDS OR LESS

Christians are free from restrictive Jewish laws.

DETAILS, PLEASE

Writing to several regional churches, Paul can only "marvel" (1:6 KJV) that Galatian Christians have turned from their freedom in Jesus back to the rules of Old Testament Judaism. Some people tried to compel Christians "to live as do the Jews" (2:14 KJV), an error even the apostle Peter made (2:11–13). Paul argued strongly "that no man is justified by the law in the sight of God. . .for, the just shall live by faith" (3:11 KJV).

QUOTABLE

> O foolish Galatians! Who has bewitched you? (3:1 NKJV).

> The fruit of the Spirit is love, joy, peace, longsuffering, gentleness, goodness, faith, meekness, temperance: against such there is no law (5:22–23 KJV).

UNIQUE AND UNUSUAL

One of Paul's closing comments, "See what large letters I use as I write to you with my own hand!" (6:11 NIV), makes some believe that poor eyesight was the apostle's "thorn in the flesh" (2 Corinthians 12:7 KJV).

SO WHAT?

Old Testament rules don't control Christians' lives—but God's Spirit should: "Walk in the Spirit, and you shall not fulfill the lust of the flesh" (5:16 NKJV).

READ GALATIANS 1–2.

● One-Month Course: your next reading is on page 228.   →

● Three-Month Course: your next reading is on page 228.   →

● Six-Month Course: your next reading is on page 225.   →

CLOSER LOOK

GRACE, NOT LAW

Many thousands of believers in Judea were "zealous for the law" (Acts 21:20 NKJV). Even those who knew they were saved by grace alone still felt it was *beneficial* for Jews to observe the Law. But certain Pharisees who were believers maintained that all Christians *had* to keep the Law. Some of them arrived in Antioch and taught that believing in Jesus wasn't enough, that unless the Greeks became circumcised and kept the Law of Moses, they couldn't be saved.

Paul and Barnabas went to the apostles and elders in Jerusalem to discuss this. There, certain believers insisted, "It is necessary to. . .command them to keep the law of Moses" (Acts 15:5 NKJV). Peter, however, said that even Jews weren't saved by keeping the Law, so the apostles wrote an official letter about this to all the churches. That letter settled the dispute for most disciples—but certain people weren't convinced.

Paul and Barnabas, who taught that believers must follow the gospel of Christ, are depicted in *Paul and Barnabas at Lystra* by Nicolaes Pietersz Berchem (1620–1683).

They then taught their doctrine in Galatia, north of Antioch. When Paul learned of this, he wrote to the Galatians, telling them, "Some people are throwing you into confusion and are trying to pervert the gospel of Christ." He called their doctrine "a different gospel—which is really no gospel at all" (Galatians 1:6–7 NIV). Paul said that those people were eager to persuade the Galatians, not to benefit them, but to make them into their disciples. But Paul declared that the Law brought people under a curse and that people who preached salvation by keeping the Law were also cursed (Galatians 1:8–9; 3:10–13).

READ GALATIANS 3 AND ACTS 15.

● Six-Month Course: your next reading is on page 226.   →

CLOSER LOOK

Love Fulfills the Law

In his letter to the Galatians, Paul wrote, "For the entire law is fulfilled in keeping this one command: 'Love your neighbor as yourself'" (Galatians 5:14 NIV). Paul was building on Jesus' teachings that "whatever you want men to do to you, do also to them, for this is the Law and the Prophets" (Matthew 7:12 NKJV). Jesus later said that the two greatest commands were, "You must love the LORD your God with all your heart," and "Love your neighbor as yourself." He concluded, "The entire law and all the demands of the prophets are based on these two commandments" (Matthew 22:37–40 NLT).

Paul stressed this message in his epistles as well, saying, "Owe nothing to anyone except to love one another; for he who loves his neighbor has fulfilled the law. . . . Love does no wrong to a neighbor; therefore love is the fulfillment of the law" (Romans 13:8, 10 NASB). All the many commandments of the Law were fulfilled by keeping that one brief command. The apostle James echoed this teaching, saying, "If you really fulfill the royal law according to the Scripture, 'You shall love your neighbor as yourself,' you do well" (James 2:8 NKJV).

It's important to believe the right things and to have correct doctrine, but it's also vitally important that our hearts be filled with God's love. If they are, then all our actions, everything we do, will be motivated by that love.

READ GALATIANS 5 AND PROVERBS 29.

● Six-Month Course: your next reading is on page 228.

THE FRUIT OF THE SPIRIT

Paul stated that "the fruit of the Spirit is love, joy, peace, forbearance, kindness, goodness, faithfulness, gentleness and self-control" (Galatians 5:22–23 NIV). These fruits are direct evidence that the Holy Spirit resides and reigns in our hearts. Just as a pear tree bears pears, someone joined to the Spirit bears the fruit of the Spirit. These are the signs of a transformed life. "Anyone who belongs to Christ has become a new person. The old life is gone; a new life has begun!" (2 Corinthians 5:17 NLT). Don't worry if the fruit doesn't all immediately spring forth, fully formed. God does some initial work quickly, but it takes time for most fruit to bud then come to perfection. But you must give Him free rein to work in your heart.

READ GALATIANS 4 AND PSALM 73.

YOU REAP WHAT YOU SOW

Paul wrote, "Whatsoever a man soweth, that shall he also reap" (Galatians 6:7 KJV). We often think of this as a law of repercussions: if you do bad to others, bad will come back to you. And there's truth in that. As Job said, "Those who plow evil and those who sow trouble reap it" (Job 4:8 NIV). But this verse

in Galatians is primarily talking about reaping life. As Paul goes on to say, "Whoever sows to please their flesh, from the flesh will reap destruction; whoever sows to please the Spirit, from the Spirit will reap eternal life. Let us not become weary in doing good, for at the proper time we will reap a harvest" (Galatians 6:8–9 NIV). Let's not forget this meaning as well.

Paul's writings remind believers to always work to do good so that we can "reap a harvest" (Galatians 6:9).

READ GALATIANS 6 AND PSALMS 75–76.

BASIC SURVEY

EPHESIANS

AUTHOR: The apostle Paul (1:1).

DATE: Around AD 62, when under house arrest in Rome.

IN TEN WORDS OR LESS

Christians are all members of Jesus' "body," the Church.

DETAILS, PLEASE

Paul had started the church in Ephesus (Acts 19) and now explains in detail the church members' relationship to Jesus Christ—so that they "may grow up into him in all things, which is the head, even Christ" (4:15 KJV). Through Jesus, God has reconciled both Jews and Gentiles to Himself (2:11–18). This new life should result in pure, honest living in the Church and in the home (chapters 4–6).

QUOTABLE

> For by grace you have been saved through faith, and that not of yourselves; it is the gift of God, not of works, lest anyone should boast (2:8–9 NKJV).

> Put on the full armor of God, so that you will be able to stand firm against the schemes of the devil (6:11 NASB).

UNIQUE AND UNUSUAL

Paul tells servants (slaves, in today's language) to "be obedient to them that are your masters" (6:5 KJV). Why? Because God will reward such behavior (6:8).

SO WHAT?

"Through [Jesus] you Gentiles are also being made part of this dwelling where God lives by his Spirit" (2:22 NLT).

READ EPHESIANS 1 AND PSALMS 81–82.

- One-Month Course: your next reading is on page 231. →
- Three-Month Course: your next reading is on page 231. →
- Six-Month Course: your next reading is on page 229. →

CLOSER LOOK

Not Grace and Works

Paul taught that our salvation is a free gift from God, dependent completely upon His good graces and not upon our personal merit or righteous deeds. "For it is by grace you have been saved, through faith—and this is not from yourselves, it is the gift of God—not by works, so that no one can boast" (Ephesians 2:8–9 NIV).

Some people think, however, that God's grace *plus* our good deeds save us, but Paul asserted that it's either one or the other, not a mixture of the two. "And if by grace, then it is no longer of works; otherwise grace is no longer grace. But if it is of works, it is no longer grace; otherwise work is no longer work" (Romans 11:6 NKJV).

Yet James said, "If someone says he has faith but does not have works . . .can faith save him? . . . Faith by itself, if it does not have works, is dead" (James 2:14, 17 NKJV). There's no contradiction, however. When you truly believe in Jesus, you don't just believe that He exists. After all, even the devils believe that much (James 2:19). Rather, you must make Jesus the center of your life. You must sincerely love God, and when you love God you obey Him (1 John 5:1–3). "The only thing that counts is faith expressing itself through love" (Galatians 5:6 NIV).

So although good deeds can't save you, if you have true faith it will cause you to do good works. That's the proof that you have genuine faith.

READ EPHESIANS 2–3.

 Six-Month Course: your next reading is on page 231.   →

WATCH WHAT YOU SAY

God approves of humor and laughter and merriment, but Christians are to know the difference between wholesome and unacceptable speech. Paul tells us, "Don't use foul or abusive language. Let everything you say be good and helpful, so that your words will be an encouragement to those who hear them. . . . Obscene stories, foolish talk, and coarse jokes—these are not for you. Instead, let there be thankfulness to God" (Ephesians

4:29; 5:4 NLT). In another epistle, he writes, "Put them all aside: anger, wrath, malice, slander, and abusive speech from your mouth" (Colossians 3:8 NASB). The following verse gives the reason for watching what we say: "Avoid godless chatter, because those who indulge in it will become more and more ungodly" (2 Timothy 2:16 NIV).

As Christians, we must guard our tongues. We must avoid obscene speech and focus on wholesome words that praise God.

READ EPHESIANS 4–5.

THE ARMOR OF GOD

Paul tells us that we're fighting "against spiritual hosts of wickedness" and urges us twice, "Put on the *whole* armor of God." Ephesians 6:14–18 describes the separate, individual pieces of armor and weaponry, and you need *every* piece of them so "that you may be able to stand against the wiles of the devil. . .that you may be able to withstand in the evil day" (Ephesians 6:11, 13 NKJV, emphasis added). You need truth, righteousness, the Gospel of peace, faith, salvation, the Word of God, and prayer. It's not enough to have the sword of the Spirit but to lack the shield of faith. You need the *whole* armor of God if you are to withstand the enemy's attacks.

READ EPHESIANS 6 AND PSALM 84.

BASIC SURVEY

PHILIPPIANS

AUTHOR: The apostle Paul, along with Timothy (1:1).

DATE: Probably the early AD 60s.

IN TEN WORDS OR LESS

"Friendship letter" between the apostle Paul and a beloved church.

DETAILS, PLEASE

With sixteen references to "joy" and "rejoicing," Philippians is one of the apostle Paul's most upbeat letters—even though he wrote it in "bonds" (1:13 KJV). Paul thanks the church at Philippi for its support (1:5) and encourages its people to "rejoice in the Lord always: and again I say, Rejoice" (4:4 KJV).

QUOTABLE

> For to me to live is Christ, and to die is gain (1:21 KJV).

> I press toward the mark for the prize of the high calling of God in Christ Jesus (3:14 KJV).

> Be anxious for nothing, but in everything by prayer and supplication, with thanksgiving, let your requests be made known to God (4:6 NKJV).

UNIQUE AND UNUSUAL

Though unity is a common theme in Paul's letters, he singles out two Philippian women, Euodia and Syntyche, pleading that they "be of the same mind in the Lord" (4:2 KJV).

SO WHAT?

When you live in the joy of the Lord, "the peace of God, which surpasses all understanding, will guard your hearts and minds through Christ Jesus" (4:7 NKJV).

READ PHILIPPIANS 1 AND ISAIAH 45:14–25.

● One-Month Course: your next reading is on page 235.   →

● Three-Month Course: your next reading is on page 235.   →

● Six-Month Course: your next reading is on page 232.   →

SETTING ASIDE DIVINE POWER

Jesus is the Son of God, and before being born as a human being, He shared all God's glory and power. When praying to His Father, Jesus mentioned "the glory I had with you before the world began" (John 17:5 NIV). So how could the omnipotent, omnipresent God become a mortal man? How could infinite deity be contained in a finite human body?

Paul tells us that Jesus had to empty Himself of His divine power and attributes. "Christ Jesus. . .although He existed in the form of God, did not regard equality with God a thing to be grasped [held on to], but emptied Himself, taking the form of a bond-servant, and being made in the likeness of men" (Philippians 2:5–7 NASB).

After becoming a limited, mortal man, Jesus experienced hunger and thirst and weariness. He was subject to human limitations. God is all-present, but Jesus could only be in one place at a time. God is all-knowing, but Jesus could no longer know everything (Mark 13:32). God is all-powerful, but Jesus could no longer do everything (Mark 6:5–6). He only did miracles by the power of God's Holy Spirit. As He explained, "I can of Myself do nothing" (John 5:30 NKJV).

Before Jesus could walk the earth as a human, He had to empty Himself of all divine power.

After Jesus resurrected from the dead, His body became powerful and eternal (Revelation 1:12–18). Only such a body could contain the full glory and power of God. Jesus was once again all-powerful and all-knowing. Paul declared, "For in Him dwells all the fullness of the Godhead bodily" (Colossians 2:9 NKJV).

READ PHILIPPIANS 2 AND PSALM 88.

● Six-Month Course: your next reading is on page 235.   →

CHRISTIAN UNITY

In Philippians, Paul not only stressed the importance of Christian unity, but outlined practical steps we can take to make it happen. He wrote, "Make me truly happy by agreeing wholeheartedly with each other, loving one another, and working together with one mind and purpose. Don't be selfish; don't try to impress others. Be humble, thinking of others as better than yourselves. Don't look out only for your own interests, but take an interest in others, too" (Philippians 2:2–4 NLT). That's already plenty to digest, but Paul also urged unity in Romans 12:16 (NIV), saying, "Live in harmony with one another. Do not be proud, but be willing to associate with people of low position. Do not be conceited." (See also Romans 15:5–6; 1 Corinthians 1:10.)

READ PSALM 89 AND PROVERBS 30.

PRAISE GOD DESPITE DIFFICULTIES

It's only natural to complain when trouble hits, but the Bible gives a surprising alternative: "Rejoice in the Lord always. I will say it again: Rejoice!" (Philippians 4:4 NIV). We can choose to be happy in Him in *all* circumstances. But it might take some doing. In Psalm 42:5 (NKJV) King David asked himself, "Why are you cast down, O my soul?" Then he commanded himself, "Hope in God, for I shall yet praise Him." However, David acknowledged in the next verse that he *still* felt miserable, confessing, "O my God, my soul is cast down within me." David poured out his heartfelt complaint—to *God*, not people—then in verse 11 (NKJV) declared *again*, "Hope in God; for I shall yet praise Him."

READ PHILIPPIANS 3 AND PSALM 42.

DON'T BE ANXIOUS

Paul was under house arrest in Rome, about to appear before Emperor Nero to face the charges against him. His future was uncertain, but at this very time Paul advised believers, "Do not be anxious about anything, but in every situation, by prayer and petition, with thanksgiving, present your requests to God" (Philippians 4:6 NIV). The NLT states it this way: "Don't worry about anything; instead, pray about everything. Tell God what you need, and thank him for all he has done." Church historians tell us that Paul was released, continued his missionary work, and was only rearrested and executed some years later. But *whatever* the outcome of that initial trial might have been, Paul refused to become anxious about it.

Even when Paul was imprisoned, he encouraged believers to turn their worries over to God. Rather than dwelling on his fears, Paul prayed and thanked God.

READ PHILIPPIANS 4 AND PSALMS 97–99.

FOCUSING ON VIRTUOUS THINGS

The Bible doesn't teach "the power of positive thinking." Rather, as we focus on our mighty God and pray for His help, *He* sends peace into our hearts and resolves our difficult situations (Isaiah 26:3; Philippians 4:7). But when it comes to moral issues, we *are* told to focus on positive, virtuous thoughts: "Whatever things are true, whatever things are noble, whatever things are just, whatever things are pure, whatever things are lovely, whatever things are of good report, if there is any virtue and if there is anything praiseworthy—meditate on these things" (Philippians 4:8 NKJV). It also helps to pray, "Let the words of my mouth and the meditation of my heart be acceptable in Your sight, O LORD" (Psalm 19:14 NKJV).

READ PSALM 19 AND ISAIAH 26.

BASIC SURVEY

COLOSSIANS

AUTHOR: The apostle Paul, along with Timothy (1:1).

DATE: Probably the early 60s.

IN TEN WORDS OR LESS

Jesus Christ is supreme—over everyone and everything.

DETAILS, PLEASE

False teaching ("enticing words," 2:4 KJV) had infiltrated the church at Colosse, apparently causing some people to add unnecessary and unhelpful elements to their Christian faith. Paul sent this letter to remind Christians of the superiority of Jesus over Jewish rules and regulations (2:16), angels (2:18), and anything else. Jesus is "the image of the invisible God, the firstborn of every creature" (1:15 KJV).

QUOTABLE

> We have not stopped praying for you since we first heard about you (1:9 NLT).

> Set your affection on things above, not on things on the earth (3:2 KJV).

> Let the peace of God rule in your hearts, to which also you were called in one body; and be thankful (3:15 NKJV).

UNIQUE AND UNUSUAL

Paul mentions a letter to Laodicea (4:16) that apparently was lost, and therefore not included as New Testament scripture.

SO WHAT?

"Beware lest any man spoil you through philosophy and vain deceit, after the tradition of men. . .and not after Christ" (2:8 KJV).

READ COLOSSIANS 1 AND PSALMS 85–86.

● One-Month Course: your next reading is on page 238.   →

● Three-Month Course: your next reading is on page 238.   →

● Six-Month Course: your next reading is on page 236.   →

CLOSER LOOK

CHRIST'S PREEMINENCE

The short book of Colossians has a deep, powerful message: Jesus Christ is God incarnate, and He's *all* we need! Who exactly is Jesus? He "is the image

of the invisible God, the firstborn over all creation. For by Him all things were created. . . . And He is before all things, and in Him all things consist. And He is the head of the body, the church, who is the beginning, the firstborn from the dead, that in *all* things He may have the preeminence" (Colossians 1:15–18 NKJV, emphasis added).

In Paul's letter to the Colossians, he encouraged the believers to stay connected to Christ by avoiding the deceptive shadows of reality.

Other things may have *some* value, but if they detract from faith in Jesus, or attempt to displace Him in any way, they're worthless and less than worthless. Paul warned the Colossians against being led by "philosophy and empty deception" rather than by Christ. "For in Him all the fullness of Deity dwells in bodily form, and in Him you have been made complete" (Colossians 2:8–10 NASB). Why choose mere philosophy over the Spirit of Christ dwelling inside us and working powerfully in our lives?

In addition, Paul told the Colossians not to worry about legalistic people judging them for not celebrating holy days or ceremonies or Sabbaths. Why? Because these things "are only shadows of the reality yet to come. And Christ himself is that reality." In the same way, Paul advised Christians not to focus on pious self-denial or to overemphasize the importance of angels, but rather to focus on being "connected to Christ" (Colossians 2:17, 19 NLT).

READ COLOSSIANS 2 AND ISAIAH 49.

● Six-Month Course: your next reading is on page 238.   →

HIDDEN TREASURE

DYING TO SELF

Paul had a blunt message to those tempted to indulge in sinful ways: "Put to death, therefore, whatever belongs to your earthly nature: sexual immorality, impurity, lust, evil desires and greed, which is idolatry. . .anger, rage, malice, slander, and filthy language." We once used to indulge in those things and thought nothing of it, but Paul warns, "But now you must also rid yourselves of all such things as these" (Colossians 3:5, 8–9 NIV). Paul was clearly echoing Jesus' words: "If anyone desires to come after Me, let him deny himself. . . . For whoever desires to save his life will lose it, but whoever loses his life for My sake will find it" (Matthew 16:24–25 NKJV). Sinful habits hinder *real* life and are worth losing.

READ COLOSSIANS 3 AND PSALMS 100–101.

HIDDEN TREASURE

PUTTING UP WITH OTHERS

Christians aren't perfect. Many times we have bad habits that we still need to overcome or a fault or "sin that so easily trips us up" (Hebrews 12:1 NLT). Even if we aren't deliberately sinning, we're still capable of being insensitive, overbearing, nitpicking, demanding, ungrateful, and downright aggravating. Paul recognized this, which is why he wrote, "Make allowance for each other's faults, and forgive anyone who offends you. Remember, the Lord forgave you, so you must forgive others" (Colossians 3:13 NLT). Because we're still human, we constantly need forgiveness—and we need to constantly forgive those who offend *us* as well. Jesus warned, "But if you refuse to forgive others, your Father will not forgive your sins" (Matthew 6:15 NLT).

READ COLOSSIANS 4 AND PSALM 117.

BASIC SURVEY

1 THESSALONIANS

AUTHOR: The apostle Paul, along with Silvanus (Silas) and Timothy (1:1).

DATE: Early 50s—perhaps Paul's earliest letter.

IN TEN WORDS OR LESS

Jesus will return to gather His followers to Him.

DETAILS, PLEASE

In this letter to another church he helped found (see Acts 17), Paul teaches on the second coming of Christ, apparently an issue of some concern to the Thessalonians. Paul describes *how* Jesus will return, but doesn't say exactly *when*. The important thing, in his words, is "We. . .urged you to live your lives in a way that God would consider worthy. For he called you to share in his Kingdom and glory" (2:12 NLT).

QUOTABLE

> For the Lord himself shall descend from heaven with a shout, with the voice of the archangel, and with the trump of God: and the dead in Christ shall rise first (4:16 KJV).

> The day of the Lord will come like a thief in the night (5:2 NIV).

UNIQUE AND UNUSUAL

First Thessalonians contains two of the Bible's shortest verses: "Rejoice evermore" (5:16 KJV) and "Pray without ceasing" (5:17 KJV).

SO WHAT?

If it was important for the Thessalonians to live right in view of Jesus' coming return, how much more so—with the passage of two thousand years—is it for us today?

READ 1 THESSALONIANS 1–2.

● One-Month Course: your next reading is on page 241.   →

● Three-Month Course: your next reading is on page 241.   →

● Six-Month Course: your next reading is on page 239.   →

CLOSER LOOK

CHRISTIANS SUFFERING PERSECUTION

From time immemorial, righteous men and prophets have suffered persecution. Jesus Himself was persecuted, and the early Christians in Jerusalem suffered as well. Paul was repeatedly maligned and attacked as he preached the Gospel from city to city. When he was in Thessalonica, he warned the Christians that they, *too*, would be persecuted—and they were.

"We sent Timothy. . .to strengthen and encourage you in your faith, so that no one would be unsettled by these trials. For you know quite well that we are destined for them. In fact, when we were with you, we kept telling you that we would be perse-

Caravaggio (1571–1610) painted *Crucifixion of Saint Peter*, which illustrates the persecution that many of the early Christians faced.

cuted" (1 Thessalonians 3:2–4 NIV). *Destined* to be persecuted? Yes. "All who desire to live godly in Christ Jesus will be persecuted" (2 Timothy 3:12 NASB).

Persecution comes in many forms. When it's most severe, disciples are tortured and martyred for their faith (John 16:2). In many nations, Christians are despised, oppressed, imprisoned, denied justice, and treated like second-class citizens. Even persecution in its mildest manifestations is painful to those experiencing it: former friends mock them, exclude them, and lie about them, and enemies deliberately make their lives more difficult (Luke 6:22).

Christians are not to go looking for persecution. Paul urged believers to pray "that we may lead a quiet and peaceable life" (1 Timothy 2:2 NKJV), and added, "If it is possible, as much as depends on you, live peaceably with all men" (Romans 12:18 NKJV). And when we *aren't* being persecuted, we must remember to pray for those who are (Hebrews 13:3).

READ 1 THESSALONIANS 3 AND PSALM 108.

● Six-Month Course: your next reading is on page 241.   →

THE GENTLE APOSTLE

Paul had founded the church in Thessalonica. He was the indisputable spiritual leader and could've made demands upon the disciples. Instead, he wrote, "But we were gentle among you, just as a nursing mother cherishes her own children. So, affectionately longing for you, we were well pleased to impart to you. . .our own lives, because you had become dear to us" (1 Thessalonians 2:7–8 NKJV). What a picture of tender, selfless love! In taking on such a sacrificial, self-effacing attitude, Paul was living out what Jesus had said: "Those who are the greatest among you should take the lowest rank, and the leader should be like a servant" (Luke 22:26 NLT). In fact, we should *all* "by love serve one another" (Galatians 5:13 KJV).

Paul wrote that we should display the same gentleness to other people that a nursing mother shows her infant. *The Young Mother* by Charles West Cope (1811–1890) helps us to visualize this type of affection.

READ 1 THESSALONIANS 4 AND JOHN 13.

NO VENDETTAS ALLOWED

One of the most powerful things about Paul's epistles is not his deep theology and explanations of complicated spiritual subjects—but how he constantly emphasizes the most basic principles that Jesus taught. For example, Paul wrote the Christians in Thessalonica, "Make sure that nobody pays back wrong for wrong, but always strive to do what is good for each other" (1 Thessalonians 5:15 NIV). Jesus had said, "Love your enemies, do good to those who hate you, bless those who curse you, pray for those who mistreat you" (Luke 6:27–28 NIV). (In Romans 12:14 Paul quotes Jesus almost word for word.) Paying back wrong for wrong, getting even, seems like the "right" thing to do—but for Christians, it's definitely the wrong course of action.

READ 1 THESSALONIANS 5 AND PSALMS 110–112.

BASIC SURVEY

2 THESSALONIANS

AUTHOR: The apostle Paul, along with Silvanus (Silas) and Timothy (1:1).

DATE: Early 50s—perhaps Paul's second oldest letter.

IN TEN WORDS OR LESS

Christians should work until Jesus returns.

DETAILS, PLEASE

Shortly after writing 1 Thessalonians, Paul dictates a follow-up. Apparently, a letter falsely claiming to be from Paul had left the Thessalonians "shaken in mind. . .troubled" (2:2 KJV) at the thought that Jesus had already returned. Paul assures them that the event is still future—and urges everyone to live positive and productive lives until the second coming. "If any would not work," Paul commands those who have become idle in anticipation of Jesus' return, "neither should he eat" (3:10 KJV).

QUOTABLE

> You who are troubled rest with us, when the Lord Jesus shall be revealed from heaven with his mighty angels (1:7 KJV).

> Brethren, do not grow weary in doing good (3:13 NKJV).

UNIQUE AND UNUSUAL

It is clear that Paul dictated this letter from his comment, "The salutation of Paul with my own hand. . .so I write" (3:17 NKJV).

SO WHAT?

As with all of the Christian life, balance is key: we should always look forward to Jesus' return, but we should also be busy doing good while we're here on earth.

READ PSALMS 114–116.

- One-Month Course: your next reading is on page 244. →
- Three-Month Course: your next reading is on page 244. →
- Six-Month Course: your next reading is on page 242. →

The Great Apostasy

After Paul wrote his first letter to the Thessalonians, he penned a second epistle in which he discussed "the coming of our Lord Jesus Christ and our gathering together to Him." He said, "Let no one deceive you by any means; for that Day will not come unless the falling away comes first, and the man of sin [the Antichrist] is revealed" (2 Thessalonians 2:1, 3 NKJV).

The "falling away" is called the "apostasy" in the NASB, the "rebellion" in the NIV, and the "great rebellion against God" in the NLT. Many Christians believe that in the end time much of the church will backslide from God. This will fulfill Titus 1:16 (NLT), "Such people claim they know God, but

they deny him by the way they live. They are. . .disobedient, worthless for doing anything good." They will then come up with deceptive doctrines to justify their disobedience. "The Holy Spirit tells us clearly that in the last times some will turn away from the true faith" (1 Timothy 4:1 NLT). (See also 2 Timothy 4:3–4.)

The apostasy is a rebellion against God. Giotto (c. 1267–1337) painted *Kiss of Judas*, which is one example of how a believer, Judas, fell away from God.

In many ways, the great apostasy is *already* here. It's been a fact of life for the church for much of the last two thousand years. Even in the early church, some Christians claimed to be spiritually alive yet were actually dead (Revelation 3:1). Rather than listing the ways that a Christian society and different churches fall short, Christians do well to examine their *own* lives and make sure that *they* are truly loving and obeying God.

READ 2 THESSALONIANS 2 AND PSALM 135.

 Six-Month Course: your next reading is on page 244.   →

THE WICKED WILL BE PUNISHED

The Christians of Thessalonica were being persecuted, so Paul wrote that God would reward them *and* would punish their enemies. "It is only just for God to repay with affliction those who afflict you, and to give relief to you who are afflicted. . .dealing out retribution" (2 Thessalonians 1:6–8 NASB). By patiently suffering, and even loving their enemies, the Thessalonians had fulfilled this passage: "Do not take revenge, my dear friends, but leave room for God's wrath, for it is written: 'It is mine to avenge; I will repay,' says the Lord" (Romans 12:19 NIV). Some people think that it's even wrong for *God* to judge, but the Bible reminds us: "True and righteous are Your judgments" (Revelation 16:7 NKJV).

READ 2 THESSALONIANS 1 AND REVELATION 20.

AN HONEST DAY'S WORK

Paul taught that those who preached the Gospel full-time should earn their living from it. He also said that if people benefited spiritually from a preacher, then he had a right to expect financial benefits in return (1 Corinthians 9:1–12). However, some Christians in Thessalonica were abusing this principle. They had stopped working for a living and were simply going from house to house sharing their so-called "revelations"—and mooching off those who held regular jobs. Paul himself had never done this (Acts 20:33–35; 1 Corinthians 9:12–18; 2 Thessalonians 3:7–9). So he reminded the Thessalonians, "For even when we were with you, we commanded you this: If anyone will not work, neither shall he eat" (2 Thessalonians 3:10 NKJV).

READ 2 THESSALONIANS 3 AND ISAIAH 62.

BASIC SURVEY

1 TIMOTHY

AUTHOR: The apostle Paul (1:1).

DATE: Approximately AD 63.

IN TEN WORDS OR LESS

Pastors are taught how to conduct their lives and churches.

DETAILS, PLEASE

The first of three "pastoral epistles," 1 Timothy contains the aging apostle Paul's insights for a new generation of church leaders. Timothy had often worked alongside Paul, but was now pastoring in Ephesus (1:3). Paul warned him against legalism and false teaching (chapter 1), listed the qualifications for pastors and deacons (chapter 3), and described the behavior of a "good minister of Jesus Christ" (4:6 KJV) in the final three chapters.

QUOTABLE

> Christ Jesus came into the world to save sinners; of whom I am chief (1:15 KJV).

> Here is a trustworthy saying: Whoever aspires to be an overseer desires a noble task (3:1 NIV).

UNIQUE AND UNUSUAL

First Timothy seems to command good pay for pastors: "Let the elders that rule well be counted worthy of double honor. . . . The labourer is worthy of his reward" (5:17–18 KJV).

SO WHAT?

Though it's a letter to a pastor, Paul's teaching "that you may know how you ought to conduct yourself in the house of God" (3:15 NKJV) can speak to the rest of us, too.

READ 1 TIMOTHY 1 AND PSALM 136.

● One-Month Course: your next reading is on page 247.   →

● Three-Month Course: your next reading is on page 247.   →

● Six-Month Course: your next reading is on page 245.   →

TIMOTHY—PAUL'S HELPER

About AD 50, Paul and Silas were traveling through Galatia (in southeast Turkey), and when they came to the city of Lystra, they met a young man named Timothy (*timo-theos*—"honoring God"). Timothy's grandmother

was a believing Jewess named Lois, and her daughter, Eunice, had married a Greek (2 Timothy 1:5). Thus, although he was Jewish, Timothy had never been circumcised.

Timothy became a Christian and was well respected by the believers. He was naturally shy, but was very pleasant and faithful, so Paul decided to take him on his missionary journeys as a personal aide. Because they'd be often preaching to Jews, Paul circum-

Rembrandt (1606–1669) painted a young Timothy at the foot of his grandmother in the painting *Timothy and His Grandmother.*

cised Timothy (Acts 16:1–3). Paul and the elders of the church laid hands on Timothy, bestowing a spiritual gift on him (1 Timothy 4:14; 2 Timothy 1:6). Paul became like a father to Timothy and called him "a true son in the faith" (1 Timothy 1:2 NKJV).

Paul still referred to him as a "youth" fifteen years later (1 Timothy 4:12 NKJV). Timothy persevered, despite his shyness and frequent stomach problems (1 Timothy 5:23), so that Paul said with great admiration, "Timothy has proved himself, because as a son with his father he has served with me in the work of the gospel" (Philippians 2:22 NIV). Paul frequently sent Timothy to churches to check up on them and to encourage and strengthen them. For most of his life, Timothy was not a leader, but a faithful follower. However, Paul later made him the overseer of all the churches of Ephesus (1 Timothy 1:3).

READ 1 TIMOTHY 2–3.

● Six-Month Course: your next reading is on page 247.   →

DOCTRINES AND HERESIES

Paul warned Timothy that "the time will come when they will not endure sound doctrine; but. . .shall they heap to themselves teachers, having itching ears" (2 Timothy 4:3 KJV). Even some believers would end up following "doctrines of demons." For this reason, Paul urged Timothy to be "constantly nourished on the words of the faith and of the sound doctrine which you have been following" (1 Timothy 4:1, 6 NASB). While it's important not to be stuck only on the basic milk of the Word, but to progress to a mature understanding of Christian doctrine (Hebrews 5:12–14), we should "not be carried away by all kinds of strange teachings. It is good for our hearts to be strengthened by grace" (Hebrews 13:9 NIV).

READ 1 TIMOTHY 4 AND HEBREWS 13.

COMMANDS TO THE RICH

Christ and the Rich Young Ruler was painted by Heinrich Hofmann (1824–1911). Christians are commanded to freely give our riches to people in need.

Paul wrote, "Command those who are rich in this present world not to be arrogant nor to put their hope in wealth, which is so uncertain, but to put their hope in God. . . . Command them to do good, to be rich in good deeds, and to be generous and willing to share" (1 Timothy 6:17–18 NIV). One way that rich people can prove that they "hope in God" is to be generous with money—sharing with the needy and giving to worthy causes. They should do this even when they long to hold on to it with a tighter fist. They can do this only if they're trusting God most of all. A related verse says, "If riches increase, set not your heart upon them" (Psalm 62:10 KJV).

READ 1 TIMOTHY 5–6.

BASIC SURVEY

2 TIMOTHY

AUTHOR: The apostle Paul (1:1).

DATE: Probably the mid-60s.

IN TEN WORDS OR LESS

The apostle Paul's final words to a beloved coworker.

DETAILS, PLEASE

Second Timothy is the last known letter of Paul. Addressed to "Timothy, my dearly beloved son" (1:2 KJV), the book warns the young pastor against false teaching and urges him to live a life of purity before his congregation. Timothy should expect trouble ("All that will live godly in Christ Jesus shall suffer persecution," 3:12 KJV), but God will be faithful ("The Lord shall deliver me from every evil work, and will preserve me unto his heavenly kingdom," 4:18 KJV). Paul begs Timothy to join him as quickly as possible, as "the time of my departure is at hand" (4:6 KJV).

QUOTABLE

> You therefore must endure hardship as a good soldier of Jesus Christ (2:3 NKJV).

UNIQUE AND UNUSUAL

Paul tells where the Bible comes from in 2 Timothy: "All scripture is given by inspiration of God" (3:16 KJV). The connotation of the word *inspiration* is "breathed out."

SO WHAT?

We should all live life in a way that we can say, like Paul, "I have fought a good fight, I have finished my course, I have kept the faith" (4:7 KJV).

READ 2 TIMOTHY 1 AND PSALMS 137–138.

● One-Month Course: your next reading is on page 250.   →

● Three-Month Course: your next reading is on page 250.   →

● Six-Month Course: your next reading is on page 248.   →

CLOSER LOOK

PAUL'S ROMAN IMPRISONMENTS

After Paul arrived in Jerusalem in AD 57, he was in the temple when some of his enemies saw him and stirred up the crowd. They dragged Paul out and began to beat him, but the Roman soldiers entered the crowd, arrested Paul, and bound him with chains. From there he was transported to the Roman city of Caesarea, where he spent the next two years in prison.

Governor Festus asked Paul if he was willing to go back to Jerusalem and stand trial, but Paul answered: "I have not done any wrong to the Jews. . . . No one has the right to hand me over to them. I appeal to Caesar!" (Acts 25:10–11 NIV). Roman citizens had the right to be tried by Caesar himself, so Paul was shipped to Rome, where he spent two years under house arrest (Acts 28:30). When he appeared before Emperor Nero in AD 62, Nero was still under the influence of wise counselors, so he released him.

Paul, who is depicted here in *Saint Paul* by Bartolomeo Montagna (1450–1523), was beheaded shortly after he wrote his second epistle to Timothy.

Paul had previously planned on evangelizing Spain (Romans 15:24, 28), and indeed the Muratorian Canon (an early Christian document) says that "Paul went from the city of Rome to Spain." After evangelizing there, Paul returned to the eastern Mediterranean. He was arrested in Troas (2 Timothy 4:13) and was taken to Rome in chains. The city had burned in AD 64, and Nero had accused the Christians of starting the fires.

Paul was sitting in the Mamertine dungeon in AD 67, facing the end, when he wrote his second epistle to Timothy. Not long after, he was beheaded.

READ 2 TIMOTHY 4 AND PSALM 119:137–176.

● Six-Month Course: your next reading is on page 250.   →

HIDDEN TREASURE

TEACHING OTHERS

Paul wrote Timothy, "You have heard me teach things that have been confirmed by many reliable witnesses. Now teach these truths to other trustworthy people who will be able to pass them on to others" (2 Timothy 2:2 NLT). In that day, most Christians were illiterate, so they depended on word-of-mouth teaching to help them grow in their understanding of the faith. Paul said to make sure to pass on solid biblical teaching. Today, most Christians are literate and can read the Bible themselves. But we still need Bible studies by competent, godly teachers—not only to ground us in the Word, but to teach us genuine Christianity by their personal example. "Be an example to the believers in word, in conduct" (1 Timothy 4:12 NKJV).

READ 2 TIMOTHY 2 AND EXODUS 18.

HIDDEN TREASURE

THE INSPIRATION OF SCRIPTURE

Paul reminded Timothy, "All Scripture is inspired by God and profitable for teaching, for reproof, for correction, for training in righteousness" (2 Timothy 3:16 NASB). The NIV translates the opening phrase literally from the Greek, stating, "All Scripture is God-breathed." What this means is that scripture is inspired because it comes from the very mouth of God. It is the very word of God. That's why it can accurately instruct us how to live righteous lives. Here's another verse that brings out the Bible's divine inspiration: "Prophecy never came by the will of man, but holy men of God spoke as they were moved by the Holy Spirit" (2 Peter 1:21 NKJV). (See also 1 Thessalonians 2:13.)

READ 2 TIMOTHY 3 AND PSALM 139.

BASIC SURVEY

TITUS

AUTHOR: The apostle Paul (1:1).
DATE: Approximately AD 63.

IN TEN WORDS OR LESS

Church leaders are instructed on their lives and teaching.

DETAILS, PLEASE

On the Mediterranean island of Crete, Paul left Titus to "set in order what remains and appoint elders" (1:5 NASB) for the fledgling church. Known for their poor behavior (see "Unique and Unusual" below), the people of Crete needed the kind of church leader who would hold fast to "the trustworthy message he was taught. . .to encourage others with wholesome teaching and show those who oppose it where they are wrong" (1:9 NLT).

QUOTABLE

> Not by works of righteousness which we have done, but according to his mercy he saved us, by the washing of regeneration, and renewing of the Holy Ghost (3:5 KJV).

UNIQUE AND UNUSUAL

Paul quotes a Cretan philosopher in this letter: "One of Crete's own prophets has said it: 'Cretans are always liars, evil brutes, lazy gluttons'" (1:12 NIV). The quotation is from Epimenides, of the sixth century BC.

SO WHAT?

Though church leaders are held to a high standard, so are the people in the pews. What's good for the pastor is good for everyone else.

READ TITUS 2 AND PSALM 66.

● One-Month Course: your next reading is on page 253.   →

● Three-Month Course: your next reading is on page 253.   →

● Six-Month Course: your next reading is on page 251.   →

CLOSER LOOK

SETTING CHURCHES IN ORDER

As an apostle and evangelist, Paul's top priority was preaching the Gospel. However, it was also important for converts to be grounded and deeply rooted in the truths of the faith. For this reason Paul also made it a priority to organize the new believers and to appoint elders to teach them and oversee them (Acts 14:21–23).

While preaching always remained a priority, as the years went on, problems and questions arose, and false teachers caused divisions, so it

These are the ruins of the Celsus Library in Ephesus, Turkey, one of the places where Paul traveled as he established churches.

became important to have mature elders and wise bishops (overseers) in place to protect the church. Paul told Titus, "For this reason I left you in Crete, that you should set in order the things that are lacking and appoint elders in every city as I commanded you. . . . For a bishop [overseer] must be blameless, as a steward of God. . . holding fast the faithful word as he has been taught, that he may be able, by sound doctrine, both to exhort and convict those who contradict" (Titus 1:5, 7, 9 NKJV).

Paul warned about "idle talkers and deceivers. . .whose mouths must be stopped" (Titus 1:10–11 NKJV). From Crete, Paul traveled to Ephesus. Years earlier he had warned the elders there that false teachers would arise (Acts 20:29–31). And now he wrote Timothy, "When I left for Macedonia, I urged you to stay there in Ephesus and stop those whose teaching is contrary to the truth" (1 Timothy 1:3 NLT). Christians are warned to "contend earnestly for the faith" (Jude 1:3 NKJV).

READ TITUS 1 AND MATTHEW 22.

● Six-Month Course: your next reading is on page 253. →

QUOTING POETS AND PHILOSOPHERS

Paul frequently quoted Greek poets and philosophers to prove a point. For example, he wrote, "One of them, a prophet of their own, said, 'Cretans are always liars, evil beasts, lazy gluttons.' This testimony is true" (Titus 1:12–13 NKJV). Paul was quoting *Cretica* by Epimenides (500s BC), a Cretan poet said to have made several true predictions. Does this mean Paul endorsed everything Epimenides said? By no means. Two lines later in *Cretica*, Epimenides said of Zeus, "Thou livest and abidest forever." In Acts 17:28, when speaking to the philosophers of Athens, Paul again quoted Epimenides, as well as citing the Cilician poet Aratus (315–240 BC). In 1 Corinthians 15:33 he quoted the play *Thais* by the Greek playwright Menander (342–291 BC).

READ TITUS 3 AND JEREMIAH 10:1–16.

TRANSFORMING HEARTS AND LIVES

Some people took Paul's message of "salvation by grace alone, not works" to unhealthy extremes, teaching that as long as a person professed "faith" in Jesus, they could continue living in sin like the pagans around them and God would ignore it. But Paul warned against this kind of deception (Ephesians 5:3–7). He taught that Jesus "gave Himself for us, that He might redeem us from every lawless deed and purify for Himself His own special people, zealous for good works" (Titus 2:14 NKJV). Jesus came to cleanse us from all corrupt deeds. Also, Paul stated that when we're born again we're "created in Christ Jesus unto good works, which God hath before ordained that we should walk in them" (Ephesians 2:10 KJV).

READ 2 CORINTHIANS 12–13.

BASIC SURVEY

PHILEMON

AUTHOR: The apostle Paul (1:1).

DATE: Probably around AD 63, when Paul was imprisoned in Rome.

IN TEN WORDS OR LESS

Paul begs mercy for a runaway slave converted to Christianity.

DETAILS, PLEASE

Philemon is a "fellow worker" (1:1 NIV) of Paul, a man who has "refreshed" (1:7) other Christians with his love and generosity. But the apostle writes with a deeper request—that Philemon forgive and take back a runaway slave, who apparently accepted Christ under Paul's teaching: "my son Onesimus, whom I have begotten in my bonds" (1:10 KJV). "If then you count me as a partner," Paul wrote to Philemon, "receive him as you would me" (1:17 NKJV).

QUOTABLE

> I always thank my God as I remember you in my prayers, because I hear about your love for all his holy people and your faith in the Lord Jesus (1:4–5 NIV).

> Having confidence in your obedience, I write to you, since I know that you will do even more than what I say (1:21 NASB).

UNIQUE AND UNUSUAL

With only one chapter and twenty-five verses, Philemon is the shortest of Paul's letters in the Bible.

SO WHAT?

Christians are called to forgive, and here's a practical example to consider. With God's help, will you let go of your grudges?

READ PHILEMON 1 AND PSALM 59.

● One-Month Course: your next reading is on page 256. →

● Three-Month Course: your next reading is on page 256. →

● Six-Month Course: your next reading is on page 254. →

CLOSER LOOK

SLAVERY IN THE NEW TESTAMENT

Paul encouraged his friend Philemon to free the slave who had run away and welcome him as a fellow Christian.

Christians recognize that slavery is morally repugnant, and Christians led the emancipation of slaves, yet Paul wrote, "Slaves, obey your earthly masters in everything you do. Try to please them all the time, not just when they are watching you. Serve them sincerely" (Colossians 3:22 NLT). Does this mean that slavery was a God-ordained institution?

No. These statements were made within a specific cultural context. Also, slavery in the Roman Empire, in Paul's day, was not as harsh as what existed in America. Emperor Claudius (before AD 54) ruled that a master who killed a sick or worn-out slave could be charged with murder. When Paul wrote to the Colossians in AD 60, Emperor Nero had just granted slaves the right to lodge complaints against their masters in a court of law for unfair or cruel treatment.

This is not to say that slavery was a desirable state even then. It wasn't! But Paul couldn't openly call for empire-wide emancipation without being arrested and executed for stirring up a slave revolt. Nevertheless, he advised, "Were you a slave when you were called? Don't let it trouble you—although if you *can* gain your freedom, *do so*" (1 Corinthians 7:21 NIV, emphasis added).

And in a letter to his wealthy Roman friend, Philemon, Paul not only asked him to forgive a runaway slave named Onesimus, but requested that he set him free: "He is no longer like a slave to you. He is more than a slave, for he is a beloved brother. . . . Welcome him as you would welcome me" (Philemon 1:16–17 NLT).

READ NEHEMIAH 5 AND JEREMIAH 34.

● Six-Month Course: your next reading is on page 256.   →

A CONSIDERATE FRIEND

Philemon was a wealthy man of Colosse, and Paul had apparently led him to the Lord, since Philemon owed him his very soul (Philemon 1:19). When Philemon's runaway slave Onesimus ended up in Rome, and Paul led him to faith in Christ also, Onesimus proved so helpful that Paul wished he could simply keep him. But instead he asked Philemon to allow him to stay. As Paul wrote, "I could demand it in the name of Christ because it is the right thing for you to do. But because of our love, I prefer simply to ask you." Paul explained, "I didn't want to do anything without your consent. I wanted you to help because you were willing, not because you were forced" (Philemon 1:8–9, 14 NLT).

READ ISAIAH 25 AND 28:9–29.

PRAYING FOR SPIRITUAL LEADERS

Paul wrote Philemon, "Prepare a guest room for me, because I hope to be restored to you in answer to your prayers" (Philemon 1:22 NIV). Philemon, and undoubtedly many others, had been praying unceasingly for Paul to be released from prison—and he eventually *was*! Paul realized the value of prayer and often requested others to pray for him. Years earlier he had written to the Thessalonians, asking them to pray that God would bless his ministry *and* protect him from his enemies: "Brothers and sisters, pray for us that the message of the Lord may spread rapidly and be honored, just as it was with you. And pray that we may be delivered from wicked and evil people" (2 Thessalonians 3:1–2 NIV).

READ ISAIAH 32–33.

BASIC SURVEY

HEBREWS

AUTHOR: Not stated; Paul, Luke, Barnabas, and Apollos have all been suggested.

DATE: Sometime before AD 70, since Hebrews refers to temple sacrifices. The temple was destroyed by the Romans in AD 70.

IN TEN WORDS OR LESS

Jesus is better than any Old Testament person or sacrifice.

DETAILS, PLEASE

Written to Jewish Christians (hence the name "Hebrews"), this letter emphasizes the superiority of Christianity to Old Testament Judaism. Jesus is "so much better" (1:4 KJV) than angels, Moses, and animal sacrifices. Jewish Christians, some of whom were apparently wavering in their commitment to Jesus, are reminded that Christ "is the mediator of a better covenant, which was established upon better promises" (8:6 KJV)—a once-for-all sacrifice on the cross that provides "eternal redemption for us" (9:12 KJV).

QUOTABLE

> Let us strip off every weight that slows us down, especially the sin that so easily trips us up. And let us run with endurance the race God has set before us. We do this by keeping our eyes on Jesus, the champion who initiates and perfects our faith (12:1–2 NLT).

UNIQUE AND UNUSUAL

Hebrews is one of only two New Testament letters (the other being 1 John) that includes no greeting or hint of its author.

SO WHAT?

"Let us draw near with a true heart in full assurance of faith, having our hearts sprinkled from an evil conscience" (10:22 KJV).

READ HEBREWS 2–3.

● One-Month Course: your next reading is on page 261.   →

● Three-Month Course: your next reading is on page 257.   →

● Six-Month Course: your next reading is on page 257.   →

HEART OF THE BOOK

THE EXALTED SON OF GOD

Some Jewish believers in Rome were getting the idea that Jesus the Messiah had made some improvements to Judaism—but since they had suffered so much rejection and persecution for following Him, they began wondering if the differences were really *that* great and whether they might be as well off returning to Jewish worship.

The writer of the epistle to the Hebrews set out to encourage and educate them. He began by stating that Jesus was God's own Son "through whom also he made the universe," and that He continues "sustaining all things by his powerful word." How can He do this? Because He, too, is divine. "The Son is the radiance of God's glory and the exact representation of his being" (Hebrews 1:2–3 NIV).

The writer also made it clear how unique Jesus is. "He became as much superior to the angels as the name he has inherited is superior to theirs." Jesus is so exalted, in fact, that scripture states, "Let all God's angels worship him" (Hebrews 1:4, 6 NIV).

The writer to the Hebrews went even further, stating, "To the Son He says:

The writer of the book of Hebrews encouraged faltering believers to fortify their faith and emphasized the fact that Jesus is God's Son.

'Your throne, O God, is forever and ever; a scepter of righteousness is the scepter of Your kingdom. . . . Therefore God, Your God, has anointed You" (Hebrews 1:8–9 NKJV). He first pointed out that Jesus is called God, then states that "God, Your God" (the Father) anointed Him. This explains why, when Jesus was on the earth, He prayed to God His Father and called Him "My God" (Mark 15:34; John 20:17).

READ HEBREWS 1 AND 5.

● Three-Month Course: your next reading is on page 261.   →

● Six-Month Course: your next reading is on page 258.   →

CLOSER LOOK

What Is Faith?

Many people wonder what exactly faith is. The Bible says, "Now faith is the substance of things hoped for, the evidence of things not seen" (Hebrews 11:1 NKJV). The Greek word translated as "substance" is *hupostasis*, and in the NIV Interlinear Greek-English New Testament its meaning is given as "reality." Thus, "faith is the *reality* of things hoped for."

The Amplified Bible gives further insight: "Now faith is the assurance (the confirmation, the title deed) of the things [we] hope for, being the proof of things [we] do not see and the conviction of their reality" (Hebrews 11:1 AMP).

A title deed is an authoritative document. While it's only a piece of paper and not the actual house or property that it speaks of, if a person's name is on a title deed and it's notarized by the proper authorities, it's proof that they own tangible real estate. If they haven't seen the properties yet—say they received them as an inheritance—they aren't revealed to the senses, but the person can still be convinced that they own them. Why? Because they have the title deed.

Faith is a very solid reality, but this raises the question why it doesn't seem to work for some people. They believe for a while, then give up without receiving what they were praying for. Why is this? Often it's because they have, at some point, discarded their title deed. "So do not throw away this confident trust in the Lord. Remember the great reward it brings you!" (Hebrews 10:35 NLT).

READ HEBREWS 11 AND JOB 13:1–15.

● Six-Month Course: your next reading is on page 259.   →

CLOSER LOOK

God's Loving Chastisements

Some Christians had the idea that after they were saved, Jesus would solve all their problems, bless them abundantly financially, and remove all sickness. So they became confused and distressed when they suffered troubles. But the apostle Peter said, "Beloved, think it not strange concerning the fiery trial which is to try you, as though some strange thing happened unto you" (1 Peter 4:12 KJV).

The writer to the Hebrews asked, "Have you forgotten the encouraging words God spoke to you as his children? He said, 'My child, don't make light of the LORD's discipline, and don't give up when he corrects you. For the LORD disciplines those he loves, and he punishes each one he accepts as his child'" (Hebrews 12:5–6 NLT). He then asked, "Who ever heard of a child who is never disciplined by its father?" (v. 7).

He also explains the reason God allows difficulties and hardships: "He disciplines us for our good, so that we may share His holiness. All discipline for the moment seems not to be joyful, but sorrowful; yet to those who have been trained by it, afterwards it yields the peaceful fruit of righteousness" (Hebrews 12:10–11 NASB).

In the book of Revelation, Jesus told straying Christians, "As many as I love, I rebuke and chasten: be zealous therefore, and repent" (Revelation 3:19 KJV). God disciplines us when we get out of line, but His purpose is not simply to punish us. The literal meaning of the word *discipline* is "to train."

READ HEBREWS 12 AND JOB 14.

● Six-Month Course: your next reading is on page 261.

GROWING UP SPIRITUALLY

A number of Christians in the early church, after finding salvation, never really hungered to learn more about their faith and didn't take the opportunity to study the scriptures, so they never grew up spiritually. As a result, they remained baby Christians. The writer of Hebrews noted, "Though by this time you ought to be teachers, you need someone to teach you the elementary

truths of God's word all over again. You need milk, not solid food! Anyone who lives on milk, being still an infant, is not acquainted with the teaching about righteousness. But solid food is for the mature" (Hebrews 5:12–14 NIV). Back then there were very few copies of the Gospels and the epistles of the apostles—but today we have an abundance of the Word to feed on.

The book of Hebrews states that we must start with spiritual milk so that we can progress and grow spiritually.

READ HEBREWS 6–7.

THE THRONE OF GRACE

The book of Hebrews tells us some very good news: "Jesus the Son of God . . .was in all points tempted as we are, yet without sin. Let us therefore come boldly to the throne of grace, that we may obtain mercy and find grace to help in time of need" (Hebrews 4:14–16 NKJV). Since Jesus was repeatedly tempted to sin, just like we are, He knows what it's like to suffer. That's why Christians can *confidently* come before His throne to ask for His mercy, forgiveness, and grace to help them during times of testing. He understands. Notice that He sits, not on a throne of judgment—to condemn believers who struggle with sin—but on a throne of grace. And He dispenses not punishment but strength and mercy.

READ JOB 9:1–20 AND HEBREWS 4.

BASIC SURVEY

JAMES

AUTHOR: James (1:1), probably a brother of Jesus (see Matthew 13:55; Mark 6:3).
DATE: Approximately AD 60.

IN TEN WORDS OR LESS
Real Christian faith is shown by one's good works.

DETAILS, PLEASE
Though the apostle Paul clearly taught that salvation is by faith alone and not by good works (see Romans 3:28), James clarifies that good works will *follow* true faith: "What good is it, my brothers and sisters, if someone claims to have faith but has no deeds?" (2:14 NIV). James encourages Christians, in everyday life, to view trials as opportunities for spiritual growth, to control their tongues, to make peace, to avoid favoritism, and to help the needy. The bottom line? "Remember, it is sin to know what you ought to do and then not do it" (4:17 NLT).

QUOTABLE
> Draw near to God and He will draw near to you (4:8 NKJV).
> The prayer of a righteous person is powerful and effective (5:16 NIV).

UNIQUE AND UNUSUAL
For those who think it's enough just to believe in God, James says, "The devils also believe, and tremble" (2:19 KJV). Life-changing faith in Jesus is the key.

SO WHAT?
Want practical wisdom for living the Christian life? You'll find it all through the book of James.

READ JAMES 1–2.

● One-Month Course: your next reading is on page 264.   →

● Three-Month Course: your next reading is on page 264.   →

● Six-Month Course: your next reading is on page 262.   →

CLOSER LOOK

RESISTING THE DEVIL

Many Christians don't understand what's happening when they come under spiritual attack. They assume that all those dark thoughts originate in their

own minds, so they're not only shocked but feel condemned. They think they're hopelessly sinful and that God can't forgive them. But often such thoughts are blatant demonic attacks that must be rejected. They're "fiery darts of the wicked one" that must be stopped by "the shield of faith" (Ephesians 6:16 NKJV).

Peter warns, "Your adversary the devil walks about like a roaring lion, seeking whom he may devour," and urges, "Resist him, steadfast in the faith" (1 Peter 5:8–9 NKJV). Resisting the devil once is often not

James wrote that we should resist the devil and trust that God will give us the strength we need to stand strong.

enough. We must usually take a stand and steadfastly, repeatedly reject his dark thoughts.

James shares a key thought: "Submit to God. Resist the devil and he will flee from you. Draw near to God and He will draw near to you" (James 4:7–8 NKJV). Christians are promised that if they resist the devil, he *will* flee. Psalm 91:1 (NASB) also promises, "He who dwells in the shelter of the Most High will abide in the shadow of the Almighty." To be sheltered by God, to enjoy His protection, we must draw close to Him and submit to Him. We can't expect His full protection if we're running around outside His will, not yielding to Him.

But if we *do* yield, "the Lord is faithful, and he will strengthen you and protect you from the evil one" (2 Thessalonians 3:3 NIV).

READ JAMES 4 AND PSALMS 29–30.

● Six-Month Course: your next reading is on page 264.   →

TEMPTATIONS VERSUS TESTS

There's a *big* difference between being tempted and being tested. James writes, "Let no one say when he is tempted, 'I am tempted by God.' . . . But each one is tempted when he is drawn away by his own desires and enticed. Then, when desire has conceived, it gives birth to sin" (James 1:13–15 NKJV). Some people, however, quote Genesis 22:1 (KJV), which says, "And it came to pass. . .that God did tempt Abraham." But the NKJV, NIV, and NASB translate this more accurately as "God tested Abraham." God often *does* test His people to make it plain what's in their hearts (see Deuteronomy 8:2)—and to demonstrate their weaknesses to *them* so that they can take necessary steps to change in that area.

READ JAMES 5 AND ISAIAH 35.

THE TONGUE

James gives a clear warning about thoughtless, foolish speech, saying, "See how great a forest is set aflame by such a small fire! And the tongue is a fire. . .and sets

on fire the course of our life" (James 3:5–6 NASB). Solomon agreed, saying, "A fool's mouth is his destruction, and his lips are the snare of his soul" (Proverbs 18:7 KJV). What we say betrays what's lurking in our hearts, for "out of the abundance of the heart the mouth speaks" (Matthew 12:34

James' writing reminds us that we must be careful about the things we say so that our speech reflects our faith in God. Our words can trap us.

NKJV). And as James says, our tongue often reveals our hypocrisy: "With it we bless our Lord and Father, and with it we curse men" (James 3:9 NASB). But if we yield our hearts to God's cleansing Spirit, our words will change.

READ JAMES 3 AND PROVERBS 18.

BASIC SURVEY

1 PETER

AUTHOR: The apostle Peter (1:1), with the assistance of Silvanus (5:12).
DATE: Approximately AD 65.

IN TEN WORDS OR LESS
Suffering for the sake of Jesus is noble and good.

DETAILS, PLEASE
As the early church grows, the Roman Empire begins persecuting Christians—and Peter assures them that God is still in control: "Beloved, think it not strange concerning the fiery trial which is to try you, as though some strange thing happened unto you" (4:12 KJV). What is the proper response to such suffering? "Rejoice to the extent that you partake of Christ's sufferings, that when His glory is revealed, you may also be glad with exceeding joy" (4:13 NKJV).

QUOTABLE
> Be alert and of sober mind. Your enemy the devil prowls around like a roaring lion looking for someone to devour (5:8 NIV).

UNIQUE AND UNUSUAL
Peter clarifies exactly how many people rode out the great flood on Noah's ark: eight (3:20). Genesis indicates "Noah and his [three] sons and his wife and his sons' wives" (Genesis 7:7 NIV) were in the boat.

SO WHAT?
Life may be hard, but God is always good. And for Christians, there's a much better day ahead.

READ 1 PETER 1–2.

- One-Month Course: your next reading is on page 267.   →
- Three-Month Course: your next reading is on page 265.   →
- Six-Month Course: your next reading is on page 265.   →

HEART OF THE BOOK

THE APOSTLE PETER

The apostle Peter (also called Simon and Cephas) was one of Jesus' earliest disciples, and along with his brother Andrew, was a fisherman. He first met

Jesus along the Jordan River where John was baptizing (John 1:40–42) and traveled with Him through Galilee for a time. Then he went back to fishing. Later Jesus called him to full-time discipleship, saying, "Come, follow me, and I will show you how to fish for people!" (Matthew 4:19 NLT).

Peter was a fisherman who was commissioned by Jesus to become a disciple. He is depicted here in *Christ Calling the Apostles Peter and Andrew* by Duccio di Buoninsegna (1255–1319).

The disciples realized from the beginning that Jesus was the Messiah, the Son of God (John 1:41, 49), but many lost faith during trying times. But Peter never doubted. After many disciples turned back, Peter declared his faith (John 6:66–69). Later, he once again clearly stated his certainty that Jesus was the Son of God (Matthew 16:13–17).

Peter was the most impetuous, outspoken of Jesus' twelve apostles. For example, when Jesus revealed that He would be crucified, Peter took it upon himself to rebuke Him, saying, "God forbid it, Lord! This shall never happen to You" (Matthew 16:22 NASB).

Peter was so sure of himself that he boasted that even if all the other disciples abandoned Jesus, he'd never do so. But when confronted, he denied that he even *knew* Jesus (Mark 14:27–31, 66–72). God allowed this to show Peter that he needed the strength of the Spirit to make it. Later, when Jesus restored him and he received the Holy Spirit, Peter became one of the foremost leaders of the early church.

READ 1 PETER 3 AND LUKE 5.

● Three-Month Course: your next reading is on page 267.   →

● Six-Month Course: your next reading is on page 267.   →

REJOICING DESPITE TROUBLES

In the middle of Nero's savage persecution, Peter wrote, "In this you greatly rejoice, even though now for a little while, if necessary, you have been

distressed by various trials." He added that Christians should "greatly rejoice with joy inexpressible." Peter first acknowledged that the persecution caused Christians intense distress, then expected them to greatly rejoice. How? He knew that enduring such trials was proof that their faith was genuine, and would "result in praise and glory and honor at the revelation of Jesus Christ" (1 Peter 1:6–8 NASB). As Paul said, "The sufferings of this present time are not worthy to be compared with the glory which shall be revealed in us" (Romans 8:18 NKJV).

Even when Peter was being persecuted by Nero, who is pictured here with his mother, Agrippina, he praised and glorified God.

READ 1 PETER 4 AND LUKE 17.

RESISTING FLESHLY LUSTS

Peter wrote, "Beloved, I beg you as sojourners and pilgrims, abstain from fleshly lusts which war against the soul" (1 Peter 2:11 NKJV). Giving in to lusts literally destroys and eats away the spiritual power in a Christian's life. One good thing about suffering—it makes people serious about their faith and gets them seeking God's will, not casually playing around with temptation and sins such as "lewdness, lusts, drunkenness, revelries, drinking parties." As Peter explained, "He who has suffered in the flesh has ceased from sin, that he no longer should live the rest of his time in the flesh for the lusts of men, but for the will of God" (1 Peter 4:1–3 NKJV).

READ 1 PETER 5 AND PSALM 50.

BASIC SURVEY

2 PETER

AUTHOR: The apostle Peter (1:1).

DATE: Probably the late AD 60s, shortly before Peter's execution.

IN TEN WORDS OR LESS

Beware of false teachers within the church.

DETAILS, PLEASE

The Christian qualities of faith, virtue, knowledge, self-control, patience, godliness, and love (1:5–8), coupled with a reliance on scripture (1:19–21), will help believers avoid the false teachings of those who "secretly bring in destructive heresies, even denying the Lord who bought them" (2:1 NKJV).

QUOTABLE

> We have not followed cunningly devised fables, when we made known unto you the power and coming of our Lord Jesus Christ, but were eye-witnesses of his majesty (1:16 KJV).

> The Lord is not slack concerning his promise, as some men count slackness; but is longsuffering to us-ward, not willing that any should perish, but that all should come to repentance (3:9 KJV).

UNIQUE AND UNUSUAL

Peter wrote this letter knowing his death was near: "The laying aside of my earthly dwelling is imminent, as also our Lord Jesus Christ has made clear to me" (1:14 NASB).

SO WHAT?

"Beware lest you also fall from your own steadfastness, being led away with the error of the wicked" (3:17 NKJV).

READ 2 PETER 1 AND PSALM 109.

- ● One-Month Course: your next reading is on page 270.   →
- ● Three-Month Course: your next reading is on page 270.   →
- ● Six-Month Course: your next reading is on page 268.   →

CLOSER LOOK

THE TEACHING OF BALAAM

By AD 68, the message of salvation through Jesus had spread throughout most of the eastern Roman Empire, and there were churches in every major city. But in recent years teachers with destructive doctrines had also risen, and some of their teachings were a licentious distortion of the pure Gospel of Jesus Christ.

Peter warned that "there will also be false teachers among you, who will secretly introduce destructive heresies" (2 Peter 2:1 NASB). In fact, some taught that since Christians were under grace, not the Law, they were now free to commit sexual immorality. Peter said, "Many will follow their sensuality, and because of them the way of the truth will be maligned" (v. 2 NASB). Peter explained that these teachers had "eyes full of adultery that never cease from sin, enticing unstable souls. . .forsaking the right way, they have gone astray, having followed the way of Balaam" (vv. 14–15 NASB).

Christ referred to a temptress as "Jezebel" and stated that she was leading His servants to sin.

Indeed, less than thirty years later, Jesus rebuked the church of Pergamos, saying, "There are some among you who hold to the teaching of Balaam, who taught Balak to entice the Israelites to sin so that they. . .committed sexual immorality" (Revelation 2:14 NIV). And a so-called prophetess (whom Christ called "Jezebel") was in nearby Thyatira. Jesus said, "By her teaching she misleads my servants into sexual immorality" (Revelation 2:20 NIV).

So often—both then and in modern times—destructive doctrines arise because people desire a "Gospel" that allows them to indulge their flesh and live the way *they* choose to live.

READ 2 PETER 2 AND PROVERBS 5.

● Six-Month Course: your next reading is on page 270.   →

THE GOSPEL ISN'T A FABLE

Most educated Greeks and Romans recognized that the stories about their gods and goddesses were simply clever fables invented by men. Jesus Christ, on the other hand, was a real historical figure who had lived, died, and resurrected in the days of the Roman governor Pontius Pilate. And there were many witnesses to this. The writers of the Gospels had either personally witnessed the events they described or carefully interviewed those who *had* seen them (John 19:32–35; 21:24; Luke 1:1–4). That's why Peter wrote, "For we did not follow cunningly devised fables when we made known to you the power and coming of our Lord Jesus Christ, but were eyewitnesses of His majesty" (2 Peter 1:16 NKJV).

READ LUKE 3 AND ISAIAH 41.

THE NEW TESTAMENT IS SCRIPTURE

At what point did the Church recognize that the New Testament was scripture? About AD 64, Paul equated the written Gospels with the Law of Moses. He stated, "For the Scripture says, 'You shall not muzzle an ox while it treads out the grain,' and 'The laborer is worthy of his wages'" (1 Timothy 5:18 NKJV). The first passage quoted was Deuteronomy 25:4. The second passage was Luke 10:7. Also, around AD 68, Peter wrote, "Those who are ignorant and unstable have twisted his [Paul's] letters. . .just as they do with other parts of Scripture" (2 Peter 3:16 NLT). By saying "*other* parts of Scripture," Peter was acknowledging that Paul's epistles were *also* scripture. (See also 1 Corinthians 14:37.)

Peter, who is represented in the painting *Saint Peter* by El Greco (1541–1614), stated that the Gospels are just as important as the laws of Moses.

READ 2 PETER 3 AND ISAIAH 42.

BASIC SURVEY

1 JOHN

AUTHOR: Not stated, but according to church tradition the apostle John.

DATE: Approximately AD 92.

IN TEN WORDS OR LESS

Jesus was real man, just as He is real God.

DETAILS, PLEASE

First John tackles the Gnostic heresy that claimed Jesus had been on earth only in spirit, not in body: "Every spirit that does not acknowledge Jesus is not from God. This is the spirit of the antichrist" (4:3 NIV). John wrote that he knew Jesus personally: "We saw him with our own eyes and touched him with our own hands" (1:1 NLT). And that knowledge leads to a saving belief in Jesus. Saving belief leads to obedience, but even when we sin, we know that God "is faithful and just to forgive us our sins" when we confess (1:9 KJV).

QUOTABLE

> Beloved, let us love one another: for love is of God. . . . God is love (4:7–8 KJV).

UNIQUE AND UNUSUAL

First John includes none of the usual features of a Bible letter—greetings, identification of the author, etc. But it's a very warm, compassionate letter nonetheless.

SO WHAT?

"These things have I written. . .*that ye may know that ye have eternal life*" (5:13 KJV, emphasis added).

READ 1 JOHN 1; PSALM 5; AND PROVERBS 17.

● One-Month Course: your next reading is on page 274. →

● Three-Month Course: your next reading is on page 271. →

● Six-Month Course: your next reading is on page 271. →

HEART OF THE BOOK

THE APOSTLE JOHN

John was the brother of James, and they worked in their father's fishing business, together with Peter and Andrew (Luke 5:9–10). John, Peter, and James were

Jesus' three closest disciples, constantly with Him (Mark 5:37; 9:2). And John and Peter were not only constant companions, but the two most outstanding leaders of the Jerusalem church (John 20:1–8; Acts 3:1; Galatians 2:9).

John was known as "the disciple whom Jesus loved" (John 13:23; 19:26 NIV), and this is very likely because, despite his youth, he was a deeply spiritual man. He would later write the Gospel of John, emphasizing that Jesus is the Son of God who is one with His Father—and John penned the words, "God is love" (1 John 4:8). John grasped these powerful facts and declared them more clearly than any of the other disciples.

Jesus named John and James *Boanerges*, which means "Sons of Thunder" (Mark 3:17). This is probably a reflection of their quick tempers. For example, one day when a Samaritan village refused to receive Jesus, John and James wanted to call lightning down upon them, to destroy

Albrecht Dürer (1471–1528) painted *The Four Holy Men* (*John the Evangelist and Peter*). John was a deeply spiritual man and was among Jesus' closest disciples.

them (Luke 9:51–56). John eventually outgrew his rash temperament to write the epistle of 1 John, emphasizing love for God and fellow men.

In his later years, John moved north to Ephesus, where he served as an overseer and wrote the Gospel of John. He was later briefly exiled to the island of Patmos during Domitian's persecution, and it was there that he received the book of Revelation (Revelation 1:9).

READ JOHN 18–19.

● Three-Month Course: your next reading is on page 274.   →

● Six-Month Course: your next reading is on page 274.   →

DON'T LOVE THE WORLD

John wrote, "Do not love the world or anything in the world. If anyone loves the world, love for the Father is not in them. For everything in the world— the lust of the flesh, the lust of the eyes, and the pride of life—comes not

from the Father but from the world" (1 John 2:15–16 NIV). But some people ask, "But doesn't God *want* us to love the world? After all, doesn't John 3:16 (NASB) say, "God so loved the world"? There's a difference. In John 3:16, John is referring to God loving the *people* who live in the world, but in 1 John he's talking about the corrupt societies and worldly values in which these priceless souls are trapped.

John warned us to avoid placing too much value in worldly possessions or beliefs.

READ 1 JOHN 2 AND ISAIAH 43.

LOVE YOUR BROTHER

John gives a startling message about loving our fellow man: "If someone says, 'I love God,' and hates his brother, he is a liar; for he who does not love his brother whom he has seen, how can he love God whom he has not seen? And this commandment we have from Him: that he who loves God must love his brother also" (1 John 4:20–21 NKJV). Some people still have difficulty believing how important it is to love others, but John stated that it was a command and is inseparably linked to having faith in Jesus. He said in one breath, "And this is his commandment: We must believe in the name of his Son, Jesus Christ, and love one another" (1 John 3:23 NLT).

READ 1 JOHN 3 AND ISAIAH 46.

THE GNOSTIC HERESY

Many ancient Greeks believed that all physical matter was evil and that only spiritual things were good. This is why they didn't believe that God would ever resurrect a dead body and reunite it with a spirit (Acts 17:32). They thought that death was a good thing, because then the "pure spirit" was finally free of the body. For this reason, they couldn't believe that the Son of God had ever had a physical body.

The Greeks, who built the famous Parthenon, did not believe that dead bodies would be resurrected. This is why they didn't believe Jesus had risen from the dead.

Surely He must only have *appeared* to be physical. But John warned, "Every spirit that confesses that Jesus Christ has come in the flesh is from God; and every spirit that does not confess Jesus is not from God; this is the spirit of the antichrist" (1 John 4:2–3 NASB).

READ 1 JOHN 4 AND ISAIAH 48.

GOD IS LOVE

Many people consider these three words to be the very heart of the Bible: "God is love" (1 John 4:8 KJV). And they are! They categorically define the very *nature* of God and are foundational to understanding what God thinks about us. It comes as no surprise to learn that God loves us—since He *is* love. And this explains why Jesus died for us: "For God *so loved* the world that he gave his one and only Son, that whoever believes in him shall not perish but have eternal life" (John 3:16 NIV, emphasis added). No wonder the greatest commandment is to love God in return. "We love him because he first loved us" (1 John 4:19 KJV; see also Romans 5:5 NIV).

READ 1 JOHN 5 AND ISAIAH 50.

BASIC SURVEY

2 JOHN

AUTHOR: The apostle John, according to church tradition. The author is identified only as "the elder" (2 John 1:1 KJV).

DATE: Approximately AD 92.

IN TEN WORDS OR LESS

Beware false teachers who deny Jesus' physical life on earth.

DETAILS, PLEASE

Addressed to "the elect lady and her children" (2 John 1:1 KJV), perhaps an actual family or, figuratively, a church, 2 John tackles the heretical idea that Jesus had not been physically present on earth. The letter was most likely a reaction to the Gnostics, who taught that Jesus was spirit only and just appeared to suffer and die on the cross. This teaching, of "a deceiver and an antichrist" (1:7 KJV), should be avoided at all costs—to the point of barring one's door against those who believe it (1:10).

QUOTABLE

> Now I ask you, lady, not as though I were writing to you a new commandment, but the one which we have had from the beginning, that we love one another (1:5 NASB).

> This is love, that we walk after his commandments (1:6 KJV).

UNIQUE AND UNUSUAL

Second John, one of the New Testament's four single-chapter books, is the shortest by verse count: 13.

SO WHAT?

Just as in John's time, false teachers spread dangerous ideas in today's world. Every teaching should be weighed against scripture, 2 John says. "He that abideth in the doctrine of Christ, he hath both the Father and the Son" (1:9 KJV).

READ 2 JOHN 1 AND PSALM 8.

- One-Month Course: your next reading is on page 276. →
- Three-Month Course: your next reading is on page 276. →
- Six-Month Course: your next reading is on page 276. →

REPEATING BASIC TRUTHS

John wrote to a friend, "And now I plead with you, lady, not as though I wrote a new commandment to you, but that which we have had from the beginning: that we love one another" (2 John 1:5 NKJV). Why did John feel it necessary to tell her something so very basic—which he admitted they'd all known from the beginning? Because this truth is so important and foundational that it was important to always seek new ways to obey it. For this same reason, the apostle Peter wrote, "I will always remind you of these things, even though you know them and are firmly established in the truth you now have. I think it is right to refresh your memory" (2 Peter 1:12–13 NIV).

READ ISAIAH 51 AND 54.

DEALING WITH HERETICS

John wrote that a so-called Christian who denied that Jesus had a physical body and died on the cross was actually an antichrist (2 John 1:7). He warned, "Do not receive him into your house nor greet him; for he who greets him shares in his evil deeds" (2 John 1:10– 11 NKJV). How then do we obey Jesus' command to "love your enemies" and give food to our enemy if he's hungry (Matthew 5:44; Romans 12:20 NKJV)? Well, we can still give him food, but

John warned against receiving or enjoying fellowship with those who do not believe that Jesus had a physical body and died for our sins.

we're not to invite him into our home to eat and to fellowship with us. Paul listed other serious sins of people who claimed to be Christians, then said, "Don't even eat with such people" (1 Corinthians 5:11 NLT).

READ 1 CORINTHIANS 5 AND ISAIAH 56.

BASIC SURVEY

3 JOHN

AUTHOR: The apostle John, according to church tradition. The author is identified only as "the elder" (3 John 1:1 KJV).

DATE: Approximately AD 92.

IN TEN WORDS OR LESS

Church leaders must be humble, not proud.

DETAILS, PLEASE

Addressed to a believer named Gaius, 3 John praises those (like Gaius and another Christian named Demetrius) who led in "love before the church" (1:6 NASB). But 3 John also has harsh words for Christians like Diotrephes, "who loves to have the preeminence" (1:9 NKJV) and refused to show kindness and hospitality to traveling evangelists.

QUOTABLE

> I have no greater joy than to hear that my children walk in truth (1:4 KJV).

> Anyone who does what is good is from God. Anyone who does what is evil has not seen God (1:11 NIV).

UNIQUE AND UNUSUAL

Third John, one of four single-chapter books in the New Testament, is the second-shortest by verse count. Its fourteen verses are one more than 2 John.

SO WHAT?

Hospitality isn't just for the Martha Stewarts of the world—Christians are expected to feed, house, and encourage other believers, especially those who minister full-time for God. Humble service to others follows the example of Jesus Himself (see John 13:14).

READ 3 JOHN 1 AND PSALM 21.

● One-Month Course: your next reading is on page 278.   →

● Three-Month Course: your next reading is on page 278.   →

● Six-Month Course: your next reading is on page 278.   →

PROSPERING IN EVERY WAY

John wrote, "Beloved, I pray that in all respects you may prosper and be in good health, just as your soul prospers" (3 John 1:2 NASB). The most important thing for believers is our spiritual life. Whatever state our health or our finances are in, it's important that our soul prospers. But John didn't believe in embracing poverty and sickness. He prayed that the recipient of his letter would not only prosper spiritually, but be in good physical health and prosper "in all respects." This surely included having sufficient finances. This is not (contrary to what some people think) advocating a selfish, materialistic lifestyle, but is praying for God to bless people in every area and to supply their every need (Philippians 4:13).

READ ISAIAH 57–58.

POWER-HUNGRY LEADERS

We should focus on serving other people rather than trying to control them.

Unfortunately, there were power-hungry shepherds in the early church as well. John mentioned one such person, saying, "Diotrephes, who loves to be first, will not welcome us." John added that he was "spreading malicious nonsense about us. Not satisfied with that, he even refuses to welcome other believers. He also stops those who want to do so and puts them out of the church" (3 John 1:9–10 NIV). These were serious sins. Diotrephes was a classic example of a control freak who insisted on having his way instead of humbly serving others. He used his position of leadership to squelch all dissenting voices and exclude those who disagreed with him. Eventually things catch up with such people, however.

READ ISAIAH 59 AND 63.

BASIC SURVEY

JUDE

AUTHOR: Jude (1:1), possibly Jesus' half brother (see Matthew 13:55; Mark 6:3).

DATE: Approximately AD 82.

IN TEN WORDS OR LESS

Beware of heretical teachers and their dangerous doctrines.

DETAILS, PLEASE

Jude tackles the same problems Peter did in his second letter: false teachers who were leading the early church astray. "Murmurers" and "complainers" who were "walking after their own lusts" (1:16 KJV) were apparently using the grace of God as a cover for their sinful lifestyles—and encouraging Christian believers to do the same. True believers, Jude said, reflect God's love, show compassion, and work to pull sinners "out of the fire" (1:23 KJV).

QUOTABLE

> Contend earnestly for the faith which was once for all delivered to the saints (1:3 NKJV).

UNIQUE AND UNUSUAL

Jude provides details of two Old Testament events not recorded in the Old Testament: the archangel Michael's fight with Satan over the body of Moses (1:9) and Enoch's prophecy of God's judgment (1:14–15).

SO WHAT?

Satan tries to sneak "secret agents" into God's church to confuse and ultimately crush true believers. It's the job of every true Christian to "earnestly contend for the faith" as passed down by Jesus' disciples and recorded in the Bible.

READ JUDE 1 AND PSALM 145.

● One-Month Course: your next reading is on page 280.   →

● Three-Month Course: your next reading is on page 280.   →

● Six-Month Course: your next reading is on page 280.   →

CONTEND FOR THE FAITH

Jude wrote a short, urgent epistle to sound the alarm about a heresy making headway in the church. He described "certain men [who] have crept in unnoticed. . .who turn the grace of our God into

lewdness" (Jude 1:4 NKJV). Jude called this "the error of Balaam" (Jude 1:11 NKJV). This is the same heresy described in "The Teaching of Balaam" (see page 268). Jude stated, "I found it necessary to write to you exhorting you to contend earnestly for the faith which was once for all delivered to the saints" (Jude 1:3 NKJV). The true faith—the pure Gospel of Jesus Christ—had been given "once for all," and it didn't need any improvements or revisions. Believers simply needed to stand up and defend it and "contend earnestly" for it.

The book of Jude emphasizes the importance of standing firm in our beliefs so that others cannot try to improve or revise the Gospel of Jesus Christ.

READ PSALMS 142–143.

THE WORLD'S FALSE GOSPEL

Jude reminded believers that the apostles of Christ had warned them, saying, "In the last time there will be mockers, following after their own ungodly lusts." That time had now come. Jude explained that these people were "worldly-minded, devoid of the Spirit" (Jude 1:18–19 NASB). Today there are many teachers following their carnal lusts instead of the Spirit of God. They lack the Holy Spirit because they're preaching a modified Gospel and mocking *true* believers. Their warped Gospel doesn't resemble what Jesus taught, but is tailor made for the worldly and resonates with many people: "Those people belong to this world, so they speak from the world's viewpoint, and the world listens to them" (1 John 4:5 NLT).

READ ISAIAH 64 AND PSALMS 70 AND 77.

BASIC SURVEY

REVELATION

AUTHOR: John (1:1), probably the apostle John.
DATE: AD 96.

IN TEN WORDS OR LESS

God will judge evil and reward His saints.

DETAILS, PLEASE

Jesus Christ arranges for John to receive a "revelation" of "things which must shortly come to pass" (1:1 KJV). Jesus then breaks seven seals from a scroll, unleashing war, famine, and other disasters. A dragon and two beasts arise to demand worship, and seven "vials of the wrath of God" (16:1 KJV) bring plagues, darkness, and hailstones on earth. The upheaval destroys "Babylon the great," the world system, just before an angel seizes Satan and imprisons him for one thousand years. After a brief release to instigate a worldwide war, Satan is thrown into "the lake of fire and brimstone" (20:10 KJV). God then unveils "a new heaven and a new earth" (21:1 KJV).

QUOTABLE

> Worthy is the Lamb that was slain to receive power, and riches, and wisdom, and strength, and honour, and glory, and blessing (5:12 KJV).

UNIQUE AND UNUSUAL

Revelation is an example of "apocalyptic literature." *Apocalyptic* implies "revealing secret information." The book of Revelation identifies Jesus Christ as the "Alpha and Omega" (1:8 KJV) and reveals the number 666 as a sign of "the beast" (13:18 KJV).

SO WHAT?

"I've read the back of the book," an old southern gospel song says, "and we win!" The curse of sin will be gone, we'll live in perfect fellowship with the Lord Himself, and we will "reign for ever and ever" (22:5 KJV).

READ REVELATION 10–11.

● Three-Month Course: your next reading is on page 281.   →

● Six-Month Course: your next reading is on page 281.   →

HEART OF THE BOOK

THE GLORIFIED CHRIST

In John's vision, he saw that Christ has been glorified, and he stated that we will be able to see all His power and glory radiating from Him.

Jesus appeared to John on the island of Patmos, and this is John's amazing description: "I saw one like a son of man, clothed in a robe reaching to the feet, and girded across His chest with a golden sash. His head and His hair were white like white wool, like snow; and His eyes were like a flame of fire. His feet were like burnished bronze, when it has been made to glow in a furnace, and His voice was like the sound of many waters. . . . And His face was like the sun shining in its strength" (Revelation 1:13–16 NASB).

Jesus was still recognizably the carpenter from Nazareth, the son of Mary, but His physical body was now resurrected and glorified. It had to be to contain the fullness of deity. Jesus was still able to appear like a normal human. That's how He looked when He appeared to His disciples after His resurrection. But John's vision shows what Jesus *actually* looked like in His full glory.

And the good news for us is that we, too, shall one day have glorified bodies: "Beloved, now we are children of God; and it has not yet been revealed what we shall be, but we know that when He is revealed, we shall be like Him, for we shall see Him as He is" (1 John 3:2 NKJV). And in that day, like John, we shall see Jesus in His exalted state, with all the power and glory of God radiating from His presence.

READ REVELATION 1 AND 19.

●   Six-Month Course: your next reading is on page 282.   →

CLOSER LOOK

ADMONITIONS TO THE CHURCHES

Many people are tempted to skip over the letters to the seven churches to quickly get to the "good stuff"—details about the end time—but some of the most potent information in Revelation is found here. To "endure unto the end" (Matthew 24:13 KJV), we need to truly *know God*, because "the people that do know their God shall be strong, and do exploits" (Daniel 11:32 KJV).

Jesus' admonitions to the churches tell us how to "know God." He told the Christians of Ephesus, "You have persevered and have endured hardships for my name, and have not grown weary. Yet I hold this against you: You have forsaken the love you had at first. . . . Repent and do the things you did at first" (Revelation 2:3–5 NIV). They had done *so* much good, been *so* faithful, yet were in danger of losing it all.

Jesus rebuked other churches for tolerating teachers who promoted sexual immorality (vv. 14, 20). This insidious teaching is infecting churches today as well, like yeast working its way through dough (1 Corinthians 5:1–9).

Jesus warned the Christians in Sardis, "I know your deeds; you have a reputation of being alive, but you are dead. Wake up! Strengthen what remains and is about to die" (Revelation 3:1–2 NIV). Jesus called the believers in Laodicea lukewarm because material affluence had blinded them. They said, "I am rich; I have acquired wealth and do not need a thing." But they failed to see that they were actually "wretched, pitiful, poor, blind and naked" (Revelation 3:16–17 NIV).

READ REVELATION 2–3.

● Six-Month Course: your next reading is on page 283.   →

CLOSER LOOK

END-TIME EVENTS

It has been said that there are as many interpretations of Revelation as there are Christians. This book, filled with vivid, highly symbolic imagery, has been used to "prove" that two of Oliver Cromwell's guards were the end-time witnesses of Revelation 11, that Adolf Hitler was the Antichrist of Revelation 13, that Iraq was the final Babylon of Revelation 18, and that Russia is Gog and Magog. And quite a few people lock onto their unique interpretations dogmatically and get quite hot under the collar with those who disagree.

So some people give up on reading Revelation entirely—but this is a mistake. There is much that Christians can agree on, and much that is clear in the big picture, if not in every detail. For example, whether the bizarre "locusts" of Revelation 9:1–11 are supernatural beings, genetically engineered monsters, or some kind of deadly drone technology, Christians can be glad that they will be spared their attacks.

And even the most skeptical among us can see that this world can't last much longer, but is headed to a terrific climax and doom. Many secular scientists admit that, the way things are going, the Bible's statement that "every living creature in the sea" will die is not so far-fetched (Revelation 16:3 NKJV). And apart from Preterists (who think that the end time was fulfilled in the judgment of Jerusalem in AD 70), most Christians agree that Christ will one day return—perhaps in our lifetime—set up His kingdom on earth, reward the righteous, and punish the wicked.

READ REVELATION 8–9.

 Six-Month Course: your next reading is on page 284.   →

CLOSER LOOK

HEAVEN ON EARTH

John described how, at the end of the reign of Christ in the Millennium, the wicked nations, spurred on by the devil, surrounded Jerusalem to attack it, but "fire came down from heaven and devoured them" (Revelation 20:9 NASB).

This fire will be global in scope and its heat intense. It will dissolve the entire earth and vaporize its oceans and atmosphere: "But the day of the Lord will come. . .in which the heavens will pass away with a great noise, and the elements will melt with fervent heat both the earth and the works

This fourteenth-century tapestry *The New Jerusalem (Tapestry of the Apocalypse)* is an artist's interpretation of what heaven on earth may look like.

that are in it will be burned up" (2 Peter 3:10 NKJV). As a result, "the old heaven and the old earth. . .disappeared," John said. "Then I saw a new heaven and a new earth" (Revelation 21:1 NLT).

Right now the abode of God, heaven, the eternal city called New Jerusalem, is in the spiritual dimension somewhere above the earth. Paul called it "the Jerusalem above" (Galatians 4:26 NKJV). Presently, Christians who die live with God in an invisible spiritual dimension, but God's ultimate plan is for us to rule and reign with Him on this earth forever and ever.

Our entire planet will be renewed and transformed into a global paradise, and God's city will emerge from the heavenly dimension and descend. John wrote, "I saw the Holy City, the new Jerusalem, coming down out of heaven. . . . 'God's dwelling place is now among the people, and he will dwell with them'" (Revelation 21:2–3 NIV).

READ REVELATION 21–22.

INVITING JESUS INTO YOUR HEART

This verse is often used to explain how we can invite Christ to save us: "Behold, I stand at the door and knock. If anyone hears My voice and opens the door, I will come in to him and dine with him, and he with Me" (Revelation 3:20 NKJV). While this was originally written to those who were already Christians, who needed to commune with Christ (v. 19), it actually *does* explain how we can invite Jesus into our hearts. After all, Galatians 4:6 (NLT) states, "And because we are his children, God has sent the Spirit of his Son into our hearts." And Ephesians 3:17 (NLT) states, "Christ will make his home in your hearts as you trust in him."

READ REVELATION 5 AND ISAIAH 11.

HEAVEN'S JOYS

The Bible describes heaven, saying, "Behold, a great multitude which no one could count, from every nation and all tribes and peoples and tongues. . . . They will hunger no longer, nor thirst anymore." Jesus Himself "will be their shepherd, and will guide them to springs of the water of life; and God will wipe every tear from their eyes" (Revelation 7:9, 16–17 NASB). Jesus promises, "I will give of the fountain of the water of life freely to him who thirsts" (Revelation 21:6 NKJV). What beautiful promises! We have a wonderful hope, which is why Paul states that we should give "joyful thanks to the Father, who has qualified you to share in the inheritance of his holy people in the kingdom of light" (Colossians 1:12 NIV).

READ REVELATION 4 AND 7.

THE MARK OF THE BEAST

William Blake (1757–1827) painted *The Number of the Beast Is 666*. The Bible is unclear about whether the mark of the beast will be physical or spiritual.

According to one common interpretation, the mark of the Beast will be a computer chip inserted under the skin of someone's right hand or forehead, linking them to the Antichrist's global 666 computer system and allowing them to do financial transactions. Others believe that it will involve even more invasive nanotechnology. Some people, however, say that just as the "seal of God" placed on the foreheads of the redeemed (see Revelation 7:2–3) is a spiritual mark, so the 666 mark is spiritual, not anything physical. Whatever the mark of the Beast is, Christians can agree that materialism and "covetousness. . .is idolatry" (Colossians 3:5 NKJV) and that we should trust in God, not worldly riches (1 Timothy 6:17).

READ REVELATION 13–14.

BABYLON THE GREAT

John describes Babylon as "that great city" that "made all nations drink of the wine of the wrath of her fornication" (Revelation 14:8 KJV). An angel described this city as a "great prostitute" and added, "I saw a woman sitting on a scarlet beast that had seven heads." Then he explained, "The seven heads of the beast represent the seven hills where the woman rules" (Revelation 17:1, 3, 9 NLT). Some people think this woman is the Catholic Church based in Rome, since the ancient heart of Rome is the Seven Hills. But it's more likely that this woman represents the global commercial system that ruled the seven great world empires of history, since all the earth's merchants become rich through her (Revelation 18:15, 19).

READ REVELATION 17–18.

Art Credits

Alvesgaspar/WikiMedia: 23 (top)
Brooklyn Museum/WikiMedia: 73 (bottom)
Calvin/WikiMedia: 60
Carlos Delgado/Wikimedia: 266
David Castor/WikiMedia: 79
Deror avi/WikiMedia: 136
GoShow/WikiMedia: 62
FranzMayerstainedglass/WikiMedia: 194
gugganij/WikiMedia: 23 (bottom)
Kimon Berlin/WikiMedia: 284
Marie-Lan Nguyen/WikiMedia: 71
Marku1988/WikiMedia: 80
WikiMedia: 9, 10, 12 (top), 13, 16, 17, 18, 20 (top), 20 (bottom), 22, 26, 27, 28, 29, 32 (bottom), 33, 35, 36, 39, 41, 42, 43, 44, 45 (top), 45 (bottom), 47, 48 (top), 48 (bottom), 50, 51, 52, 53, 59 (top), 63, 64, 65, 66, 69, 73 (top), 75 (bottom), 76, 82, 84, 91, 92, 94, 95, 97, 98 (top), 98 (bottom), 101, 107, 115, 119, 120, 121, 122, 125, 126, 127, 132, 138, 141, 143, 144, 154, 158, 171, 174, 178, 179, 186, 198, 200, 203, 205, 206, 208, 213, 217, 223, 225, 239, 242, 245, 246, 248, 265, 268, 269, 271, 273, 286
Shutterstock: 12 (bottom), 19, 24, 31, 32 (top), 37, 38, 55, 56, 59 (bottom), 67, 72, 75 (top), 85, 88, 89, 102, 103, 104, 105, 108, 109, 110, 112, 113, 116, 134, 146, 147, 150, 152, 156, 160, 163, 166, 168, 175, 181, 184, 188, 190, 192, 211, 214, 216, 218, 222, 227, 230, 232, 234, 236, 251, 254, 257, 260, 262, 263, 272, 275, 277, 279, 281
Valerie McGlinchey/WikiMedia: 240
Xena Sheikh Yousef/WikiMedia: 149